BRENT LIBRARIES

Please return/renew this item
by the last date shown.
Books may also be renewed by
phone or online.
Tel: 0333 370 4700
On-line www.brent.gov.uk/libraryservice

'An artful mix of lyrical writing and assured analysis that
amounts to a quiet manifesto for action'

Financial Times

'There is so much that is of outstanding quality in this book: the way Cocker draws the reader into understanding the extent, range and significance of the issues; the exquisite pieces of classical "nature writing", gems of intimate description; the quality of in-depth historical research; the intellectual sense-making that draws on wider ecological theory; the sheer elegance of the writing sustained over 300 pages. Maybe most refreshing is Cocker's willingness to "speak truth to power", to name names, to point to stupidities in policy and in action'

Shiny New Books

'What a relief it is to have this subject explored without the usual diatribes and righteous hysteria. Cocker's quiet tone carries great authority and *Our Place* deserves to command respect and wide attention'

Literary Review

'Fascinating... *Our Place* is a brave book... It will undoubtedly ruffle what few figurative feathers we have left'

Caught by the River

'This is the best book on the state of nature since George Monbiot's *Feral* and deserves to be read just as widely'

Mark Avery

'Devastatingly perceptive'
Herald Scotland

'This book contains some exquisite writing about nature, but it is always powerfully and insistently ground in "its cause"... A radical polemic in the tradition of Hazlitt and Cobbett'

The Week

MARK COCKER

Mark Cocker is an author, naturalist and environmental activist whose ten books include works of biography, history, literary criticism and memoir. His book *Crow Country* was shortlisted for the Samuel Johnson Prize in 2008 and won the New Angle Prize for Literature in 2009. With the photographer David Tipling he published *Birds and People* in 2013, a massive survey described by the *Times Literary Supplement* as 'a major literary event as well as an ornithological one'.

ALSO BY MARK COCKER

*Loneliness and Time: British Travel Writing
in the Twentieth Century*

*Rivers of Blood, Rivers of Gold: Europe's
Conflict with Tribal Peoples*

Birders: Tales of a Tribe

Birds Britannica

A Tiger in the Sand: Selected Writings on Nature

Crow Country

Birds & People (with David Tipling)

Claxton: Field Notes from a Small Planet

MARK COCKER

Our Place

Can We Save Britain's Wildlife
Before It Is Too Late?

VINTAGE

1 3 5 7 9 10 8 6 4 2

Vintage
20 Vauxhall Bridge Road,
London SW1V 2SA

Vintage is part of the Penguin Random House group
of companies whose addresses can be found at
global.penguinrandomhouse.com

Penguin
Random House
UK

First published in Vintage in 2019
First published in hardback by Jonathan Cape in 2018

penguin.co.uk/vintage

A CIP catalogue record for this book is available from
the British Library

ISBN 9781784701024

Printed and bound in Great Britain by Clays Ltd, Elcograf S.p.A.

Penguin Random House is committed to a sustainable future
for our business, our readers and our planet. This book is
made from Forest Stewardship Council® certified paper.

This book is dedicated to my mother Anne Marjory Cocker (née Simpson) who gave me the gift of birds and flowers, and also to our much-missed grandad, George Bramwell Simpson, 1896–1972, who loved to take his grandchildren in the back of his Mini Clubman to visit the farmers and farms of Reaps Moor, north Staffordshire.

The question of all questions for mankind – the problem which underlies all others and which is more deeply interesting than any other – is the ascertainment of the place which man occupies in nature.

Thomas Huxley

By the side of religion, by the side of science, by the side of poetry and art stands natural beauty, not as a rival to these, but as the common inspirer and nourisher of them all.

George Macaulay Trevelyan

The explicit acceptance of the view that the world does not exist for man alone can be fairly regarded as one of the greatest revolutions in modern Western thought.

Keith Thomas, *Man and the Natural World*

To renew the living fabric of the land so that it also replenishes the spirits of its human inhabitants seems to me as close as one can come to a single expression of the aims of a total conservation policy.

Richard Mabey, *Common Ground*

A thing is right when it tends to preserve the integrity, stability and beauty of the biotic community. It is wrong when it tends otherwise.

Aldo Leopold, *A Sand County Almanac*

As long as nature is seen as something outside ourselves, frontiered and foreign, *separate*, it is lost both to us and in us.

John Fowles, *The Tree*

Contents

FOREWORD

This book had its origins in the wish to write a short polemical work on the state of British nature, whose declining fortunes I have observed and endured for most of my life. I quickly learned that I am constitutionally incapable of polemic, but the idea of saying something about the origins of environmentalism – its achievements and failures during the twentieth century – and about the state of the British countryside has remained.

Instead of pronouncing from a soap-box I have tried to present the subject in the form of a physical journey, partly because I thought it might help to hold the reader's interest if I could evoke something of the British wildlife and British places that motivate all our efforts, alongside the more technical material about countryside history and politics. In the end, I also found that presenting the book as a personal journey closely mirrored my own evolving relationship to its subject.

While I have been attached to the more-than-human parts of life since my earliest childhood in Buxton, Derbyshire, I have found it complicated to unravel why the state of nature in this country is as it is, but also to work out what I think and feel about this unfolding story. Progress has been slow, and the book has cost me proportionately more hard labour than any other I have written. On occasions, it has felt like a physical voyage.

I should explain some of the book's limitations. There is precious little on marine conservation. I have no excuse for this except that it is a massive subject in its own right, and it has been well covered by the likes of Callum Roberts in his wonderful *The Unnatural History of the Sea*. He is a professor of marine conservation; I am a landlubber from Derbyshire with no special knowledge of sea life. Nor have

I covered the long history of ideas, dating from the early modern period and even back to Classical times, which has brought us to our present engagements with nature.

Even the full story of British conservation could only truly be told in a multi-volume work running to many hundreds of thousands of words. You have only to scan the fastidious volumes of environmental history by John Sheail to appreciate this. Mine is no more than a watercolour of the full panoramic picture. I have provided an outline of the rise and work of the chief voluntary organisations, along with the forty-year fortunes of the statutory conservation body, the Nature Conservancy (Council). Yet I have attempted to search the landscapes themselves and sift an almost overwhelming mass of material on these themes to find a series of fundamental, interlocking truths, an understanding of which is essential to any grasp of the British countryside in the early twenty-first century.

Finally, I should say a word more about the choice of format. For better or for worse I am usually branded a 'nature writer'. Whatever that means, I am committed to the literary genre in which I operate. It is a book form usually viewed as a merging of lyrical responses to nature with the political, scientific and ethical materials that arise from our relationship with the other parts of life: a blend of the private and the public, the emotional and the technical.

In an earlier book, *Crow Country*, I tried to unite a piece of genuine natural-historical research with a personal memoir in a hybridised format that I call 'the poetry of fact'. It is in the same spirit of experimentation that I now offer this book, because *Our Place* is an attempt at a similar fusion, between an autobiographical narrative of place and a historical exploration of how and why the British countryside has come to look as it does. I think of this book as one that operates in non-linear ways, and I describe it as a work of the 'ecological imagination'.

It would have been completely impossible to get to grips with any of it without help from all sorts of people. They include Mark Avery,* Helen Baczkowska, Patrick Barkham, Charlie Barnes of the Greater Lincolnshire Nature Partnership, John Birks, Margaret Bradshaw,* Nigel Brown, Andrew Chick, Mike Clarke,* Andy Clements,* Tim Dee, Jeremy Deller, Michael Dower, Euan Dunn, Jim Egan, Jonathan Elphick,

John Fanshawe, Jake Fiennes,* Ian Findlay,* Colin Ford, the late Dr Martin George, Bob Gibbons, Adam Gretton,* Richard and Helen Grimmett, Anna Guthrie, Mark Hancock,* Mike Harding, Martin Harper,* Sarah Henderson, Stephanie Hilbourne, Greg Hitchcock, Julian Hoffman, Rob Hume, Colin Jones, Tony Juniper,* Dr Paul Kemp, Eugene Kielt, Osbert Lancaster, Ian Langford, Richard Lindsay, Sir John Lister-Kaye,* Richard Mabey, Michael McCarthy, Chris McCarty, Peter Marren,* Pete Mayhew,* Matt Merritt, Chris and Doris Murphy, Jeremy Mynott, Derek Niemann,* David North, Peter Phillipson, Katrina Porteous, Dame Fiona Reynolds,* Ian Rotherham, Tim Sands, Matt Shardlow,* Marion Shoard,* John Sizer, John Snape, Andy Stoddart, Pete Styles, Moss Taylor, Adrian Thomas, Des Thompson, Mike Toms, Merlin Waterson, Brett Westwood and Andy Wightman.* Of these, Jim Perrin will know his major contribution to the format of the book and I bless him for it. An asterisk after a name indicates that the person has kindly submitted to a formal recorded interview and/or relentless enquiries on a spectrum of subjects. I also wish to single out Alistair Elliot, Matt Howard, Matt Merritt and Giles Watson and thank them deeply for permission to include in the book their superb poetry.

I switched agents during the course of the book, but I thank both Gill Coleridge and Patrick Walsh for their wonderful, continuous and harmonious support. Not too many authors can say that they have had the same editor for more than thirty years. Fewer still can acknowledge three decades of guidance from an editor as talented, patient and as skilled as Dan Franklin. I also wish to thank his colleagues at Cape including Clare Bullock, Joe Pickering and Anthony Hippisley. For the book's wonderful cover I am deeply indebted to my friend, the artist Jonny Gibbs, and to Mathew Broughton of Cape, who oversaw its production. My partner Mary Muir is the rock on which all my achievements are founded (it must be said, however, that there was a slight increase in the 'I-can't-wait-for-this-book-to-be-finished' moments!). No more need be said, except to offer her my heartfelt thanks and love.

I am sorry if I have left unacknowledged anyone who should have been mentioned. I also apologise in advance for any errors, which are mine alone.

Claxton, October 2017

I

MY PLACE

to cast a tool of ash and hooked iron
to take care in boots at the edge of standing water
to throw from the shoulder, then heave from the lumbar spine
to clear a dyke of leaf-fall and slub from the past three decades
or further
to feel a suck and pop of sedge-roots tearing from bog
to spit splash-back of festered water from one's lips
to retch one's balance of vows and curses where no one else is
listening
to imagine a cut of clearer water
to haul deeper with long-drawn tines
to blister then callus both hands in unfavourable conditions
to consider the phased wing-strokes of dragonflies
to listen to the short, descending arc of willow warbler song whilst
working
to see sunlight on the nodes of a Norfolk hawker's forewing
to act with the whole body and mean it

Matt Howard, 'Crome'

Blackwater is our place. I bought it in the spring of 2012, largely on the proceeds of my previous book *Birds and People*. It's a fraction over 5 acres – two fields called Oak Meadow and Sallow Fen – in the floodplain of the Yare, just before the river cuts a long slow curve under the village of Brundall, then heads south-east across the great flatlands of Halvergate, there finally to be extinguished in the shallow blue maw of the North Sea.

Blackwater lies in the parish of Postwick in a south-pointing spur of the river's north bank, exactly opposite the Ferry Inn, an old red-brick public house that leans drunkenly where the foundations have sunk into the underlying peat. In the spring of 2013 a couple of young friends and I were digging a pond at Blackwater when we unearthed a 4-pound chunk of ancient rusted metal. It was part of a massive chain, a ferry chain perhaps, a reminder of how the people of east Norfolk once outflanked the impediment of this awkward river.

Taken together the two fields, whose outlines are clearly visible on an OS map of 1879, are roughly rectangular in shape, but towards their northern end the east and west boundaries push slightly outwards, then turn sharply to a point so that the bloc of land looks to be capped by a pitched roof. In my happier moments the outline reminds me of a tall beehive. When the work seems momentarily overwhelming and Blackwater lays me low, it feels like a coffin.

The toughest of the work involves the dykes, which both separate the two fields and bound the whole perimeter. On an aerial photograph of 1946 you can see these rectilinear water channels, maybe six feet deep at their middles, as clearly as if they had been ruled in thick pen. There are no obvious trees on Blackwater, just two small bushes at the centre of Sallow Fen. Otherwise the fields are clear. Then all agricultural activity must have ceased, because a later sequence of aerial photographs, given to me by a friend from the Environment Agency, reveals what happened over the intervening years. By 1978 all the boundary dykes are blotched with sallow and alder. Come 2011 the eastern boundary has a continuous canopy and the central and southern dykes are obliterated by tree cover. Blackwater is falling down to woodland.

A single hectare of trees produces about 5 tonnes of debris a year.[1] Slowly, autumn after autumn, vast quantities of leaves fluttered down from those trees and entered my dykes, creating a dark, loose, stinking soup of anoxic sludge. Stick in a pole or rake and stir the turbid drain and great foul gloops of marsh gas engulf you. No wonder they named it Blackwater. Where the tree cover is thickest, the sense of hard-brewed lifelessness in those dykes is total.

My first two seasons of work, which were fitted around the 400,000 words of *Birds and People*, were devoted merely to halting the deterioration. Over that whole first winter, each weekend, I cut and cleared tonnes of invasive scrub. One redeeming element in the process was the towering piles of sallow that have kept our woodburner supplied ever since. Felling the trees on the dry banks is a steady, pleasant form of labour, the chainsaw making light work of the softwood trunks. At the end the logs are stacked, the big branches are piled high as brashing and the lesser stuff is burned off.

Yet sallow loves water and is happy to sink roots deep into the heart of the dyke. In many places the trees are entirely aquatic in lifestyle, growing and rotting in the fetid mulch of their own making. Were I to leave that process uninterrupted and had I the luxury of two centuries – climate change and sea-level rises notwithstanding – my guess is I'd have a nice patch of relatively dry alder and oak woodland bisected by nothing more than shallow muddy troughs where the dykes once cut their course. And the biodiversity of Blackwater would be restored. In the absence of an oak tree's life expectancy, I am returning the place to its original condition.

In truth, I'm looking to create four distinct habitats in two fields: first, open clear-water dykes throughout, rich in invertebrates and damp-loving plants like purple loosestrife and water soldier. At Sallow Fen I'm happy to operate a laissez-faire policy so that the tree cover can expand and rise. On Oak Meadow, however, I'm clearing it systematically to give ground to the tall herb dominated by reed sweet grass, hemp agrimony, great hairy willowherb and meadowsweet. In late summer this herb layer is a lush, chest-high rainforest beloved of whitethroats and elephant hawkmoths. In some years I have the zany invertebrate churn of grasshopper warblers rising from its Amazonian depths.

Then on the close-cropped stretch along the south dyke at Oak Meadow, where I first cleared-felled those sallow thickets, my aim is for something more delicate. Repeat mowing is intended to re-create what may well have been there when Sir Thomas Browne studied the birdlife of the Norfolk Broads – a wet meadow filled with marsh orchids and the starburst blooms of ragged robin. All of this is the plan. For now, I do battle with those dykes.

Two winters ago, I set out not only to strip sallow off the sides, but also to winkle out any last trees that had burrowed beneath the foot of the drains. Getting at the submerged stumps is ghastly work. Manoeuvring a chainsaw in a bog is dangerous, and the task must be done mainly by hand. I regularly operate clad in waders with water up to my waist. Any exertion while effectively wrapped in plastic is sweaty and unpleasant.

The alternatives are worse. I've fallen in so often I always now carry spare leather boots in the car. Some pairs of wellingtons have been so routinely filled with fetid water that they're almost beyond use. You have to wash the insides and then stand them to air and dry sometimes for weeks. They're fine the moment you put them on, then your feet cook, and by the time you take them off again there blossoms once more the old stench of anaerobic slub. Only now it is ripe with age and fermentation.

There have been days when I have fallen in, changed my clothes, fallen in again and changed once more. Then I've promptly fallen in a third time. After that I worked with my feet sloshing in half-filled boots. On one occasion I slipped and fell to my thighs, filled both wellingtons and completely submerged the chainsaw. There was also a strange moment when I was stripped naked, wrestling with the cold clag of soaked clothes and socks; just minutes later two women wandered through, thinking Blackwater was a footpath.

Clearing out the trees from the dykes is only the first part of the challenge. The most gruelling of tasks involves hauling the floating mats of vegetation off the surface using an old claw-headed Norfolk implement, bought for me by a friend, called a crome. It's like a long-shafted garden fork, but the tines extend and curve right round and hook backwards. It's designed specifically for pulling weed from dykes, but it can also feel like an instrument of torture.

Decades of neglect have allowed the phragmites reed and the sedge to smother the surface completely in some sections. The phragmites is the worst. Where it vanishes into the dyke is a dense boll of accumulated sludge bound together by reed root. From this upper layer the plants then send down longer tuberous rhizomes that get further purchase in the mud below. They look like fleshy white ropes, or perhaps the small intestines of some carnivorous triffid, and they make reeds incredibly tenacious. They literally cling to life.

I pull and pull, my feet sinking in the quagmire edge, and at times it feels as though my exertions are met by a counter-effort from the reed itself. I heave. It pulls. Any minute now I could easily fall over backwards. Or fall forwards into the water. More often the crome pulls loose from its hold and I am sprayed with black water, so that when I get home at night my clothes are bespattered with dried mud and my face is encrusted in salt. But when a clump finally works free and I land it on the bank like a great slippery mud fish, all gleaming and running dark ooze, there is that countervailing sense of achievement. Sometimes the sod can weigh anything up to thirty pounds and is 2 feet in depth with great dangling white barbels of root around its mud mouth, yet the space it leaves in the dyke seems only 7–8 inches across. Back I go to repeat the process again and again.

It is surely not unnatural, as I mop the sweat and pause to quiet the air rasping in my lungs, to ask also why on Earth I do it. Why did I spend so much money – the largest purchase in my life after our Claxton house – on 5 acres of hard labour? To what end do I work? What is it I hope to achieve? And for whom?

My guess is you already know the kinds of rationalisations I could give you. After all, conservation efforts like mine are nothing new. People have been restoring environments, making of them suitable habitats for wildlife, for about a century. It's this social and cultural context that lends my actions a veneer of normality. Think about it: I'm doing all this work for other species. There's no material profit to be had, not much practical benefit and little obvious reward. I do get firewood, but I could buy better-quality pre-chopped logs for £100 a ton. My aim isn't really fuel.

It's emperor moths in my tall herb and Norfolk hawker dragonflies in the dykes. I dream one day that those freshwater strips might become home to a real star like the fen raft spider, a creature that until recently had only three breeding sites anywhere in Britain. However, in any other age, had a man laboured simply to create a future living space for an arachnid called *Dolomedes*, he would either be canonised or carted off to Bedlam.

Humankind and its hominid ancestors have been on this planet for about 4 million years. For something like 3,999,850 of those years hardly any human ever devoted himself to the prosperity of another species. There were occasional anomalies. The earliest record I know dates to about 400 BC. The Greek historian Herodotus suggested that sacred ibises were protected by law in pharaonic Egypt. Infractions were even punishable by death. But this early legislation was almost entirely motivated by human self-interest, given that millions of the ibises were harvested from special compounds (*ibiotropheia*) and then slaughtered for mummified interment in ibis shrines. They were a functioning part of Egypt's hydra-headed religious life.[2]

The idea that other animals were protected solely for themselves, so that they might multiply and thrive, was not considered until the nineteenth century. In fact, in the 3 billion years of life on our planet no single species of any description has ever made the survival of another species its deliberate priority. Until we did.

So we are odd. And in many ways, this is a very odd age – the environmental age. Wildlife conservation is among the largest social and cultural developments of our time. Green ideas, green initiatives, green organisations are the very bread and butter of the mainstream. The Green Party has just begun to make headway, even in a change-averse political system like ours. Some of the key conservation charities are household names and part of the essential fabric of British life. The National Trust – with its sister charity, the National Trust for Scotland – has more than 5 million members. That's one in thirteen of all the people in this country. It's one in ten of all voters.

I personally have never known anything other than the environmental age. It's the period in which I grew up and to which my adult life has been largely devoted. The book that is most often associated with the birth of environmentalism is Rachel Carson's minatory study on the effects of pesticides, *Silent Spring*. It was published in 1962 when I was still in nappies. In the spring of 1971, when I did my eleven-plus, Friends of the Earth was founded. The *Ecologist* magazine, with its groundbreaking special edition 'Blueprint for Survival', which spoke of 'the irreversible disruption of the life support systems on this planet', sold 750,000 copies in the year I went up to Buxton Grammar School, 1972. In a sense my search for the origins, meaning and background to environmentalism is an autobiographical journey. We have co-existed all our lives.

The real question that Blackwater prompts is not, why do I care, but why do *we* care? What has happened in this country to precipitate this massive upheaval that affects us all? Blackwater is in some ways a symptom of our collective transformation. This book is an attempt to explore our new place in the world and how we have got here. Yet it's still a personal book. I speak for no official organisation. While I consulted or interviewed a whole suite of key thinkers and activists in the realm of 'nature' politics, the biases, like the errors, are mine.

I also acknowledge that there is already a vast library of books on British conservation. My only excuse for adding to it is to offer a simple single volume that summarises the story clearly and engagingly. I am not the first to attempt it. That task has been well done by others: Max Nicholson (*The Environmental Revolution*, 1970), Bill Adams (*Future Nature*, 1996), Peter Marren (*Nature Conservation*, 2002) and Rory Spowers (*Rising Tides*, 2002). I can, however, bring it up to date.

Our Place is not even a conventional account of nature conservation – a linear chronology of the major developments since 1894 (the beginning of the National Trust), or 1889 (foundation of the Royal Society for the Protection of Birds) or even 1865 (the Commons Preservation Society). Many of these key moments are described, but we will meet them along the way, so to speak, because the book is shaped around a series of imaginative journeys through six landscapes that have been central either to me or to the environmental story in general.

The path will meander and we will encounter the stories several times, but coming from different directions. The overall goal is to evoke some of the most distinctive landscapes in Britain, but it is also to examine why they are important and – a very different question – how we have come to see them as important.

Fundamentally the book will seek to unravel a central paradox of British environmentalism that has dogged me for years. But its full force was only truly spelt out with the first publication of the *State of Nature* (2013) report. It is a remarkable, and remarkably troubling, document, not least because it involved the collaboration of twenty-five different environmental organisations. It summarises all manner of expertise from mycologists (fungi) to herpetologists (amphibians/ reptiles), and looked at organisms you've probably neither heard of (bryophytes), nor seen (liverworts). But it also covers birds, bumblebees, bats, bugs and butterflies. It investigated the health and prospects of British wildlife in a way that had never been attempted before. Its editors pulled together population data from a huge suite of different organisms – 3,148 species, to be precise – and it concluded that of these, 60 per cent had declined in the last half century, and 31 per cent had declined badly. More than 600 species were considered to be threatened with extinction.[3]

It is important first to underline how significant are those findings. There have been many attempts to measure how nature fares in Britain for almost all my life. The index of farmland birds, for example, has been a critical tool to observe changes in our agricultural environment for the last forty-five years. In brief, it attempts to calculate the changing fortunes of the birds to gain insight into the natural health of their home, the farmland landscapes of crops and pasture. However, it only uses as a measuring stick the populations of about twenty bird species specialising in these sorts of habitats.

Let's not overlook that those findings alone are profoundly alarming. Once common inhabitants of arable fields (the grey partridge) and of hedgerows (the turtle dove) have been reduced to a dismal rump – less than one-tenth of the total numbers that existed in 1970. Their losses exceed 90 per cent. The farmland bird index has been utilised right across Europe, and Britain has the worst statistics of any of the countries.[4]

Yet public perception is odd. We hear the evidence of the formal study, but we like to counter it with our own more informal and intuitive sources of information. It's exactly the same with the evidence for climate change: everyone hears the global science, but each of us has a theory about their weather. So, grey partridges and turtle doves may be going, but what about the explosive increases in little egrets or red kites? People now see and count red kites as they head down the M4. They've even reached the outskirts of London.

Buzzards were once confined to the western extremities of Britain. Many people saw them only on rare visits to the Scottish Highlands and often mistook them for eagles. Now buzzards are in virtually every parish and are the country's commonest bird of prey, increasing more than sixfold in thirty years. These ups and downs among British wildlife are assumed to be part of the give and take – the eternal ebb and flow – of natural systems, and they seem to rebalance the overall equation. People are alarmed, but they are also consoled.

The *State of Nature* report allows for no such wriggle room. It spread its nets wider than every previous investigation of our wildlife. The more species you include in your study, the more finely grained is the resulting picture. Every one of those animals and plants will have slightly different ecological requirements. Measuring the fortunes of so many meant that the *State of Nature* report interrogated every nuance of British countryside. It was unprecedented and it is incontrovertible. In the teeth of its grim message we cannot simply point out that long-tailed tits have increased in our gardens, or that speckled wood butterflies are now common in Scotland, where once they were absent.

To drain the cup to the bitter end, we need to recognise that the bottom-line figures in the *State of Nature* report measure not just the scale of loss, but the rate of decline. They don't indicate the bottom of a curve: they chart the direction of an arrow. It means that, however bad things are, they will get worse without major change. Nature is slipping away from these islands; slowly, steadily, inexorably, field by field, dyke by dyke. I know it; we now know it. There can be no dispute. Not since the last ice age has Britain been so stripped bare of its natural inhabitants.

That realisation brings us face to face with a fundamental conundrum. If we now measure affairs in this country by public preparedness to join environmental organisations, then we are the most nature-obsessed nation on the planet. In fact, never have people seemed to care more. The National Trust is the giant of the membership bodies – remember those 5 million – but it is just one of several. The RSPB has 1.2 million members, while the Wildlife Trusts have 800,000. Then there are twelve other organisations all with substantial support: Friends of the Earth UK (300,000), the Woodland Trust (227,516, and claims 500,000 supporters), Wildfowl and Wetland Trust (over 200,000), Greenpeace (120,000), Campaign to Protect Rural England (over 60,000), Butterfly Conservation (26,000), Whale and Dolphin Conservation (19,586), British Trust for Ornithology (17,265), PlantLife (11,000), the John Muir Trust (more than 10,000), Hawk and Owl Trust (7,000) and Marine Conservation Society (5,500).

Leaving aside the fact that many people are members of more than one organisation, we can see that the figures add up to 8,026,852. That's almost one in eight of us. In comparison, in August 2016 the shared membership of the Labour (515,000), Conservative (149,800) and Liberal Democrat parties (76,000) was only 730,800.

To put some of this into a comparative context, it is useful to look at an institution called BirdLife International. It's a federation made up of separate national ornithological organisations, and it coordinates global efforts for bird conservation. Its UK representative is the RSPB. If we look at the size of the counterpart bodies we find that the French equivalent (*League pour la Protection des Oiseaux*) has 46,000 members. The German counterpart (*Natürschutzhund Deutschland*) has 478,000. The RSPB's Dutch sister (*Vogelbescherming Nederland*) has 154,000, while the Spanish version (*Sociedad Espanola de Ornitologica*) has 12,000. To understand these figures truly we need to see them as a proportion of their national populations. When this has been factored into the figures, the UK membership is more than twice the size of the Dutch and more than three times the size of the German. It is an astonishing 25 times greater than that of the French and 87 times more than the Spanish partner.

So there it is. The British love wildlife, and they appear to love it more than others. Yet in the last half-century we have failed it, and we are still losing it day after day. How can that have happened? And why? But, also, why do we care? Who inspired us to think that this is an important matter? And can anything really turn it around? Is there any hope to be found? These are the questions that have shaped the book you're about to read.

2

A VERY BIG THING

If you want to see and talk about the impact of environmentalism in Britain then there are few better places to start than north Norfolk. It has almost every kind of protective designation. It's a Ramsar site, a Biosphere Reserve, a Special Protection Area (SPA), a Special Area of Conservation (SAC), and 19,000 acres of it are a Site of Special Scientific Interest (SSSI). It is, in addition, an Area of Outstanding Natural Beauty (AONB). Its coast is a 28-mile-long ribbon of reserves owned by most of the main voluntary and statutory conservation groups in this country, but particularly the National Trust, the Norfolk Wildlife Trust and the Royal Society for the Protection of Birds. It is also entwined with the earliest years of the first, and it is a birthplace for the second. In some ways it is the history of environmentalism converted to soil and seashore.

For me it is more than that. It is also one of my ur-landscapes: the place that determined where I went to study for my degree. Most people choose a course when they go to university. I chose a landscape. I made all of my five selections to study English literature based on their proximity to bird habitats. North Norfolk was the first choice. I came here in 1978; I've never left. I now no longer live on the coast, but it altered the course of my life.

This book could be written entirely around the issues that flow from a walk through north Norfolk. I shall return to it again and again but, most important, it enables me to introduce the key dramatis personae in the story: the organisations, even the individuals, that have shaped our responses to the natural environment.

If you're walking the whole coastal path in north Norfolk and begin in Hunstanton, then there is value in that preliminary mile from the old lighthouse to the first nature reserve. If, like me, you choose to go in wintertime, you'll pass the café and shop, with their boarded windows and that winter air of vanquished jollity, a sign announcing to the deserted car park, 'Buckets and Spades, Beach Toys & lots more'.

Heading for Holme Dunes you carry on by the beach huts, locked now and salt-lashed, through the bushes where black scrotal sacks of dog shit have been snagged at intervals by dog walkers on the bare spines of the buckthorn bushes. Then come the golf clubhouse and the course itself, with its shorn monoculture of hand-laid turf, broken only by flags to mark the putting greens that are devoid even of worm-casts.

At least this short stretch, with all its conventional touristic and recreational features, allows a visitor tramping the next thirty miles of this magnificent shore to see just what has been saved by *not* developing it. For north Norfolk has been described as 'the finest complex of sand flats, marshes, shingle ridges and dunes in this country'.[1] It is one of the most natural coasts in Europe and, while long settled in a series of small fishing villages from Hunstanton to Cromer, development has been carefully contained.

Most of the shore is now in the hands of conservation bodies – a jigsaw pattern of reserves belonging to the National Trust, the Norfolk Wildlife Trust, the Norfolk Ornithologists' Association and the RSPB. Where their boundaries are exposed Natural England and the Environment Agency pick up the baton, preserving the integrity of the dunes as a major part of the coastal sea defences. Today the whole area is wrapped about with protective legislation and official designations. My guess is that, were the legionaries who built the Roman fort at Branodunum to return and sail up Brancaster creek, they would find all the landscape features that they had originally encountered in the third century AD.

It is at Holme Dunes, a reserve of the Norfolk Wildlife Trust, that you really start to sense the presence and power of its dominant landform: saltmarsh. You walk past the freshwater pools, where the natterjack toads breed, and across the dunes to the pines, all the while savouring a winter song of the breeze, played through the skeletal elder trees and blended with the calls of curlew rising off the marsh. By the time you get beyond the ridge of pine at Holme and look east towards Thornham and Titchwell, the saltmarsh is all before you.

It is the one habitat that binds the coast together, interlinking the more prominent and famous features – the freshwater scrapes at Cley Marshes, the shingle spit at Blakeney, the brooding pine-topped dunes between Holkham and Wells, with their magnificent 5-mile stretch of grazing marsh, and then the dune system on Scolt Head Island. Saltmarsh is the matrix and the connective tissue of the coast and its appeal, like its beauty, is elusive.

As the name suggests, it is a niggardly land form. There are no primary colours, no contours, few buildings and barely any trees. It is laid down by tidal action in layers of silt, which are then colonised by pioneer grasses and plants. Over decades the mud and the salt-tolerant vegetation build upwards, until only the very highest tides can reclaim the oldest saltmarshes briefly for the sea.

Its tallest plant is called suaeda or shrubby seablite, whose dense waxy thickets come no higher than a man's chest, although they can be as impenetrable as jungle. Like the sea purslane, which is its constant companion, suaeda is so quietly green it is only just this side of a chromatic boundary that separates dead from living vegetation. Saltmarsh in winter grey falls softly upon the human eye.

The boldest topography is not any form of relief above the horizon: it is the negative space of the wriggling creeks that cut down into the saltmarsh flats. To these sunken channels – loose and sticky, treacherous underfoot – are attached a larger, crazier circulatory system of mud gutters and dripping gullies that spread and carry the pulse of seawater in and out two times a day, like capillaries through the body of the marsh.

Other than the creeks' tidal pattern, there is too little contrast and detail for the mind to get real purchase upon this place. Saltmarsh bulks large and level, but its sameness is resistant to the eye and even to language. An area like Warham, fifteen miles to the east of Holme, has the clarity and space of desert. The odd wrecked ship or boat may have its rotting vestige of human story, but this is often the closest it comes to companionability. This landscape is as wild as rainforest. Its awkwardness and inhumanity are its salient features.

Wading birds are its most conspicuous and vocal inhabitants, yet even they are often out of view as they wander below the flats among the network of incised creeks. Occasionally, when the sky is free of cloud and the mud sheen carries a faint bluish cast, a rush of winter light reveals the crisscrossing trails pricked into the loose slop by the birds' feet, whose owners have since wandered round the bend or flown away. Then the creek walls trap their sounds, narrowing and distorting the natural range of curlew or redshank notes so that the voices seem remote, as if piped up out of the mud by megaphone.

One of the most routine dwellers in Norfolk saltmarsh is now the little egret, and it is remarkable how these arriviste herons, which colonised Britain from continental Europe only in the 1990s, not only thrive but also manage to stay so clean in all this loose-silted English muck. The egrets' whiteness out-dazzles even swan white. The birds flush out the creeks, necks extended and broad wings pulsing gracefully, then they pitch down and vanish to feed once more. That sudden coming-up of something so pure from such a blur of winter grey has the power of a revelation.

If saltmarsh is the matrix habitat of the north Norfolk coast, it's also the least visited. People flock to the birding hotspots at Cley and Titchwell; holidaymakers troop down Lady Ann's Drive all summer long to play on the sandy flats of Holkham Beach, but the saltmarsh, which runs without interruption from Thornham to Burnham Overy and then again from Wells to Cley, is relished by few. You can walk the 10-mile stretch between the two last-named locations and barely meet another soul. In fact, at a place like Stiffkey Greens it is difficult even to recognise you are overlooking a nature reserve at all. However, almost all of it belongs to the first major dramatis persona of this book: the National Trust.

Almost as far as the eye can see, east and west, the landscape is the property of the National Trust. Glance north at the tall dune ridge dominating Blakeney Point and you are looking at one of the earliest landscapes it ever acquired, and one of the oldest properties in British environmental history. It is also among the first major coastal sites acquired by any organisation. Wicken Fen in Cambridgeshire and a handful of others pre-date it, but these were often only tiny parcels. Blakeney Point runs for more than three and a half miles.

A quirk of cartography means that the Ordnance Survey chops the spit in two between sheets 133 and 134. In the Explorer Series you have a full sense of its unity, but also of its strangeness. A slender finger of shingle, heaped and relentlessly re-configured by the tide, reaches out towards the North Sea before thickening and curling south-west back towards land in a hooked tip. In shape it reminds me of a bird's abnormally long toe – say the middle digit and pectinate claw of a bittern – but don't get too carried away by the exact configuration recorded on paper. The beauty of Blakeney the place is its mobility. Like the sea itself, this ridge of sand and pebble is always mutating, and its present shape defies all but the most recent two-dimensional versions. If a single land feature had to stand for this whole coast it would have to be this moon-moulded curve of stone.

Today the National Trust is the major stakeholder in north Norfolk, and that relationship began with Blakeney in 1912. The acquisition, which occurred only seventeen years after the organisation had been created, illuminates perfectly the originating principles of the three Victorians credited with the National Trust's foundation. They are Octavia Hill (1838–1912), Sir Robert Hunter (1844–1913) and Hardwicke Rawnsley (1851–1920).

The alphabetic order in many ways measures their relative inputs, although in his book, *Founders of the National Trust* (2002), Graham Murphy argues for a more even, three-way division of credit. It was certainly true that the first two were dead within a year of Blakeney's purchase, but their mark on National Trust policy was already indelible. What the last figure, Hardwicke Drummond Rawnsley, brought to the process was raw energy and unflinching enthusiasm for the cause. A friend who knew all three suggested that while Hill and Hunter, in confronting an obstacle, would recognise it as such, then devise a route around it, the good Canon Rawnsley 'didn't know the meaning of the word "No", and it would be his way to have said, "There is no obstacle there; go on."'[2] *

My guess is that, could any of these three people be resurrected miraculously and permitted to see their legacy, they would be astonished at how their offspring has prospered. Yet one wonders whether they would be equally convinced by its commitment to their original founding vision.

Today we perhaps don't always think of the National Trust as first and foremost an environmental body, rather as a preserver of British cultural heritage, the quintessence of conservative values, the default recipient of former aristocratic property. In truth the organisation has often been curiously muted on environmental politics. In the past it was regularly criticised for a lack of passion over contentious issues, such as hunting and blood sports.[†] It was more or less forced by its membership to stop the hunting of stags with hounds on National Trust property. Even today much of the farmland that it owns is managed in ways that show no or almost no concern for biodiversity. The prominent activist Mark Avery calls it 'a dozing giant', whose focus on 'nature conservation is weak and blurred'. In his book on his life in environmental politics, *Fighting for Birds*, Avery, a National Trust member, refuses to concede it is much more than 'a very good part of the entertainment industry', more concerned with offering you tea cakes in nice surroundings than changing the world.[4]

However, if we measure our top wildlife agencies purely by acreage of land secured, or simply by the numbers of people reached and persuaded, or the depth of the pockets that are perpetually emptied in nature's widest

---

* Another witness to Rawnsley's temperament was the gardener at his old church-yard, who said he was a 'peppery old swine'. A more benign image came from the parishioner who called him 'the most active volcano in Europe'.[3]

† It has been largely true of the National Trust for much of last century, but public reticence has been dropped more recently, especially under the last two Director Generals, Dames Fiona Reynolds and Helen Ghosh. The former was vociferous in opposing government proposals both to privatise the Forestry Commission and to loosen planning regulations. The latter has highlighted climate change as a major challenge for British wildlife.

cause, then the National Trust has no competitor. After the Forestry Commission it is Britain's largest single landowner: with the National Trust for Scotland* it owns 815,000 acres (330,000 ha). Judged in the round, there is something magnificent about that achievement.

If one traces the sequence of events by which it first saw light of day, it was not any of the key founders, but Octavia Hill's sister Miranda who sowed the first seed. The two women were lifelong collaborators in campaigns of social welfare for the poor, and one winter's evening, in a lecture to her own family, Miranda proposed the foundation of a 'Society for the Diffusion of Beauty'. It drew on the radical if quixotic proposal that to be truly happy humans – all humans, rich and poor – needed beauty just as much as they needed decent housing or fair wages. The better-connected Octavia, who could call on royalty to further her schemes, circulated the essay among friends and invited them all to a meeting in 1878.

The very notion that the shortcomings of Victorian society, with all its poverty, injustice and inequality, might be cured, and that you could 'save starving souls by means of pictures, parties and pianos', received a broadside from more practically minded critics.[5] But the central idea survived its baptism of fire.

All eventually agreed: beauty – in the form of gardens, window flowers and open public space – enriched the lives of all. From it grew a short-lived body called the Kyrle Society, with Octavia as its treasurer and named after a seventeenth-century philanthropist who had devoted his wealth to the good of his Herefordshire neighbours. One of the truly outstanding achievements of Miranda Hill's brainchild was the preservation of the Burnham Beeches, an ancient wood near

---

* The fact that there are two separate agencies with different histories – the NTS was founded in 1931 – is often overlooked. That its founders felt the need to create a separate institution is perhaps a measure of the quintessential Englishness of the older organisation. By 1931 the National Trust had not acquired a single Scottish property. Technically the northern version is the National Trust for Scotland for Places of Historic Interest or Natural Beauty. It fulfils an identical remit as its sister organisation in England, Wales and Northern Ireland. Membership of one, which costs substantially less north of the border, allows access to the properties of both.

the Buckinghamshire village of Burnham that had been threatened with enclosure. The team sent to persuade the Corporation of London to buy the wood – with its glorious antique pollards that survive to this day – was a twin delegation involving the Kyrle and the like-minded Commons Preservation Society (CPS). The brilliantly effective solicitor employed by the latter was Robert Hunter.

If beauty had inspired the creation of one organisation, it was a concern to secure green space for public good that had led directly to the foundation in 1865 of the Commons Preservation Society.* The great period of enclosure – roughly from 1760 until the first decade of the nineteenth century – had seen 3 million acres of wastes and common lands turned over to private farming interests. And while the process gradually slowed, it had by no means stopped in Hunter's day.[6] By 1845 the total area levered into the estates of Britain's landed classes was 6.5 million acres. In the next two decades a further half a million were privatised.[7] Hunter and the CPS sought to resist both this loss of land for the public's recreational use, and the forfeiture of individual common rights, which were often economically vital to poor landless people. Its solicitor had built up the CPS's astonishing record of success, and had overturned or defeated in open legal battle proposed enclosures at some of England's most iconic landscapes, such as Epping Forest and Wimbledon Common.

This had also attracted support from major intellectuals, including John Ruskin and John Stuart Mill. In fact, it was the Burnham campaign that triggered a Damascene conversion in Mill. From being an enthusiastic privatiser of land, the philosopher later wrote, 'The desire to engross the whole surface of the earth in the mere production of the greatest quantity of food and the materials of manufacture, I consider to be founded on a mischievously narrow conception of the requirements of human nature.'[8]

---

* The Commons Preservation Society is still in existence and still campaigning, as the Open Spaces Society. Technically it is the oldest environmental organisation in Britain. Alas, it has never expanded its membership like the other organisations, to the point where hardly anyone knows of its existence today. In many ways, its role as champion of green space for public good was superseded by its offspring, the National Trust.

The battle for Burnham Beeches might have brought Hunter and Hill into close working partnership, but they realised that there was a need not just to preserve access to open space, but also to create an institution that could buy and hold such properties in the interests of all. Hunter's original idea was a joint-stock company with the necessary economic clout and legal infrastructure to manage large tracts of land. Hill, on the other hand, favoured a trust (her proposed title was 'The Commons and Gardens Trust'), which would emphasise its benevolent purpose as opposed to its commercial acumen. At the top of her letter containing these suggestions Hunter scribbled two words: 'National Trust'. At an inaugural meeting held on 16 July 1894 the trust was born.* 'Mark my words, Miss Hill,' said the Duke of Westminster, who was its first president, 'this is going to be a very big thing.'⁹

There have been many biographies both of the National Trust's founding trio and of their famous institutional offspring. It is not an easy life story to narrate in linear form. For one thing, the organisation evolved in fits and starts, and the narrative centres on different places at different moments. Sometimes major developments occurred concurrently, but each with very different focus or consequence. But three clear elements stand out in its history.

The first is that the National Trust began life as a campaigning organisation, and open, green spaces for the usage and enjoyment of people were very much its origins. Recall Octavia Hill's initial attempt at a name: 'The Commons and Gardens Trust'.

The second salient fact was the importance of a legal entitlement framed by Sir Robert Hunter in what became known as the National Trust Act of 1907. This provision makes the organisation unique among all other environmental bodies, and a quasi-agent of the nation. From that date the Trust was allowed to confer on its property inalienable

---

* The actual date chosen by the organisation when celebrating its own centenary was 12 January 1895, which was the day its articles of association were registered under company law.

status, which meant that it could not be mortgaged, sold or taken away for other purposes. In truth, the UK government has found ways around the inalienable provision when so required. But its establishment and confirmation through subsequent National Trust Acts gave a strong guarantee to potential benefactors that their generosity could not be thwarted or overturned by life's vicissitudes. It made the gift as permanent as possible and steered the Trust towards its status as default recipient of private donations.

The third and more controversial element in its history was the marked shift during the 1930s from its original ethos to one in which the organisation became dominated by concern for built structures formerly owned by the aristocracy and landed gentry. It had always been engaged with the conservation of beautiful buildings. From the 1930s, however, the National Trust was primarily devoted to buying up or, more often, obtaining through gift, large country houses of a single powerful social group. In defence of the measures, one historian has observed that there 'was a widespread conviction that the [Second World] war would mean the end of one social order and the beginning of another'.[10] It was now or never to obtain a priceless and vanishing part of Britain's built heritage.

This change in emphasis by the National Trust was directly a consequence of what was called 'the Country House Scheme', floated by an aristocrat, Lord Lothian, whose estates included Blickling Hall, just fourteen miles from the north Norfolk coast and now the Trust's headquarters in the region. In 1934 he proposed that landowners could escape death duties, which rose from 50 per cent in his day to as much as 75 per cent by 1945 on assets valued at more than £1 million. However, if the owner left their land assets to the National Trust with its agreement, then these tax obligations could be waived, and in return they could keep part of the property as a rent-free residence. In short, they would lose their house but keep their home, and avoid the swingeing taxes into the bargain. Over the ensuing decades it led to a widespread transfer that enriched the Trust immeasurably, but it established a pattern and an image of the organisation from which it has never escaped.

Such was the attentiveness of both National Trusts to the architectural and landscape achievements of the aristocracy that, according to the historian Chris Smout, they possibly helped to smooth class relations in the twentieth century. A 'speculative case could be made', he suggests, 'that they delayed the abolition of the voting powers of the hereditary peers for nearly one hundred years.'[11]

It is certainly true that no one but its most partial devotees could deny the Trust's deep bias towards the cultural milieu of the upper classes. Its top officials, like its council members over 120 years, have been drawn from that same social cadre, many of whom were either related or family friends of one another. Famous will be the day when its chair, or even the chief executive, speaks with the traces of a working-class accent or, better still, bears evidence of a non-white ethnic descent. The National Trust is patrician in both make-up and ethos. At times, its refusal or inability to challenge the vested interest of the landed classes induces in it a form of political and cultural rigor mortis.

One obvious consequence of 'the Country House Scheme' is that the organisation now owns in excess of 200 historical properties like Blickling Hall. These places are peppered all over a National Trust map of Britain. Equally remarkable is that the Trust has probably acquired its extraordinary membership – surely the world's largest for any non-governmental 'environmental' organisation – directly *because* of its ownership of beautiful bricks and mortar. The American Paula Weideger, one of the more sceptical chroniclers of the National Trust story, has pointed out that 78 per cent of all members are recruited at properties or their associated shops. Less than one in eleven comes from its countryside or its coastal holdings.[12]

The exponential growth of the National Trust coincides precisely with this phase in its development. In 1933, just prior to the launch of the scheme, it had 2,750 members. After the war this jumped to 13,000, and there were already half a million people visiting its properties, and particularly its big posh houses.

Today the figure is in excess of 10 million. The number of subscribing members also rose rapidly with all those hordes that passed through the turnstiles. In 1950 it was 20,000, and by 1970 226,000. The first million was reached in 1981, and then the two-million mark by 1994. By 2014 this figure had more than doubled again.[13]

A more ambiguous blessing of this extraordinary process is the extent to which big houses dictated and still dictate the character of the Trust membership. Joining the organisation became a transactional arrangement. For an annual fee of around £100, a modern family gains free access to some of Britain's most important houses and their landscaped surroundings. This exchange is about value for money. For family weekend entertainment membership of the National Trust is one of the best deals in Britain. But what it quickly ceased to be about was supporting an organisation and underwriting its campaigning zeal. It was a swap rather than a cause; a purchase, not a moral statement about values.

The emphasis upon caring for Chippendale chairs as opposed to large copper butterflies may have been financially rewarding, and increased the organisation's theoretical clout by boosting membership numbers. Ironically, however, it also reduces the National Trust's actual ability to flex its membership muscle. Fear of offending its 5 million members is the tail that wags the dog.

A classic example occurred with a proclaimed return to the campaign trail under Dame Helen Ghosh, who has been the figurehead of the Trust's drive to confront climate change. Why would it not show concern about this issue? Setting aside that climate chaos threatens the very bases of our lives, the National Trust owns and manages longer stretches of vulnerable coastline than any other landowner except the Crown Estate. It possesses some of the most important land for wildlife in Britain. Why would it ignore the cardinal environmental challenge of the age?

Yet arguing for wind farms or solar panels or energy from sustainable sources is not how people wish to see the Trust use its time, resources and influence. 'To its four million members,' argued the *Daily Mail* columnist Quentin Letts in an attack on the policy shift, 'the National Trust evokes a bucolic image of the conservation of our history.' Another journalist, who claimed he would rather eat worms than renew his membership, pointed out that 'no longer, it seems, is the National Trust about preserving the glories of the English country house, connecting us with our past and conserving the 775 miles of coastline.' Implicitly, neither critic wishes to accept that the organisation has a campaigning remit. For them, the National Trust should only conserve 'our history' as if the past could be magically retained, corralled and made material. The bricks and mortar of the English country house are presumably the perfect means of connecting us with this rigorously stratified cultural past.[14]

In the same issue of the *Daily Mail* as Letts's attack was a letter from an ordinary member of the organisation, who responded thus: 'Thanks to Dame Helen Ghosh's political agenda outside of the true objectives of the National Trust, that's £100 membership saved this year.' Note here the absolute assumption that the member, far better than its director-general, knows exactly what the Trust's 'true objectives' are. Note also the repeated and explicit disavowal of campaigning that has any degree of political content.[15]

One cannot help reading of Hill's lifelong efforts for social housing, or of Hunter's tireless legal struggle to preserve open natural spaces for public use, or of Rawnsley's near-religious mission to preserve the beauty of upland landscapes, without concluding that the National Trust was born of social agitation and of cultural politics. The muddle over what precisely the National Trust stands for now and what its life mission should be has bedevilled the organisation almost since its inception.

In a curious way it somehow seems very British – absorbing fundamental contradictions and carrying on regardless in its own bumptious, brilliant, Churchillian manner. What is indisputable is both that the National Trust has always campaigned, and that one of these campaigns radically affected saltmarsh in north Norfolk.

The initiative was launched in 1963 and it was entitled Enterprise Neptune. Merlin Waterson, the Trust's former regional director in East Anglia, has called the scheme 'the most effective campaign' in its history, 'and its greatest achievement'.[16]

It is hard to disagree. I imagine that its three founders would have heartily approved not only of the scale of its ambition, but also of the quietly relentless way with which it has been pursued until the present day. At times there is something wonderfully bloody-minded about the Trust.

Essentially it began with a detailed inventory of Britain's entire coast. The findings were mixed. A third had already been completely trashed; a third was of little or no interest. The last fraction, a mere 900 miles, was to be bought for posterity. And it's still being bought.

It is perhaps more than coincidence that the first man in charge of Enterprise Neptune was none other than Commander Conrad Rawnsley, grandson to the indomitable and visionary Canon Rawnsley. His appointment, no less than his methods, was deeply controversial. In mid-campaign he had the temerity to lambast the Trust for having lost its founding ethic and zeal, especially in its concern to involve or reflect the lives of ordinary people. In Rawnsley's judgement it had become a toffs' club – complacent, high-handed, elitist. In particular, he criticised the Trust's work in the period since the 1930s when all it seemed to care about was hard-pressed aristocrats.[17]

Rawnsley's roughshod campaign may have created enemies and stirred up trouble, but it is hard to dispute that Enterprise Neptune returned the Trust to its original calling. Between 1965 and 1977 the organisation bought 199 miles of coast, to create a grand holding of 386 miles. Today, as stated earlier, it owns 775 miles.

Commander Rawnsley was eventually sacked for his insubordination and retired to north Norfolk, setting up home on the green at Burnham Market. Even into his nineties he simmered with resentment at the way the official histories had largely erased him from the Trust's collective memory. But he surely took pleasure from the fact that so much of the north Norfolk coast now has the Trust acorn on its title deeds. The grandson of Europe's most active volcano deserves immense credit.

Even before Neptune, in 1923 the National Trust had obtained a second key part of north Norfolk: Scolt Head Island. Like Blakeney, it is a stretch of high dune hemmed by creek and saltmarsh. It runs for 4 miles from directly opposite Commander Rawnsley's home in Burnham Market, right through to a point due north of Brancaster. Technically Scolt is a genuine island being encircled by tidal flow, yet you can easily walk there at low water. Its purchase protected the other key geomorphic feature in the county. Yet what really captures my imagination and illuminates the far-reaching nature of Enterprise Neptune – not to mention the radical character of the entire National Trust project – is all the further acquisition. Here are the Trust's purchases in chronological order:

Blakeney Point, 1912, 1,184 acres (479 ha)
Scolt Head Island, 1923–37, 1,621 acres (656.6 ha)
Brancaster, 1967, 2,150 acres (870 ha)
Morston Marshes, 1973–86, 588 acres (238 ha)
Stiffkey Saltmarshes, 1976, 487 acres (197 ha)
Gramborough Hill near Salthouse, 71 acres (28.6 ha)
Friary Farm, Blakeney, 1984, 80 acres (32.4 ha)
Branodunum Fort, Brancaster, 1984–5, 23 acres (9.3 ha)
Blakeney Freshes, 1986–9, 196 acres (79.3 ha)
Holme-next-the-Sea, 1991, 5 acres (2.2 ha)

I find it fascinating to reflect upon this series of purchases in north Norfolk in the light of Octavia Hill's personality and her original vision for the National Trust. Much of her reforming work was devoted not to place and nature, but to the housing and living conditions of the urban poor. However, in all fields to which she attended, she appeared to be one part fusspot nanny, one part deeply conservative Christian, but also one part radical vigilante. In the same way, her co-founding of the National Trust has about it a touch of socialism that should still astound us.[18] Speaking at an Oxford meeting about the first large parcel of land that the Trust acquired in the Lake District, Hill declared of Brandelhow, near Derwentwater:

It commands views of Skiddaw in one direction and Borrowdale in the other, from its slope you can see the whole space of the lake set with its islands, it has crag and meadow and wood, on it the sun shines, over it the wind blows, it will be preserved in its present loveliness and it belongs to you all and to every landless man, woman and child in England.[19]

There is perhaps an element of patrician condescension in her remark, yet there is also, surely, a touch of the Marxist, of the Leveller's sense of equality bound up within it.

It strikes me that there is a still strong strain of that Victorian radicalism in the Trust's determined acquisition of north Norfolk saltmarsh. In many ways it is the very antithesis of the country house and its showcase garden. For these landscapes, which were acquired without fanfare or fuss, are resistant to human access or human occupation, even at an imaginative level. By their very nature they are deceptive, churlish, dour, sometimes even positively hostile. It is one thing to buy a place that's famous, unique or conventionally beautiful. It is easy, in a way, to campaign for rare animals and unique habitats. It is not so easy, however, to champion a dripping gulley. It takes vision to see the worth of all that mind-mending mud. In a sense, saltmarshes are places for nobody. What better landscape, in a way, for us all?

Over the course of the twentieth century, conservation has become the preserve of a cadre of specialists, whose vocabulary is clogged with the technicalities of environmental science. At times the jargon seems to have become deliberately obscure. It is a language of professional exclusion. Yet something simpler is in the air tonight.

All I can tell you, as I stand at dusk on Stiffkey Greens, watching winter geese come to roost, is that immanent here is something Octavia Hill, Robert Hunter and Hardwicke Rawnsley knew in their bones. Lonely places are virtuous, and humankind is in need of them.

Of wintering wildfowl tonight there are two species. The brent geese move in tight globular units. Their contact notes seem gnarled and lowly, as if the charcoal-coloured birds have evolved vocalisations in close proximity to ground. They land among the brighter lawns of sea purslane and slowly waggle together with awkward steps; now that they are closer their calls seem chuntering, comical, familial. They have new warmth and intimacy, for the birds are, in truth, each other's neighbours or close relatives.

By contrast, the pink-footed geese fly high overhead in loose, swaying skeins that fall through the layers of sky towards the distant sea roar.

They drop into the dusk's pink afterglow over Warham, and steadily, towards the horizon, one by one, they plump down into the shadowy vegetation, their wings flickering in last light, the barking-dog notes fading and the white crescents at their tail bases marking the spot where each bird berths finally on the dark ground. The night and sky and marsh are one. I turn to go.

3

RSPB Soap

About a third of the way along the coast from Hunstanton, as you walk west to east, lies the tiny harbour of Burnham Overy Staithe. At one time this deserted creek was a key entrepôt for the international trade in wool. Throughout the medieval period boats plied out of here across the North Sea to Flanders, while another north Norfolk harbour further east at Blakeney once boasted a port more important than Great Yarmouth or Kings Lynn.

Now Burnham Overy Staithe and Blakeney are holiday resorts. At low tide in winter the pleasure yachts lie helplessly on their sides and the only sound of human origin is the insistent bell-like note of sail lines chafing on their naked masts. Stand on the deserted bank at Burnham Overy with your back to the village and you can look west all the way to the pines at Holme, close to where your walk began. Look east, and there's your destination. On the horizon the poplars march down Lady Ann's Drive, and between you and those trees is a landscape that shows what happens when saltmarsh is domesticated.

The conversion to grazing marsh began with the sea wall on which you stand. The bank was constructed in 1639 and was part of ongoing agricultural improvement in this area that was intensified by successive generations of a local dynasty, the most famous of them being 'Coke of Norfolk', Thomas William Coke, the noted agriculturalist, who was created Earl of Leicester in 1837. He had surrounded his family seat, the Palladian mansion known as Holkham Hall, with a great wooded park and planted it with 1,057,940 new trees. Not to be outdone by his illustrious father, the second earl did the same on the dune stretch that is visible on the seaward horizon. These 1.5 million plantings, mainly of Corsican pines, began in 1859 and now run in a 3-mile-long belt all the way to Wells-next-the-Sea.[1]

The trees stabilised the dunes, and the second earl then set about completing his encirclement of the Holkham saltmarsh with more seawalls on the eastern boundary. All the creeks silted up or were in-filled, while the salt-tolerant plants steadily turned to grass that sheep and stock could graze. Catch these rough and undulating pastures with the light at the right angle and you can still see traces of their wild origin. Across the fields are ridges and faint contours that mark where the tide once took its wriggling line back to sea. Should the depressions fill with winter rain all is suddenly plain: there, in the snaking rills of water, turned steely by the sun-blasted dazzle, are the ghost creeks of saltmarsh.

The bank heads north from Burnham Overy and then bends west into the dunes where the pines begin. At the start of the wood you can choose to walk by the sea, or on the landward edge. If you take the former route you will find the sand flats are sublimely empty and vast and, for those very reasons, it is headline Holkham, Hollywood Holkham too,* a beach where everyone goes.

The landward side of the dunes is a place of winter chiaroscuro – fast-flowing currents of sunlight through the trees that pool on the woodland floor or flare momentarily on the grey-flaked bases to the pines. Eventually this vertical geometry of light and shadow is lost in the dark wood, but details are particularised in such a place. There's the sharp cold call of a coal tit, the wheezy irritated notes from grey squirrels; here come a party of long-tailed tits shaped with the roundness of tiny toys, and laced together by a fabric of notes that tugs each bird from bush to bush and encircles them as a family unit.

For two summers in my twenties I worked at Holkham as assistant warden for the Nature Conservancy Council, and the whole long dark

---

* The closing scenes from *Shakespeare in Love*, where the Bard's amour, played by Gwyneth Paltrow, walks the desolate, loveless shore of a New World, were shot on Holkham beach.

stretch of trees is filled with a crop of thirty-year-old memories.* I still know the clearing in the woods where, on 25 February 1985, I saw my first arctic redpoll among an insatiably busy group of 100 common redpolls. The flock of birds, no member of which weighed more than half an ounce, was restless and unpredictable. Sometimes they could be approached to a few feet, yet one misjudged move and all would blizzard away like windblown scraps of lichen. The flock would swirl as a single organism and land in a tree, where it showered the surroundings with its nasal invertebrate buzz; or it would twist mid-flight like a sheet and return, plumping down almost exactly on the spot it had just left. Distinctly, now and then, the arctic redpoll would be among them in plain sight.

The species breeds as far north as any small bird on Earth: in northernmost Greenland and Ellesmere Island in Canada. The tiny body was almost lost in dense feathering, its bill no more than a cone poking from a feathered boa. The plumage was far thicker than that of its redpoll companions. The pin-thin black legs emerged from a swathe of loose down around the thighs which looked like long white pantaloons. Cold-coloured, a blend of tundra bryophyte flecked with snow, the bird was what it seemed – a scrap of the frozen north on Holkham's close-cropped rabbit lawns.

Where the pines finally end at Wells harbour I reach the kissing gate that leads onto the gravel car park. The details of this ordered geometric space are entirely prosaic – parking-ticket machines, tarmac, upright posts, white road markings and, across the small lake known as Abraham's Bosom, trailers crammed end to end in a caravan park that is closed for

---

* It was originally the Nature Conservancy, but changed to the Nature Conservancy Council in 1973. Its final dismemberment in 1989 gave rise to three separate offspring. They were English Nature, Scottish Natural Heritage and the Countryside Commission for Wales. In 2006 English Nature was then rebranded as Natural England and brought within the bounds of the government department for agriculture, once MAFF and renamed DEFRA in 2001 (Department for the Environment, Food and Rural Affairs). The Welsh offspring of the NCC has also changed identity once more. In 2013 it was merged with the Welsh branches of the Environment Agency and the Forestry Commission to become Natural Resources Wales.

winter. Having come to the end of the afternoon walk, people sit on the tailgates of their vehicles changing footwear, or they stow dogs on back seats before cars steadily pull away until the place is empty.

The failing light and steady drainage of human company are a stimulant to my final recollection this afternoon. For it was here, just through the gate, in this car park, that I made a first active contribution to conservation. For six weeks in February and March of 1985, earning £11 a day, I worked in tandem with a colleague – three or four days on, three days off – for the Royal Society for the Protection of Birds.

I lived in a tiny caravan that had no toilet, was lit by gas lamp and heated by a two-ring burner. My temporary home was a can of artificial warmth in a freezing cold car park. Each morning a first duty was to take my mattress outside to dry off the night's accumulated condensation. The inconveniences were part and parcel of life on the conservation frontline. I was not there for pleasure, but for the adventure.

My task was to watch over Britain's only breeding pair of a small Scandinavian bird called the parrot crossbill. The species is a specialist feeder on pine seeds in the boreal forests of western continental Europe. Occasionally, if their particular food crop fails them, parrot crossbills will wander abroad in search of new sources. A small number had been in Britain since the early 1980s, and one pair had elected to breed in trees immediately adjacent to the car park in Wells. My role was to give them a chance of success.

Wells is among the busiest walking spots in the Norfolk countryside. Even in February the cars of dog walkers arrive at dawn. All day I would be immersed in duties, a key part of which was to keep check on the birds' progress. Even more of my time was spent fielding enquiries from the steady stream of curious visitors, whose first inkling that something was afoot was my own short-lived residence at one end of the site. Therein lay a strange kind of paradox. I was, at once, to keep the celebrity nest free from disturbance, but also to broadcast the birds' presence to anyone who cared to enquire.

By day all went well, and my life was full of companionship and conversation. It was the onset of late afternoon, with its customary reassertion of winter frost, that induced the recurring melancholy. The same rituals would all unfold: a steady shrinkage of daylight, the ebbing away of visitors to the last few, the final cones of brightness from headlights as the cars tunnelled through the darkness to Wells, and then the rhythmic sea roar restoring itself as the only sound in that spot until dawn. I was cocooned once more in cold and solitude.

In 1985 the only way my partner Mary and I could talk while I was wardening was for us to coordinate our visits to our nearest respective telephone boxes. In that era before laptops and mobiles, the RSPB had however, at least worked out one hi-tech link to my avian wards. From Boots the chemists they had bought a battery-operated cot-listening device and put it at the base of the nest tree. The gizmo had originally been marketed at first-time parents, who could keep permanent tabs on their snoozing infant when in a part of the house other than the nursery. In truth, the devices were almost useless. One could barely make out anything above the crackling static of the cheap-quality microphone.

But mine was rigged up from the nest tree to the caravan, theoretic-ally to alert me if any nefarious assault were attempted by an egg collector. Nothing ever happened, and all I ever heard from the speaker, posted by my bed, was the night wind soughing through the branches, or the occasional hysteria from an oystercatcher spooked on the tideline. Yet that theoretical twenty-four-hour guard was very much part of the publicity and ethos of the protection scheme.

At that time, this was classic RSPB. In fact, it is still. For all its exist-ence the organisation has been a master both at winning attention for the lives and dramas of birds, and engendering our own emotional entanglement in their affairs. The determination to take direct action, but simultaneously to capture public attention for its effort, are both fundamental to RSPB operations on this coast, as they are elsewhere.

Just eleven miles west of Wells-next-the-Sea is Titchwell, one of the very busiest of the RSPB's 200-plus reserves nationwide. Here the subliminal messages in the service of wildlife are everywhere. As you sit in the café even the napkins continue the brand reinforcement. RSPB coffee is 'Bird-Friendly' and meets a standard designated by the Smithsonian Migratory Bird Commission. The seafood is approved by the Marine Stewardship Council; the chickens' eggs are free-range, the hot drinks Fair Trade. On the table is a laminated leaflet on RSPB volunteers, with an image of local folk smiling with TV personality Chris Packham. The RSPB blackboard by the RSPB menu asks customers to 'Vote for Bob', the RSPB's red squirrel standing up for nature at the 2015 general election.

As you walk down the track to the sea along what is surely the busiest footpath in all Norfolk, it is the deep contrast between the two sides that strikes you most forcefully. To the west, towards Thornham and Holme, is an expanse of saltmarsh, with all its remoteness and uniformity (it is one of the few large patches of the habitat that doesn't belong to the National Trust). To the east is the RSPB's Titchwell reserve, dominated by three large rectangular lagoons and overwhelmingly busy with flocks of birds. What really draws the eye, however, are those at minimum range on the edge of the scrapes by the track.

Some are the very same birds you can never quite get to see on the saltmarsh. Here, suddenly, they are at your feet: mallard, gadwall, teal, shelduck, all in quiet pairs skirting the pool edge, then a scatter of ruff, redshank, curlews and dunlins.

Almost under your nose is a pair of spotted redshanks. They are so incredibly close that you can enjoy the marginal details separating them from common redshank – the inch extra in the leg and bill and a stronger shade of grey in the upperparts – but you can also see the tiniest micro-features of individual feathers and the very light that shines in their eyes as their beaks sweep the shallows. As you watch them you cannot help but feel on intimate terms with them. It's this orchestrated entwining of bird and human experience that the organisation seeks to provide for members and visitors, and which has become a part of its institutional DNA.

It was there even at the moment the RSPB was born. Of the major charitable conservation groups, this is the oldest. That first gulp of air happened in a well-to-do suburb of south Manchester in a middle-class villa called The Croft. In 1889 the issue that had called the good ladies of Didsbury to arms was a hundred-year-old penchant for feathers in female millinery – hats, boas, ruffs, costume trimmings. At the end of the nineteenth century the fad had become a global craze, so that every tea-girl or housemaid in her Sunday best felt dowdy without at least a spray of bright birds' plumage in her costume. The effect of this was devastating. The calculated tonnage of fine feathers officially entering the fashion salons of Paris and London alone between 1870 and 1920 is just under 64,000.[2]

It translated into the slaughter of hundreds of millions of beautiful birds of all kinds – finches, hummingbirds, parrots, birds of paradise. But neither the grimy nor the downright ugly were disdained: even vultures and marabou storks were killed. The holocaust was global and, in some species, nearly terminal (the Chinese egret is still exceptionally rare today).

The most affected were the very creatures that now loom so dramatically out of the Norfolk saltmarsh: the egrets, but especially the little egret's large cousin, the great egret. In breeding dress these white herons all sport lacy diaphanous plumes on their backs, and those 'aigrettes', as they were known, were in highest demand for haute couture. Another of the birds harvested in Britain was the great crested grebe, whose density of plumage exceeds all others. 'Grebe fur' was the name for the processed skins and, while they had been used in civic costume since the Middle Ages, the Victorian craze unleashed catastrophic levels of consumption. By the 1860s Britain's grebes were down to 32 pairs (today there are 6,000).[3]

What the middle-class women of Didsbury could perhaps have never known is the power of their cause. Despite being without the vote – and, perhaps more accurately, precisely *because* they were so disenfranchised – these remarkable females took the fight to their own hat-wearing, hat-buying sex, and won. One tactic was to go to church armed with prayer book and notepad. While most were singing the words from the former they would write down in the latter the names of those with offending hats. Come Monday there would be a letter in the hall accusing them of murder. By 1921 these efforts had been pivotal to the trade being halted almost worldwide.

What is telling about this particular environmental creation myth is that the other harvests or lethal bi-products of industrialised

Britain – the whales, seals and penguins that were rendered down in their millions to produce domestic oil, the voracious consumption of countryside for factories and houses, or the raw poisons that boiled into the skies or poured into the rivers of England from Victorian industry – failed to galvanise the national imagination in quite the same way as feathers in hats. A concern about cruelty to animals of all kinds had been an expanding cause of nineteenth-century society for decades. Yet this cultural development had centred largely on domestic animals or creatures kept for entertainment, such as fighting cocks and dogs. The concern for wild birds seemed to represent a fresh departure.

However, legislation to protect birds had very deep roots in this country. It originated in the Anglo-Norman passion for hunting. In fact, the first laws that could be broadly construed as environmental were a sequence of royal decrees dating back to the twelfth century that made it an offence to take or destroy the nests and eggs of breeding birds of prey. The purpose was to preserve the basic raw materials on which the medieval devotion to falconry was founded.

Another key strand of legislation emanated from concern for the second major element of hunting – the species that served as the sportsman's target. In the modern period three birds had become a holy trinity for the landed classes: the non-native common pheasant, the native grey partridge and the so-called 'King of Game Birds', a race of willow ptarmigan endemic to Britain and known as the red grouse. The issue over who had access to these edible fowl – and more precisely, who had the right to kill them – evolved into a major anxiety. In the first sixty years of the eighteenth century there were five parliamentary acts dealing with the poaching of small game, but from 1760 to 1820 there were well over fifty such pieces of legislation.[4] Birds had become a British, but particularly an English, obsession. John Ruskin once asked mischievously, 'Have English gentlemen, as a class, any other real object in their whole existence than killing birds?'[5]

It is perhaps a smaller step than we imagine from a preoccupation with killing birds to an equally impassioned concern to halt that slaughter. The 'repentant butchers' was a semi-humorous name that early environmentalists used to describe their own Damascene conversion from one to the other. The first truly environmental legislation, whose aim was simple preservation of wild birds for their own sake, was an act of 1869, designed to spare seabirds from wanton carnage by so-called sportsmen. The Society for the Protection of Birds was born of that cultural volteface prompted, in part, by an increasing awareness that nature was finite: that feathers, especially tons of feathers, exposed limits at source.

After the society had helped to force a ban on the milliners' trade in plumes it soon began to rail against an entire repertoire of commonplace Edwardian cruelties. One long campaign was fought against the trapping of songsters – larks, linnets and goldfinches – for the thriving trade in caged birds that inserted an element of wild song into the heavy brocades and darkly varnished furnishings of the early twentieth-century parlour. Millions of male skylarks that migrated to Britain ended up in tiny cages in ill-lit living rooms, singing for their miserable lives.

What is so striking about the origins of the RSPB, which acquired its royal charter in 1904, is the extent to which it was a feminine entity. It was largely by women for women and against the consumption of birds in female costume. By 1899 it had a membership of nearly 26,000 in 152 national branches. Most of those members had to pledge that, apart from domesticated ostrich plumes, their hats were feather-free. The leading lights of the RSPB in this founding phase were also female, especially the long-serving secretary and president, respectively Margaretta Louisa Lemon and Winifred Cavendish Bentinck, the dowager Duchess of Portland, who sustained her duties for sixty-five years.

In truth, this astonishing first phase had largely run its effective course by the time the world went back to war in 1939. But the RSPB soon rose again in the hands of a new, largely male, professional conservation corps, whose successes marched in close step with three other key developments of the post-war period: increased mobility, increased income and greater leisure for a burgeoning middle class. On 20 July 1957 when the Prime Minister Harold Macmillan told a rally in Bedford that 'most of our people have never had it so good', the RSPB had 7,000 members.

Almost exactly ten years later, when the Beatles announced to the world (or, at least, to the 400 million who watched the first performance of the song) that all we needed was love, the membership had trebled. By the time I joined the Young Ornithologists' Club in 1973 aged thirteen, it had trebled again. There were now 100,000 of us.

In the period that I was enlisted in its junior ranks, one of the key mechanisms for RSPB recruitment was an annual touring film show. Up and down the country, over several nights at popular cinema or theatre venues, there would be a local screening of purpose-made RSPB films. Sometimes I would attend several nights in succession. I can still recall that in 1973 in Buxton the headline event was called *The Land of the Simmer Dim*. It was about the wildlife of the Shetland Isles, narrated in the impossibly soft and seductive accents of genuine islanders such as its legendary naturalist Bobby Tulloch. In the way of those old celluloid flicks, the landscapes and wildlife looked as if they had been hand-coloured after the footage was obtained, while the musical score overlaying those shaky images wandered in and out of key.

But to me, and to people like me, it was magical and hugely persuasive. The annual coming to town of the RSPB to show wildlife films was a highlight of our calendar. It was in the tradition of the low-church evangelists of the eighteenth century or the temperance meetings of the nineteenth. It mingled social entertainment with political and moral persuasion. Quietly, subtly, with distorted chords and blurred images, we were being asked to pledge to nature. And many of us did.

Rob Hume, the long-standing editor of the RSPB's magazine *Birds* and a former lifelong employee of the organisation, recalls how incredibly successful those film-show recruitment drives were. In big cities such as Birmingham or Sheffield it was not unusual to recruit 100 new members in a night. Over one or two evenings the films would be screened to audiences of thousands, and there would often be special matinees for schoolchildren. Simple advertisements in local newspapers to accompany the film events were equally effective. By the end of the twentieth century RSPB membership plateaued at around a million. Today it has risen again to 1.2 million.

What the new army of members licensed was the purchase of properties like Titchwell, which was bought in 1973. It means that, like me, the place is emblematic of that surging phase of RSPB growth. Yet it is still salutary to recall that the site has been under their protection for only a little over four decades. The social developments that converted Titchwell into one of the most visited portions of Norfolk coast may have their roots in an age before motor cars, but the emergence of conservation as a genuinely effective private enterprise is much more recent.

My own modest, six-week role in 1985 as part of the parrot crossbill team at Wells also speaks volumes about the entire ethos and approach of the organisation. The working model for that kind of activity – guarding rare birds in situ – was and still is, arguably, the RSPB's most celebrated project ever: the ongoing Operation Osprey at Loch Garten in the Highlands. When I sat in my caravan at Wells, the Scottish scheme was the same age as I was, twenty-five. The somewhat paramilitary-style title now seems little more than a calculated appeal to our sense of the dramatic, yet at its inception in 1959 Operation Osprey's whiff of hands-on guerrilla action for nature had real substance.

With their five-foot wingspan, ospreys are eagle-sized predators with an incomparable gift for catching fish. The bird's primary strategy, a dramatic plunge-dive after which it rises from the water amid a rainbow gauze of diamond droplets, often with a trout writhing in its talons, is one of the most unforgettable sights in all British nature. During the nineteenth century the species had bred widely in the Highlands, and prior to that date it had probably occurred throughout the whole mainland of Britain.

Persecution on account of those fish-eating habits, or merely on the grounds that they possessed the raptor's hooked beak and claw, drove them inexorably from human presence. The straths of northern Scotland eventually became their only redoubt. There they attracted the unwanted but relentless attentions of several major Victorian predators – the egg collector, the sportsman and the killer of rare creatures who helped stock the taxidermist's shop window. By 1916 their collective works had entirely eliminated ospreys from the country as a breeding species.

Following a 40-year absence, however, the birds attempted a tentative return, only to be met, time after time, with the nihilism of the nest robber. Operation Osprey was the RSPB response, a moral battle of life and death, whose genius lay not in any protective veil of secrecy, but in the flash-bulb-popping glare of publicity that they swathed around the birds' nest tree. By the end of the first year 14,000 visitors had trooped to Garten to view the celebrity birds. On its twenty-fifth anniversary, while I sat eating muesli in my Wells caravan, Operation Osprey had clocked up a million tourists.

If you visit the present project at Loch Garten, you realise what an impressive and slick piece of social theatre it is still. Each year it receives about 30,000 people and has a recruitment target of around 550 new members. It is box-office stuff, especially if you factor in that ospreys are not a particularly difficult bird to see in Britain today. There are currently 300 pairs and, with luck, you can see them on almost any Scottish loch. Last time I drove to the Highlands I chanced on three without searching hard at any known locality. A week later I saw one in Wales, because there are also several pairs in that country now, as well as a thriving introduced population in middle England. For most of Loch Garten's visitors, however, that single osprey pair is probably the first they have ever seen. The support staff works skilfully to help them feel that it is still the only one.

When I called to meet the impressive all-female crew who run the project I came away with two key reflections. Regardless of the security of its population and ongoing increase of this fish-eating bird in Britain, the organisation meticulously sustains the idea of moral mission. Every night there assembles what the staff call their 'forward team', a group of RSPB members who sleep underneath the nest just in case of some undisclosed attack. Once it was an essential tactic to thwart the efforts of egg collectors or vandals.

Now that same input serves no truly meaningful conservation purpose, except in this sense: it binds the imaginations of all those worthy unpaid people to the cause. Some of them have been coming for decades and, no doubt, each return to this wonderful place under-pins their commitment and their associated sense of camaraderie. Over its entire life, Operation Osprey must have enlisted the support of several thousand volunteers. It has turned birds' lives into an emotionally involving process, and has made nature matter to people. In a sense, Operation Osprey means nothing and everything to conservation effort in Britain.

The second reflection arose from a conversation with the young warden leading the public-engagement team. She spoke of the marginal decline in visitor interest and numbers. What would really galvanise the tourist imagination and bring the journalists back, she suggested, is some shenanigans at the osprey nest itself. Ironically, there is nothing quite like a bit of villainy to stir conservation's pulse. Once it was a hooded intruder at the nest tree's wire-wrapped base, but better still today is some illicit conduct by the avian occupants themselves.

She added that, just down the road at another well-known Scottish osprey watch point, they were in clover because the breeding pair had become a *ménage à trois*. The newspapers and television reporters were having a field day with this spicy *affaire de cœur de Balbuzard pêcheur*. The chief of operations mused wistfully on how much better it would be if only her ospreys would do something equally exotic. Alas, 'EJ' and 'Odin', as the Garten birds are known, are just your regular boring couple.

Most telling was her revelation that a raptor love triangle not only brings more visitors, but also has a directly translatable impact on the numbers of new members the RSPB can recruit at Loch Garten. In short, the closer it gets to an avian *EastEnders*, the deeper the public response. Therein lies a striking irony. So much of the RSPB's efforts over the last 130 years are about the value and importance of other species, yet the more the creatures resemble us, the more the public seems to care.

Despite that anomaly it is important to note how the organisation's attention to other species provides a fundamental distinction between itself and the National Trust. Although both have essentially devoted themselves to the preservation of semi-wild places, and while both have mass memberships and are among the largest charitable landowners in Britain (the two National Trusts combined have 800,000 acres, compared with the RSPB's 323,000 acres), and hold some of our most important, wildlife-rich countryside, they are substantially different in character and method.

What galvanised the spirit of Hill and Hunter and set Canon Rawnsley rushing to the barricades in his beloved Lakes was something essentially about us. It was the impact of open space and beautiful places, including handsome buildings, upon our experience. It was the opportunity to walk in fresh air, to feel the grass underfoot, to enjoy the scenery, to perceive beauty however it might be manifest. Their concern was to secure these as part of a birthright for Britons. And the transaction involves two components: the material landscape in which those wholesome effects are immanent, and the human spirit that responds and connects to the physical stimuli. But the process is located, measured and validated within. The National Trust's mission is rooted in the human heart.

The RSPB's philosophical position begins on the other side of this human–nature nexus. It exists to serve other species: the non-human parts of life. It campaigns to preserve wild birds and now, since it too, like the National Trust, has undergone a recent substantial shift in emphasis, the entire natural community of wild animals and plants. It lobbies at both a political and cultural level for national agricultural and planning policies to accommodate wildlife. It owns and manages land precisely to maximise the indwelling communities on each habitat. Its staff includes at least sixty professional scientists, not to mention their administrative and technical support colleagues, to shape and fine-tune their management policies on behalf of other species. The National Trust, in comparison, has only recently acquired specialised ecologists of any kind. This doesn't mean that the National Trust has not been an effective preserver of wildlife, or that the RSPB overlooks the way in which people are moved and enriched by their encounters with nature – but each organisation starts from the opposite end of this chain of cause and effect.

Another fundamental issue that separates them is their relationship with their members. As we have seen, the National Trust subscription has become largely transactional. As the eminent environmentalist Peter

Marren has noted, 'The public loves a bargain, and for the modest membership fee the whole of the Trust's vast estate is open to them.'[6] This was never the RSPB's way, and in 2007 it codified the distinction by operating without a fixed monetary figure as a fee to join. People decide for themselves what they want to pay. It places the fulcrum of connection between the individual and organisation in that precise sphere of moral choice. The question is not what your membership does for you, but what being a member *means* to you. The implicit assumption is that joining the RSPB is about caring for nature, and you place your money on the thing you hold dear.*

The insistence on values before value for money marches in close step with the organisation's entire ethos. As its former conservation director Mark Avery has noted, 'the RSPB funds all conservation work from cash flow, and its financial reserves would only run the organisation for about twelve weeks if money stopped coming in.' The RSPB lives and dies in pursuit of its mission.

It has created one fundamental dividend: in today's environmental climate, when formal government bodies like Natural England or Natural Resources Wales (even the name of the latter speaks of its emasculation) have been essentially muzzled, the RSPB is the de facto official voice of nature in Britain, and *not* the much larger, theoretically more powerful, National Trust. Both organisations are institutionalised and bureaucratic – after all, they manage memberships in seven figures – and both are conservative and cautious. In fact, a recurrent concern is that both have become morally becalmed by anxiety over upsetting their members. However, on the issue of moral commitment the RSPB overwhelms its larger sibling hands down.

Underlying its fundamental sense of purpose is the implication that the RSPB is engaged in a form of cultural struggle for nature, albeit

---

* One wonders if this moral emphasis to membership may have cost the RSPB some of the massive recruitment enjoyed by the Trust. In 1973 their respective positions were 226,000 (NT) as opposed to 100,000 (RSPB) members. Since then, and during the period of greatest expansion in all environmental organisations, the ratio has gone from about 2:1 to 4:1 in favour of the National Trust. As Peter Marren emphasised, 'the public loves a bargain.'

against some largely undisclosed opponent. So often one detects a buffering sense of sectarian belief in RSPB staff. It was powerfully in evidence at Loch Garten when I was there. Neither of the young wardens I talked to said they had ever considered a job with the National Trust: there was just too little in the latter's character to inspire them.

I probably felt the same thing thirty years ago, as I stood by my caravan in the March sun after another damp night alone in the car park. There it was the next day: a small sense of triumph when the male parrot crossbill resumed his jumbled, tuneless ditty on his favourite song perch; and from a specific spot among the trees I could see the female's bulbous grey head and her bright eye above the lip of the nest, sitting still on her eggs. There was the pallid warmth of the sun on her back as there was on mine. My shirtsleeves were rolled up; it was another day guarding nature.

4

A LARGE NUMBER OF LOCAL RESERVES

As you walk east from Wells harbour along the ten-mile stretch of saltmarsh to Cley, St Nicholas' Church on the hill at Blakeney comes to measure your westering progress. Then you finally come close to this well-known Norfolk village, and perspective causes that imposing four-toothed ecclesiastical tower to sink into its orbit of trees. And when you finally turn north from the harbour along the raised bank enclosing Blakeney Fresh Marsh, a new fixture looms on the horizon. It is just five storeys tall and stands virtually at sea-level, yet the old mill at Cley acquires monumental proportions.

It is the one significant building in this landscape, a structure visible at all times in an utterly flat place, and perhaps the only measure of singularity in what is arguably Norfolk's most famous village. However, Cley-next-the-Sea is a location that, on first acquaintance, is easy to underestimate. An old hotel called the George, a pub, the Three Swallows, four to five shops and a quaint curving street of flint-faced cottages with a shallow hem of wet grassland: it is not the most arresting settlement on the coast.

It cannot wow you with its clifftop location or topographical drama. Nor does it enfold you in the picturesque like some beauty spot in the Cotswolds or the Derbyshire Dales. There is a line of beech and sycamore on the hill behind to soften the horizon and, come spring, to mingle a primary colour into Cley's winter pastels. Until then, however, the village is dominated by the sumptuous softness of reed and the multitudinous grey shades of the bare shingle.

For all that blended ordinariness, Cley, like its immediate neighbour Blakeney Point, is woven into the creation myth of a major environmental organisation, the devolved county-based structure known collectively today as the Wildlife Trusts, and the last of the group routinely referred to as 'the big three', which includes the National Trust and the RSPB. It is the youngest of the trio, and the establishment of a nature reserve at Cley in 1926 marked its effective beginning.

What is so telling about this particular story is the way it also comments on the initial limitations of the National Trust to serve as a genuine campaigner for the environment in the early twentieth century. It also draws into its orbit the complex failures of yet another conservation pioneer, a body few can recall today but which was known as the Society for the Promotion of Nature Reserves (SPNR). Full of promise, radical and, in many ways, ahead of its time, the SPNR was eventually subsumed in the more conventional but concrete achievements that were initiated in north Norfolk in the spring of 1926. The failure of one and the success of the other are now inextricably linked in the story of the Wildlife Trusts.

Let's begin with that triumph at Cley. Like many early conservation initiatives, it has some of its origins in the killing of birds. The suaeda thickets between Blakeney and Salthouse are strategically placed to intercept and harbour waves of continental birds passing south in autumn, or, conversely, north in spring. Among the flocks of more common European migrants are occasional lost wanderers and rare visitors from Siberia or North America. In 1896 one such scrap of Asiatic feathers proved to be Britain's first ever example of a species known as Pallas's warbler.

These avian 'sports' galvanised the interests of a local sub-group in the Victorian bird-hunting tribe known as 'the Gentlemen Gunners'.*

---

* In his book *Cley Marsh and Its Birds*, Billy Bishop, the second in a family dynasty that has wardened the reserve since 1926, gives a graphic account of the ways of the Gentleman Gunners. The start of their season was fuelled by the purchase of 1,000 cartridges and good supplies of rum and beer. After a heavy night in the George or the White Horse at Blakeney, the slaughter began on 1 September and 'with first light', wrote Bishop, 'came pandemonium'. Because all that bird killing was thirsty work, the Gentlemen had pre-hidden beer supplies in convenient rabbit holes along the shore.

They were a band of upper-middle-class shooting folk who invariably sought to blast and then immortalise their finds through the arts of the taxidermist. One such stuffer of rare birds, H. N. Pashley, had set up shop in Cley, and his emporium of skins became a focal point for both this community of rarity chasers and their various avian discoveries. The Pallas's warbler of 1896, for example, was prepared by Pashley and sold for an astonishing £40, the equivalent today of about £700 per gram of this 6-gram midget.[1]

Mingled with the allure of the rarities was Cley's other major natural asset: the mixture of pools, shallows and mud fringes along Cley's coastal marsh. Go today and stand at the North Hide blind in August,* or wander out to the complex of beautifully thatched shelters in the middle of this wonderful reserve, and you get a full sense of why the place captivated so many bird-hunters.

For this is a wader spot par excellence. These birds are some of the world's great wanderers, many breeding at the northern limits of terra firma on Earth. However, come the winter they can be on the shores of Namibia, or out in the mid-Pacific. At Cley in autumn here they all are, pausing briefly amid the warm clear light of the Norfolk coast: greenshank, curlews, redshank, godwits, ruff, dunlin, wood sandpipers, knot, golden plovers, stints, whimbrel – sometimes up to twenty-five species on one pool – where their movements are relentless and fickle.

Often they sweep up in globes of anxiety, and just as suddenly they land and resume their intense mechanical up-and-down action, mud-jabbing on interweaving paths. And for now the birds look perfectly at home. As they feed, their busy reflections are mirrored precisely in the pool's still water, where they look as fragile as the September thistledown floating on its surface. Then you wake the next day and they are all gone.

For the Gentleman Gunners stalking such prey was considered grand sport, but what started in the Victorian era as recreation slowly by the

---

* The surge tide of November 2013 smashed up and carried away the substantial structure once known as the North Hide, and a substitute blind, erected by the Norfolk Wildlife Trust, now marks its former spot.

new century acquired a moral dimension. In 1901 a group of locally based enthusiasts had set up a protection society to fund and direct what were in effect professional summer wardens, known at that time as 'watchers'. (The warden's house at Cley is still known as 'Watcher's Cottage'.) Throughout the period the RSPB had used this same strategy, employing skilled field observers at ornithological hotspots such as Dungeness in Kent. By 1920 they enjoyed the services of twenty-nine such watchers in 13 locations at a cost of £405.[2]

Yet the middle-class professionals who raised the funds to secure these local services eventually came to realise that their best means of safeguarding the wildlife was also to control the land. In 1926 the opportunity arose to acquire Cley's hallowed marshes, when they came up for sale at the death of the owner. Sydney Long was a Norwich-based doctor born in Wells-next-the-Sea and already had a strong record of conservation efforts on that coast. He attended the auction and made a successful bid of £5,160 (about £282,000 in 2015 values) for the entire 407 acres.*

Who knows what mixture of bold vision and private anxiety might have gripped the good doctor once he'd raised that finger. But a week later Long, with his 'fair drooping moustache – like a gentle Viking'– gathered a few friends in the George and put to them his brainchild of a formal organisation that would work to secure properties for wildlife.[3] It was incorporated in November 1926 with Long as its honorary secretary and a title, the Norfolk Naturalists Trust.

Even in the 1920s purchasing land in the interests of nature was still a radical and daring project. As we have seen, the stock RSPB measures had been to employ watchers both to protect birds directly from disturbance, and to work within existing bird-protection legislation to prosecute those who contravened the law. During the 1920s a

---

* The exact area of Cley bought by Long is confused. Martin George uses the customary figure of 407 acres in his account of Norfolk conservation in *The Birds of Norfolk* (1999). The Trust itself in its commemorative fiftieth-anniversary history defined it as exactly 400 acres (*Nature in Trust*, p. 16), but the original poster for the auction indicates 435 acres. I am grateful to David North for showing me a facsimile of this historical document.

large 1,100-acre parcel of Dungeness in Kent had come up for sale. The site held important populations of scarce breeding birds and the RSPB had been posting their watchers to guard them for years. However, when it came to buying the place outright it could neither find the wherewithal to do so (for £5,500), nor have faith in a fund-raising campaign. It met in conference to debate the issue, where its committee concluded that Dungeness, with 'its birds and desolation would not appeal to the British public in the least'.[4]

The one organisation that had pioneered the acquisition of land was the National Trust. By 1919 it had pursued the policy over three decades and already held 63 properties and 6,000 acres. Yet it also had unique assets. It had had the initial high-profile leadership of Octavia Hill. It had a powerful network of aristocratic supporters, and it also had that special act of parliament, designed by Sir Robert Hunter, which meant that donations to the National Trust were inalienable and as secure as any property could be in such uncertain times.

In Norfolk the National Trust had set the environmental precedent in 1912, with the creation of the reserve at Blakeney. That achievement wasn't quite all it seemed. It may have been one of the Trust's most important wildlife sites to date, but the driving force behind the acquisition had been a London-based academic called Professor Francis Oliver. He, in conjunction with others including Sydney Long, had spearheaded the campaign to acquire Blakeney and Scolt Head Island for the National Trust. In effect, the latter was a beneficiary of other people's zeal, and Oliver would eventually become disillusioned with the Trust's inaction, even though he had served himself on its executive committee.

One of the major donors to the Blakeney appeal was a Northamptonshire-based banker called Charles Nathaniel Rothschild (of whom more later). For now it is sufficient to add that the National Trust was no stranger to Rothschild's brand of wildlife-inflected benef-icence. It was he who had brought about the organisation's first high-profile nature reserve, when he had given it a small area of Wicken Fen in 1899. That land had been gifted with a proviso that the Trust take account of its important population of swallowtail butterflies.

The hint of latent caution in Rothschild's caveat reflected something that came to dominate perception of the National Trust after the First World War. Naturalists increasingly recognised that the organisation could not and would not act as the default champion of nature when important wildlife areas were threatened. This was partly because the Trust had found that properties donated to it without some supporting financial legacy could be a drain on its own limited resources. It just couldn't afford to take on everyone's pet project. It was also a reflection of the fact that the board of the National Trust was not solely concerned with biodiversity.

Landscape beauty or amenity and, eventually, bricks and mortar weighed as heavily as any concern for a site's wildlife riches. In fact, after 1918 the Trust had expressed unwillingness to accept properties that were 'only of interest to the naturalist'. In 1923 it acted on this self-limiting proposition when it refused Woodwalton Fen, even after first Rothschild and then his widow offered this magnificent Cambridgeshire site (along with a handsome cash endowment). Similarly, in 1926 the National Trust rejected the idea that it assume responsibility for Cley Marsh in Norfolk.[5]

It is in light of this reluctance to act that one understands the full significance of Sydney Long's boldly raised index finger at the Cley auction in March 1926. He had decided to go it alone. In the process he founded a new way of doing nature conservation. The Norfolk Naturalists Trust drew on a number of key strengths that were to transform environmentalism in this country. One of these was something the new organisation had in common with the National Trust. Their initial strength lay in the support offered by the same cadre of upper-middle-class and aristocratic naturalists who had the education, time, money and opportunity to pursue their cultural concerns for Britain's shrinking natural heritage. They also possessed the necessary legal and business acumen to create the formal structures necessary to buy and hold land.

But a problem for the National Trust was the implication of that first word in its title: it was a countrywide project. The opportunities and challenges across the whole of Britain – and, as we know, its board more or less ignored Scotland completely in its first four decades – were many. The available resources were limited, however, a group of like-minded friends living within, and focused upon, a single county had a natural coherence. The narrower geographical compass meant that people who filled the committees and oversaw its affairs generally lived close to one another. It was practically convenient. It also tapped into that local pride and connection to place which people feel for their home county. It would prove to be an enduring and winning combination.

There was instant confirmation of this when Sydney Long's friend, a man called J. W. Castle, was inspired to stump up the lion's share of the purchase price for Cley: an extraordinary £4,000, a private gift that would be worth £207,000 today.[6] Barely eighteen months later the Norfolk Naturalists Trust was back in business, bidding for a twenty-acre patch at Martham, and by 1930 the ambition ran to the whole of Alderfen Broad, with its hinterland where swallowtail butterflies thrived.[7] The price agreed for Alderfen's seventy acres was 2.5 times more per acre than the Trust had paid at Cley. After the sale, the auctioneer quipped, 'I wish all the land in Norfolk was water!'

The Second World War slowed developments, but by 1945 the NNT held nine reserves. These included one of the most important wetlands in the region, Hickling Broad, which, at 800 acres, was twice the size of Cley. What was most telling about these early achievements was not the resumption of land acquisition at the end of the war, but the fact that the organisation had comfortably survived Sydney Long's death in 1939. Even so, it is impossible to ignore the pioneering character of his vision.

It took an entire generation before another county looked to replicate Long's successes. In 1946 the Yorkshire Philosophical Society acquired one of the last remaining fragments of old fen in the county, Askham Bog, which had been mined for peat since Roman times. The purchase followed a similar pattern to that in Norfolk. Wealthy industrialists – in this instance with fortunes founded on the nation's sweet tooth, Francis Terry and Arnold Rowntree (it is interesting to note that the man who paid for Hickling Broad in 1944 was Christopher Cadbury) – bought the site, and the Yorkshire Naturalists Trust was inaugurated to receive it as a gift. Similarly, in Cymru, the West Wales Field Society made a parallel shift from studying nature to protecting it. That change of emphasis led Max Nicholson to suggest that the Welsh organisation should be considered 'in effect the second Trust to be founded in Britain'. However, its formal incorporation did not occur until 1961.[8]

Regardless of which body deserves the runner-up slot, one thing was crystal clear. The county-based model possessed what is known in business jargon as 'scalability' – a potential for being replicated and expanded. In the 1950s Trusts began to spring up all over Britain. By 1958 there were eight, and others were in the process of formation. In 1961 alone, Sussex, Devon, Derbyshire, Suffolk, Gloucestershire and Glamorgan acquired their own, and by 1963 there were thirty-four, including representatives in Somerset and one covering the whole of Scotland.[9]

The Scottish Wildlife Trust is the ultimate in terms of size for a single trust, given that the country holds a third of the British landmass and two-thirds of its coastline, including 790 islands, but with less than one-tenth of the UK population. Since its formation in 1964 the SWT has established and now manages 120 reserves.[10] Its adaptation to the peculiar geographical parameters north of the border suggests how the trust model established in 1926 had enormous inbuilt flexibility.

So too does the formation of the Berkshire, Buckinghamshire and Oxfordshire Wildlife Trust, where the founders agreed to work in unison from the outset. Their success has long confirmed the merits of that original decision: from an original roster of just thirty individuals in 1959, BBOWT now has 50,000 members.[11]

The spread of the movement mirrors closely the rapid post-war expansions of the RSPB and National Trust. Today the Wildlife Trusts' cumulative membership stands at more than 800,000 spread over forty-seven different regions. It may still be the smallest of 'the big three' but, considering that in many counties the pioneers started from scratch just fifty years ago, it suggests a potential to outgrow both of its siblings.

Today the Norfolk Wildlife Trust (as it became in the 1990s) is still one of the more successful. Cley stands at the heart of this development even now, with a state-of-the-art visitors' centre founded in 2015. In fact, the building on the ridge behind the reserve now rivals Cley windmill as the most impressive structure in the whole landscape. In total the NWT has 34,000 members (2015) and fifty reserves covering 10,625 acres. They are impressive statistics, but they are more than matched in other counties. The Surrey Wildlife Trust, to give one example, was only born in the same year as me (1959), but today it has 31,000 members and 77 reserves.[12]

What singles out the entire Trust movement from its origins is its focus on the offshore marine environment, in which sphere it has been the dominant player. Another key aspect has been its concern for the whole of the natural environment: from vegetation and invertebrates right through to birds and mammals. There is no selectivity, although charismatic animals tend to receive most attention: bitterns, otters, swallowtail butterflies etc. Equally, its logo is one of Britain's best-loved creatures – the badger. In prioritising the nature part of the human–nature nexus, the Wildlife Trusts share the same ethical position as the RSPB. And, like the RSPB, they are distinct from the National Trust in making this emphasis.

The Wildlife Trusts have another characteristic that separates them from all other NGOs: the ability to focus efforts at the local level, which is inbuilt into the county structure but also dials down, in some instances, to an extraordinary degree. South of Norwich is an NWT reserve that embraces less than one-tenth of one acre. In it stands the remarkable 700-year-old tree known as Hethel Old Thorn. It is the smallest nature reserve in Britain, but many Trust sites protect just such pockets of wildlife that might be only the span of a churchyard or the last surviving fragment of a flower meadow. The capacity to take account of the smallest sites is reflected in the Trusts' total landholdings. If considered as a single entity the Wildlife Trusts manage 2,300 nature reserves, compared with just over 200 for the RSPB. Yet the total areas held by the two organisations are respectively 230,000 and 323,000 acres.

One other classic illustration of the Trusts' localism is their central place in the management of what are known now as Local or County Wildlife Sites. In the 1980s a national survey was initiated to locate and formally notify all those bits of Britain that are still significant for their wildlife populations, but which lie outside any formal network of reserves, or the legal framework covered by the designation known as a Site of Special Scientific Interest. Local Wildlife Sites are in some ways the residue of British wildlife once the cream has been considered. In another sense they are the final filigree.

There are more than 42,000 such places in England alone. My own Blackwater Carr is one of them. In total they cover a twentieth of England's entire landmass, or more than 1.6 million acres, and technically they are described as areas with 'substantive nature conservation value'.[13] Through partnerships with the local planning authorities, the Wildlife Trusts seek to advise or to help owners with the management of these places for nature. The designation has no formal protective mechanism, although planning authorities are required to take account of Local Wildlife Sites when considering applications for building or development.*

The entire network illustrates how the Trusts are now woven into the most detailed micro-fabric of conservation effort. They are the default organisation championing nature on the doorstep. The downside of their unitary structure based upon county or region is the level of administrative duplication, with each trust employing its own director, its own conservation officer, its own communications director and so on. It means that much more of its income goes on the replication of these personnel.

Another key challenge arising from that level of localism is the ability to act on a national stage. The Wildlife Trusts' reconciliation of forty-seven regional entities to a united vision and a single programme is a complicated process. Typically the Wildlife Trusts' quarterly publication for members, entitled *Natural World*, has suffered a chronic lack of both identity and telling content. But then how do you produce a single

---

* Alas, the process works less well in practice than it appears on paper. A large majority of the partnerships (45) reported insufficient resources to manage and protect sites, while 133 local authorities provided no financial support to the Local Wildlife Site system. Between 2009 and 2013, 707 sites were lost, partially lost or damaged.

editorial voice to meet the needs of nearly fifty separate institutions? For more than thirty years, successive editors have failed to come up with a genuine answer.* As a consequence *Natural World* looks and sounds like a publication designed by committee. It is just a single example of how, among the big three, the Wildlife Trusts are considered to punch below their true collective weight on a national stage.

The issue is an old one. As long ago as the mid-1950s the embryonic trust movement recognised the need for an overarching institution to give it an effective central voice and overall coherence. The county groups functioned as a set of hard-working limbs, but they lacked a heart and head that could coordinate their efforts. In 1958 they found a candidate to supply the missing parts. Their merger was gradual and complicated, because the organisation chosen to serve as the central office had already been in existence for more than forty-five years.

And, in its way, it had been just as pioneering as either the National Trust or the RSPB. Sadly, its founding formula had not meshed with the simple social realities of Georgian Britain and, by the 1950s, it had become virtually moribund. What gave the enterprise its meaningful future was the county-based model founded in Norfolk. It is partly for this reason that I've told the history of the Wildlife Trusts beginning with Cley. However, the organisation itself places its own creation story thirty-four years earlier, with an account of the Society for the Promotion of Nature Reserves.

It was the brainchild of none other than Charles Rothschild, the man who had kickstarted the National Trust land holdings at Wicken Fen and Blakeney Point. He was a scion of the great European banking family, but also a polymath of exceptional breadth and one who completely fulfilled the adage that if you want something done ask a busy person. Rothschild was a husband, father, financier, landowner, entomologist, author of 150 scientific papers, namer of 500 new flea

---

* Many if not all of the 47 trusts produce their own county- or regionally based publications. Alongside *Natural World* the NWT, for example, has published a quarterly newsletter for decades called *Tern*, whose content at least has the merits of local relevance and clear focus.

species and discoverer of the vector-in-chief of bubonic plague, *Xenopsylla cheopis*, the Oriental rat flea. Alas, he was also a man short of time and would take his own life at just forty-six years of age. Prior to his suicide on 12 October 1923, Rothschild had been debilitated by encephalitis that he had contracted during the Spanish flu epidemic at the close of the First World War.

In happier times he had collaborated with three close colleagues – Charles Edward Fagan (1855–1921), William Robert Ogilvie Grant (1863–1924) and Francis Robert Henley (1877–1962) – to found the Society for the Promotion of Nature Reserves. In May 1912 *The Times* carried a leader to announce its formation. Drafted partly by Rothschild himself, it read,

> The only effective method of protecting nature is to interfere with it as little as possible; and this can only be done by forming a large number of local reserves … to safeguard the varying species and types of scenery on their native ground. England is still rather behindhand in organised effort for this purpose.[14]

That last sentence oozed English understatement, given that the US government had declared Yellowstone a National Park more than forty years earlier. But it wasn't that Rothschild was weak on his history. The key element that separated the SPNR from all other contemporary conservation initiatives was that its founders had really seen and understood the future. Rather than reacting piecemeal and often ineffectually to the threats that were starting to overwhelm the British environment in the twentieth century, they planned to work strategically.

Within three years of formation they had drawn up a list of the 284 best sites across both the UK and Ireland (which was still part of the British Isles), with a plan to secure these environmental treasures in perpetuity. In 1916 they published the inventory. That programmatic identification of our finest wildlife heritage was to become a cornerstone of state conservation after the Second World War. (The philosophy that underlay it and the developments that flowed from it are all considered under the fourth landscape, Upper Teesdale.)

Unfortunately, from the outset they never planned to create a mass democratic organisation open to all comers and founded solidly upon membership subscriptions. Rather they created a council comprising fifty handpicked nominees and then a small additional number of associates, who were also co-opted by their peers. The most regrettable part of the SPNR programme was that they had no intention of seeking to purchase those 284 wildlife sites that they had identified. They might supply the vision and research, but someone else would have to do the heavy lifting to raise money and purchase land.

To its four wealthy founders it must have felt like the natural way forward. Each of them was an extremely busy professional. At that time the only others who were assumed to possess the means to implement meaningful protection of the environment were people from their own social class and background. In short, it was to be a catalytic pressure group or, less charitably, an exclusive and elitist club, made up of like-minded friends and colleagues.

On paper some of the chosen few elected to the SPNR looked hugely influential and the kind who would achieve great things, such as Sir Edward Grey, Liberal statesman and Foreign Secretary, as well as E. S. Samuel, a future Secretary of State for India. It is typical of the cultural clout exercised by the SPNR board that they held their meetings at the British Museum, where the founder Charles Fagan was second in command, or in the Speaker's rooms at the House of Commons, where the SPNR's first president, J. W. Lowther (later Viscount Ullswater), held office. The plan was to use exactly these kinds of social connections to work behind the scenes in the interests of nature.

Unfortunately there was a basic flaw in this structure. The SPNR was effectively a stylish cart without a working horse. You had to have someone to cajole or to steer to do the heavy lifting you lacked the means to implement. And the National Trust, on whom so much hope had been placed, proved to be not terribly concerned about wildlife as a primary target for its purchases. In the interwar years it would morph, as we have seen, into the default caretaker of stately homes, and for decades nature was largely off its aristocratic agenda.

And if the National Trust proved a disappointment, then there was to be no compensatory joy from the British government. In 1916 the man who became president of the Board of Agriculture, R. E. Prothero, was one of the SPNR's high-placed contacts. That appointment, unfortunately, yielded absolutely no official support for the Society's work, other than the blandest of reassurances.[15] It was early proof that an organisation founded on a principle of prodding, nudging and catalysing others to do the real tasks was set to enjoy small success. So it proved. It would take three more decades and another world war before Westminster politicians took any decisive and formal action for nature.

The third of the SPNR's fundamental miscalculations was about those privileged gentlemen of influence – and they were almost all men – who became its nominated affiliates. Perhaps it was partly the fault of the SPNR board, because in the six years after it had been founded there had been only two council meetings. It was not until 1923, a full eleven years after formation, that it communicated at all with its associate members. A good illustration of the lack of ownership or commitment shown by the neglected members was the appeal to them for funds by the SPNR council in 1927. Of the approximately 300 wealthy, privileged and influential individuals adopted into its ranks, six paid up. When the exercise was repeated a year later, the number of donors halved.[16]

What really ended all the SPNR's early promise was not the parsimony of its elect few, but the suicide of its chief architect. As the historian John Sheail has written of Charles Rothschild: 'Only he had had the resources and stature to recruit further outstanding figures to the council and win the necessary patronage.'[17] Following his death in 1923 the SPNR drifted on, but only because of its founder's parting generosity. In his will he had left the society two properties.

One was a 20-acre block of Essex saltings called Ray Island, near West Mersea. Alas, its fate followed a familiar pattern. Rothschild had originally offered it to the National Trust, but it had refused it (ironically, it does now own the island, and the Essex Wildlife Trust manages it). Two years later, after Ray Island had become the property of the SPNR, the latter sold it off, largely to raise money to look after

Rothschild's other main bequest, the 200-acre site in Cambridgeshire called Woodwalton Fen. It was one of the last British places for the large copper butterfly (and even this was a re-introduction, albeit successful, after the insect went extinct in the nineteenth century). That this major reserve, which is now part of a visionary landscape-sized scheme called the Great Fen Project and managed by the Wildlife Trusts, was saved for posterity is one of the few indisputable achievements of the Society for the Promotion of Nature Reserves.

A second indissoluble merit was the SPNR's willingness to unite with the county trust network when the call finally came in the 1950s. That it had limped on at all and for so long was itself a kind of achievement, and largely down to the doggedness of its secretary, Herbert Smith, who performed his duties until his death in 1953, by which time he had served the SPNR for forty years. Even so, when the negotiations got under way in the 1950s to bring about a merger, one of the representatives of the county trust movement noted the SPNR's genius for inaction and under-achievement. He suggested it was like 'gazing on "a very desirable mansion to which one finally gains entry only to find most of the rooms empty"'.[18] A formal union of the two was only really initiated in 1976, when the SPNR was rebranded as the Society for the Promotion of Nature Conservation.*

That same date was significant in other ways. It was, of course, important as the fiftieth birthday of both the reserve at Cley-next-the-Sea and of the Norfolk Naturalists Trust as a conservation pioneer. But I too celebrated a key anniversary in that year, for on 24 June my sixteen-year-old self stood for the first time on the hallowed turf of Cley Marshes.

---

* To make matters just a little more complicated, the SPNR would undergo two further metamorphoses: one in 1981, when it received its Elizabethan seal of approval and became the Royal Society for Nature Conservation; then a second in 2004, when it emerged finally and officially as the Royal Society of Wildlife Trusts. Tim Sands suggests that only with that second name change did the county-based structure and the old SPNR truly become a single institution.

It took a friend and me two days to hitch the 170 miles from Buxton, and halfway we were forced to camp overnight on the back lawn of a south Lincolnshire pub before our pilgrimage was complete. The temperature on that first Norfolk afternoon, in that unforgettable year, was 90 degrees Fahrenheit. In the way of teenagers independent for the first time in their lives, we sweltered under massive rucksacks. I remember my first views of Titchwell were of quaking flats simmering in heat haze.

It was only at night on Salthouse Heath, just to the east of Cley, where we set up camp, that the temperature fell and we could savour our achievements. Lying on our backs, side by side, in the starlit dark, cocooned in our emerald nylon, my companion and I luxuriated in the idea of reaching this hallowed place and, specifically, in the songs of nightingales and the unearthly electric whirr of nightjars.

By the morning, around four, the night birds had ceased on Salthouse, but another unfamiliar voice enveloped us in a softness of sound few Derbyshire boys could have known. The only prominent architecture was a wave-like pulsing quality. It was being pumped towards us and felt not so much like song, as an atmosphere akin to the lapping of warm air or warm water, washing over our dormant plot, a song without direction or clear source, reminiscent of the reel of crickets that one hears on Mediterranean nights. Yet these were indisputably birds, turtle doves in fact, and they seemed to summarise, for any northern stranger, all the otherness of this low-lying eastern county.

We walked down later that morning across the heath, and in my notebook casually I logged fifteen turtle doves for the day.* Then we cut diagonally downhill towards and through the coastal cornfields which themselves involved, for children of gritstone moor and limestone dale, a form of unfamiliarity. The bearded heads of barley and turtle-dove song partook of the same uncharted territories.

Dropping off Scrib Hill towards Great Hulver Hill, there revealed and completely renewed in that morning light, was the whole north

---

* Turtle doves may have been routine fixtures of this coast forty years ago, but not now. Less than 10 per cent of the British population survives.

Norfolk coast. From our vantage point high on the old glacial ridge, we could make out faintly the raucous gravel-toned jumble of black-headed gulls' notes. We could see the landscape curving away westwards, quivering even at this hour, and ribboned in blue or pastel where plots of reed and marsh entwined. And far off was the mill. It was Cley. I was there. It was hot. A love affair had begun.

5

A BIT OF A COMPETITOR

Today, forty years later, from those same slopes between Furze Hill and Great Hulver Hill, with my back to Salthouse Heath and all those childhood memories, I can still obtain magnificent views over this shore. I think of this prospect in many ways as an embodiment, in terms of suaeda thicket, mud-lined freshwater, grazing marsh, shingle spit, sand shoal, tidal creek and saltmarsh, of the very idea of conservation.

The whole glittering panorama suggests how our society has undergone that ethical enlargement described in the passage by the historian Keith Thomas quoted in this book's frontispiece. It says how we have come to recognise our true place on Earth, whose destiny we share with millions of other species. Without the social and cultural impacts of environmentalism, this coast would look indisputably different. Without it my life would have been entirely other. And I would certainly never be here, now, on this hill.

Almost everything I can see from this spot belongs to or is managed by one of the organisations that I have described. Due north and immediately west are all acres of the Norfolk Wildlife Trust. Just to the east and to the west, beyond Cley, where the shingle strand of Blakeney Point is clearly visible, are National Trust lands. In that indeterminate swerve of mud and sky, far on the western horizon, one can intuit even the RSPB's Titchwell and the other coastal reserves.

This prospect maps out the achievements of conservation. Paradoxically, I must concede that it also charts the profound limits to its success. For behind me, just inland from the coastal hem, is the 90 per cent of Norfolk which has no environmental designation. This is one of the most intensively agricultural counties in Britain, stigmatised sometimes as a beet-and-barley prairie. Like many generalisations, it contains a large measure of truth. Across stretches of the arable area the only meaningful habitats are the hedge boundaries, and in some parts these have gone too. The central clay lands have often been stripped down to all but the most vestigial life forms, a miserable margin of roadside weeds and then the subsoil arthropods, fungi and bacteria invisible beneath the crops. Much of the county, much of England, in fact, is like this.

The view over north Norfolk doesn't just chart the limits of environmental success as determined by the greater forces at work in the British landscape. The place also indicates some chronic failings that are internal to conservation. One can see the interlocking jigsaw pattern of reserves as an expression of the collective efforts of Britain's green movement. Yet the fact that they are a jigsaw exposes the fallacy in the very idea of unity. For there is no green movement except in name; there are just overlapping, sometimes, competing organisations.

The American transcendentalist Ralph Waldo Emerson suggested that 'There is not a passion in the human soul, perhaps not a shade of thought but has its emblem in nature.'[1] Sometimes one wonders if all those different passions haven't also generated their own specific environmental action groups in Britain. Almost every form of life – bryophytes, spiders, flies and zooplankton even – has its own club, society or online community.

Time and again those fissiparous tendencies have led to lack of clarity and absence of cohesion. It is painful to say it, not just because I have on occasions indulged such distractions myself, but also because it implies criticism, if only by implication, of many deeply admirable people who have devoted their lives to nature's cause. But just below where I now stand there is a fragment of the landscape that embodies this divisiveness.

It is the gorse-topped knoll called Walsey Hills that banks on to the coast road and faces the easternmost grazing marsh at Cley. During the seventies I camped on Walsey Hills and scoured its gorse-and-bracken slopes for adders – sudden dark zigzags of writhing silver – which seem like encoded messages from another realm.* Walsey now also features a tiny concrete bunker belonging to a body called the Norfolk Ornithologists' Association, a dedicated group that, it was always said in my teenage years, was born of opposition to what was then called the Norfolk Naturalists Trust.

I would not suggest for a moment that any such rivalry plays a role for the present members on either side, nor that the NOA's purposes are not exactly as it defines them for itself: namely the further investigation and study of bird migration. Yet one cannot visit two of the NOA's key sites – the little ringing station on Walsey and another immediately adjacent to the NWT's own reserve headquarters at Holme Dunes (close to where my walk began and which I mention on p. 12) – and not sense an underlying link between the two organisations. The proximity speaks volumes. From these two prominent NOA territories it is almost as if one is gazing over the shoulders of the larger and older wildlife institution. The gossip I heard in my teens often centred on the silent antagonisms that recurred between Cley's warden Billy Bishop and one of the NOA's prime movers, Richard Richardson.

While it may only have been hearsay, it is indubitably true that dissatisfaction with a pre-existing organisation played a part in the founding of several new breakaway bodies. One need only look over the top of Walsey Hills to see an example. The purchase of Cley Marshes and the establishment of the NWT came about, in part, because the National Trust had refused to act in 1926.

I can assert with even greater certainty that subtle rivalries exist and continue to dog the work of wildlife-oriented communities. It is a difficult subplot to narrate, because no one wishes to own to it, or to dwell on it. Privately, however, the employees of all conservation groups will admit that it occurs.

---

* The farmer, on hearing that Walsey Hills might be designated as an SSSI for its populations of reptiles (slow worms and common lizards also occur), which have massively declined nationally, instantly pre-empted any such measure and scalped the whole site, by taking a plough to most of the southern section of the hill. What remains is a relic.

A classic example is cited in the autobiography of Ted Smith, who was among the most important environmentalists of the twentieth century. This remarkable, unassuming man co-founded the Lincolnshire Naturalists' Trust and played a central role in engineering the fusion between the Wildlife Trusts as a whole and the Society for the Promotion of Nature Reserves. He was also at the heart of a failed scheme to create an overarching coalition for the entire green movement.

In more parochial times, during the 1950s, when he was trying to halt a caravan park being developed in the midst of one of the most important coastal sites in Lincolnshire, Gibraltar Point, he sought moral and political support from his existing eco-allies. All duly stepped up to the plate, with the exception of the Norfolk Naturalists Trust, whose secretary wrote to him claiming to know nothing of 'Jamaica Point' and refusing to comment.[2]

By consensus the most conspicuously branded, least collaborative and most unwilling to share credit is the RSPB, which may be the darker side of its more driven ethic and centralised structure. Some of the most admirable champions of the environment I have known have been RSPB employees.* Farmers and landowners routinely specify that their relations with junior members of the staff are often perfectly harmonious. It is when decisions are passed to senior management that problems arise. I have been present when some of the RSPB's highest-ranking officers openly conceded the existence and impact of competition. And they mean their own with others. I recall precisely a well-placed RSPB executive confessing, 'To be honest, we see the National Trust as a bit of a competitor.'

The author Julian Hoffman, researching the Welsh Labour government's scheme to drive a six-lane motorway, a 14-mile-long M4 bypass, right across the middle of the Gwent Levels, found almost universal opposition to the project. In 2015 he gathered reactions from café

---

* Nicola Crockford, Ian Dawson, Euan Dunn, Gillian Gilbert, Rob Hume, Matt Howard, Grahame Madge, the late Eric Meek, Derek Niemann and John O'Sullivan, to name just ten of the outstanding people that recur at all levels and in all parts of the organisation.

owners, taxi drivers, environmentalists, landladies, pub staff, soldiers, mothers in the streets and children pond-dipping. All but two of these objected to the road scheme on the grounds that it would violate a wonderfully open, protected landscape in south Wales, whose management dates back 1,000 years, and which serves as a refuge for a mass of rare organisms, including 144 animals and plants listed as Red Data Species,* as well the first breeding cranes in Wales for 400 years.

The Levels comprises eight SSSIs and the River Usk Special Protection Area. The motorway would damage five of these nine protected zones. When asked for an opinion at the RSPB's Newport Wetland, a reserve on the Gwent Levels but to the south of the proposed road route, its staff member said as far as she was concerned the motorway would not affect their site and might actually boost visitor numbers.[3]

Competition may be part of the very DNA of our capitalist society. Rigorous self-interest may be the lifeblood of good business. The problem is that environmentalism is not a branch of business, nor can its successes be measured in economic terms. It is a cultural movement attempting to shape social values and attitudes to the more than human parts of our world. The competitive advantage of one organisation over another will never truly advance a green cause. On the contrary, by adopting the language and attitudes of capitalism, environmentalists are defeated at source.

A detail we may actually measure on an econometric scale that fully demonstrates why competition is so unproductive is the modesty of resource at the disposal of the big three environmental organisations. In 2013/14 the income revealed by their respective annual reports suggested a conservation war chest of £704 million (National Trust

---

* A Red Data listing for any species is a designation that forms part of a wider initiative to list the world's most vulnerable organisms. The scheme was started in the 1960s by the International Union of Nature and Natural Resources (IUCN), based in Gland, Switzerland. The concept of animals or plants being red-listed has become a mainstream method of highlighting the most needy and focusing efforts upon them. British environmentalists now also draw up lists of national species that are coded red, amber and green. The aim is always to sharpen priorities and concentrate work where it is most required.

£450 million, RSPB £127 million and Wildlife Trusts £127 million).*
Even if one factors in the 15 per cent of the Common Agricultural
Policy paid by DEFRA towards rural development and environmental
improvements – a figure of £3.5 billion between 2010 and 2015 – the
grand total in cash for nature in 2014 was £1.2 billion.[4]

To put the last sum in perspective, the amount that the British
people spent on perfume in that year was £1.6 billion.[5] The figure spent
on general cosmetics, meanwhile, including fragrances, was £9.12
billion.[6] The relative figures speak for themselves.

However, we should be clear that the cardinal failing of the green
'movement' is not competition – the internal jockeying described above:
the real issue, the central problem, is the way that these lesser failings
have frustrated the creation of a deep-rooted common purpose. Why,
after 120 years of lobbying governments and campaigning among the
public, is there not a recognisable single voice for all environmentalists?
After all, even lipstick makers have their collective: the CTPA – the
Cosmetics, Toiletry, Perfumery Association.

In the past, environmentalists such as Ted Smith understood the
importance of unity, because they tried to bring it about. The most
telling moment came at a time when the county trusts and the Society
for the Promotion of Nature Reserves were undergoing their own
protracted fusion. In the late 1950s a short-lived institution entitled
the Council for Nature was also conjured into existence. One of its
key architects and proponents, Max Nicholson, whose name appears
increasingly in the context of the next two landscapes, wanted it to be
'representative of both the scientific and the widespread, but diffuse,
public and popular interest in nature conservation'.[7] There was hope
that it could underpin a 'grand alliance of naturalist and amenity bodies
acting in concert under an umbrella title'. In short, it meant everyone
with an interest in nature. One imagines it as a sort of Trades Union
Congress for all wildlife-oriented people.

---

* I am grateful to the accountants John Snape and Colin Ford, who is also Head
of Finance at the Norfolk Wildlife Trust, for unravelling the complexities of the
respective annual financial statements of the big three.

The drive to combine all forces received its most significant expression in 1969, when a concrete set of proposals from the then director of the RSPB Peter Conder sought to effect a merger between his own organisation and both the Society for Promotion of Nature Reserves and the Council of Nature. While such initiatives continued in various guises until 1973 nothing definite ever emerged.[8]

Yet the hope has never died, and found renewed expression in 1980, with the creation of a body called Wildlife Link. In 1990 it then performed its own amalgamation with another group, the similarly titled Countryside Link, to become the Wildlife and Countryside Link, or 'Link' for short. It states that its central mission is to

> maximise the efficiency and effectiveness of the environmental voluntary sector through collaboration. By bringing our members together on policy areas of interest to them, we provide them with a forum to develop a collective view on national and international issues affecting wildlife and the countryside.[9]

There is strong evidence that the desire for greater integration has never gone away in the very document with which my book begins. The *State of Nature* report of 2013, from which much current thinking on the British environment draws its urgent clarity, was a collaboration involving twenty-five separate wildlife organisations.

This historical quest for unity is telling in both directions. On the one hand it adumbrates the recurrent recognition that solidarity is a key prerequisite. On the other hand, it reminds us that true consensus has thus far proved elusive. It also sheds light on the larger and seemingly intractable complexity at the heart of the nation's encounter with nature. As I noted earlier, put any ten Britons together and you will have as many versions of what the word 'nature' really means.

The cultural commentator and literary critic Raymond Williams wrote in his book *Keywords: A Vocabulary of Culture and Society* that 'Nature is perhaps the most complex word in the language.' In his attempt to unravel the lexical knot he proposed three core areas of meaning. Nature was 'the essential quality and character of something'.

It was also 'the inherent force which directs either the world or human beings or both'. Yet it is not just 'The force that through the green fuse drives the flower', as Williams' fellow Welshman Dylan Thomas put it more memorably in his poem. Nature, according to Williams, is equally the material world itself. And that physical universe, made of nature, might, or might not, include humans too. In summary, his complex tripartite definition of nature takes it to be:

i.   the essential quality of things
ii. the creative energy that directs life
iii. the physical world itself, with or without humans

Williams further pointed out that the root of the word 'nature', the Latin *natura*, derived from a past participle of the verb *nasci*, meaning 'to be born'. At its very origins, therefore, 'nature' has been assumed to be concerned with where things come from and their original conditions. Implicit in those shades of meaning is a sense of looking back to the beginning.[10] The very word that has become synonymous with the whole cultural and political enterprise of securing wildlife and the environment – nature conservation – is steeped in the ideas of valuing the past and of securing what once existed.*

If, like Williams, we strip nature back to its very essence then we return to the primary cosmic forces that first created life: the light from the sun, and then the chemical-processing powers of green plants here on Earth and, earliest of all, of marine cyanobacteria. It is the capacity

---

* For these reasons 'conservation' is an unfortunate term. Personally, I dislike it, as do many others. I try, as far as possible, *not* to use it. (To some extent 'reserve' partakes of the same backward-looking and future-averse tone of much environmental language.) The problem is that it is so entwined in the enterprise that one almost cannot avoid it. The reason it is so unhelpful is that it suggests a concern for nature is intellectually conservative – a holding-on to the past, a refusal to admit change or novelty. Almost by default it becomes difficult to talk about the future, and invariably it puts those who advocate for nature in socially negative positions, from which they appear to oppose change or development out of instinct. In truth, environmentalism is a fundamentally positive ethic, a wish to shepherd into the future as abundant a range of life as possible.

of these organisms to turn the sun's energy into carbon compounds, through the magician's wand of photosynthesis, that has given rise to the 3-billion-year-old flush of complexity that we call life.

The problem for environmentalism is twofold. The world's human population seems now to assail the most basic machinery of life. Yet each organisation has chosen a different spot in that momentous unfolding to plant its flag. The groups have then made a case for separate and even contradictory parts. Thus, the Campaign to Protect Rural England (CPRE) has championed life at its very source.* One of its major programmes is for dark skies and the ability to see myriad stars burning out in the cosmos, free from the effects of light pollution given off by cities and towns. On the other hand, it has also campaigned for the bendiness of country roads, which it defines as an inextricable part of rural life.

To return to my place above Walsey Hills, there is another issue implicit in this landscape mosaic of reserves and official designations that speaks of the challenges of conservation. It is a problem of language.

I do not mean being lost for words to express even the simplest things about nature: the way, for example, that the winter sun plays now in the reeds. Their shared properties have transfixed me for thirty years, and I have often found myself taking and re-taking photographs, one after the other, to capture the essence. Individually the old seed heads of each phragmites stem are a glorious burnt brown, minutely tinged purple. Somehow, when the wind pushes the plants in unison,

---

* Founded in 1926 as the Council for the Preservation of Rural England by the planner Patrick Abercrombie and his friend and fellow architect Clough Williams-Ellis, CPRE mounted a decisive stand against urban sprawl, whose insidiously spreading tentacles were referenced in a book by Williams-Ellis called *England and the Octopus* (1928). CPRE now has branches in Wales and many regions or counties of England. It also has an influence in Parliament that seems bigger than its 60,000 membership. Like the National Trust it has been largely preoccupied with safeguarding landscape beauty or rural character as opposed to biodiversity. It is presently a notable champion of the Green Belt, whose institution in 1947 largely cured England of the outwardly sprawling cephalopod feared by Clough Williams-Ellis.

so that the whole bed ripples and folds, the reed crowns are suddenly – uncannily – swollen up with sunlight. Look at reeds against the sun and a billion pale hairs floss up as if illuminated from within and breathing wings of light sway and billow as the vegetation stirs.

It is not lack of words, however, that bedevils conservation. It is obscurity of meaning. To give it to you in its most condensed form: the coastline has been recognised, in part or whole, as an SSSI, AONB, NNR, LNR, SPA, SAC, a Ramsar Site and a Biosphere Reserve. Parts of it or its adjacent areas are managed by ESAs, CSS and, through rural payments from DEFRA, in the form of ELS and HLS.

Or to translate all this into a format that is barely more digestible: the coastline is recognised, in part or whole, as a Site of Special Scientific Interest, an Area of Outstanding Natural Beauty, as various National Nature Reserves and Local Nature Reserves (or, as they are called in Norfolk, and unlike most other counties, County Wildlife Sites), a Special Protection Area under the European Union's Birds Directive 2009/147/EC, a Special Area of Conservation under the European Union's Habitats Directive 92/43/EEC, a Ramsar Site under the Ramsar Convention of 1971, and a Biosphere Reserve in accordance with the Man and the Biosphere Programme 1971 of the United Nations Educational, Scientific and Cultural Organization. Parts of it, or its adjacent areas, are managed as Environmentally Sensitive Areas, Countryside Stewardship Schemes and through rural payments from the Department of the Environment, Food and Rural Affairs in the form of Entry-Level Stewardship and Higher Level Stewardship.*

Alas, my sample only hints at the real complexities. Bill Adams put it best when he spoke of the 'maelstrom of countryside designations'.[11] The business of nature is indivisible not just from acronyms, but from a writing style that is well illustrated by the passage quoted above from the Wildlife and Countryside Link website (see p. 67).

Here are two more from the same source:

---

* In fairness, I should point out that, after ten years of operation, both ELS and HLS are in the process of being replaced by Mid- and Higher-Tier Countryside Stewardship, which should simplify things!

The Agriculture Working Group works to support and deliver a sustainable, high-quality, multi-functional rural environment through influencing and monitoring policy on rural development, agri-environment, bioenergy, and animal welfare standards.

The Legal Strategy Group seeks to improve the creation, implementation and enforcement of English Law to better protect the natural environment by bringing together legal experts from across the NGO community to identify and take opportunities to provide support to members and working groups in the implementation, defence and development of environmental law. The group will also consider access to environmental justice issues.[12]

This is the classic argot of official nature. Anyone who has ever had to wade through an internal document by any eco-group will know the recurrent qualities: multi-syllabic words entrained in unwieldy colloquy, the passive voice or lack of specific agency, the overly long sentences, the worthiness of tone, lack of clarity and, sometimes, the absence of meaning. A friend of mine once wrote a spoof of the genre that he called 'Towards Focusing'. His title was perfect. While the content often wishes to suggest that many actions will flow from the utterances, the tone, syntax and rhythms convey exactly the opposite sense. It is a prose style of very little action. In large part, it is a language of powerlessness.

This is not to blame environmentalists: we have to recognise that often the cards are stacked against them. Environmentalism is essentially about land and how it is managed. Alas, more than 53 million of us in Britain own an average of just seven-hundredths of one acre. More than almost any other in Europe, this is a nation of landless people. In fact, one wonders at times if the green lobby is a latent response to the ongoing impacts of nineteenth-century enclosure and the many forms of dispossession they entailed. My guess is that most green organisations are staffed with people who are professional, middle-class and landless.

The country's actual terra firma is concentrated in the hands of a tiny minority. And that dispensation has existed for a thousand years. In 1072, prior to the drawing-up of William the Conqueror's Domesday project, 4.9 per cent of England's eleventh-century population controlled 99 per cent of its land. Today just 0.3 per cent of Britain's 65 million own 69 per cent of it all.[13]

Such is the regressive nature of its land tax regime and subsidy system – an injustice, incidentally, which until the Brexit decision of June 2016 was guaranteed by EU agricultural policies – that those who own most land receive the most in direct payments through another acronym, the CAP (Common Agricultural Policy). In his brilliant analysis of land ownership in Scotland, *The Poor Had No Lawyers*, Andy Wightman pointed out that in 2009, of £591 million doled out to landowners, just 1,032 individuals were in receipt jointly of £177.7 million of taxpayers' money. It means that the Duke of Buccleuch, Britain's pre-eminent baron, with 241,887 acres – and more land than all the properties belonging to the Wildlife Trusts combined – is probably in receipt of monies in the form of subsidy from the poorest taxpayers: the working men and women of Blackpool or Thanet.[14] Wightman points out that individual farmers (often disguised under anonymous legal trusts) received £8,553,490.76 of public money from 2000 to 2009; for no reason other than the fact that they are the wealthiest, largest landowners in the country.[15]

It is axiomatic that whoever owns the land largely controls its use and has most impact upon its management. Those long-entrenched landed interests which, until recently, enjoyed preponderant representation in the House of Lords and major influence in the Commons, the judiciary and in various forms of local councils and fora, have been able to shape environmentalism in their own image or neutralise and even cancel its impact. It is not a coincidence that many of the major initiatives – national parks and SSSIs are two good examples – were launched without powers of compulsion or even minimal legal means of enforcement. Nor is it unrelated that for British citizens the right to roam upon unproductive lands was an initiative launched in 1884. It required another 116 years and more than twenty-five legal attempts to secure it.

It is hardly surprising that the main currency of conservation has not been action and the exercise of power. Words, ideas, knowledge and slow persuasion have been its chief weapons. The downside has been a tendency to presume – 'hope' might be a better word – that recasting the language will somehow reshape the landscape in all its senses. Time and again new initiatives, groundbreaking reports or break-through schemes have given rise to whole new ways of doing business. Just to give a sense of the ongoing turnover of good ideas: in the 1990s it was all about Biodiversity Action Plans, in the 2000s it was landscape-scale conservation and in the 2010s it has been re-wilding.

To give a little background: Biodiversity Action Plans followed the enormously successful UN conference on Environment and Development in Rio de Janeiro in 1992. It is often referred to as Rio '92. From that major event, which 178 nations attended, came binding obligations to abide by the principles of sustainable develop-ment. Each country had to draft its own Agenda 21 (named after the forthcoming century), and from it, in the UK, emerged the Biodiversity Action Plan (BAP for short; one still hears conservationists talking of BAP species, by which they mean animals or plants covered by their own specific remedial plans).

A steering group was founded to draw up the so-called '59 steps' which were the very fabric of the plan, and which the government committed to implement. There were sub-sections to the Biodiversity Action Plan, which focused on individual organisms (116 of them including anything from bitterns to natterjack toads, and covered by SAPs – Species Action Plans) and on fourteen habitats that were in need of urgent help. Alas, the BAP scheme was discontinued in 2010.

However, in the new millennium another less official but all-consuming priority was identified. Ecologists had come to appreciate that preserving pockets of habitat in reserves, no matter how diligently, often did not secure the important populations of plants and animals that had led to any site's initial establishment. The reason is that ecosystems and their associated organisms function at the scale, not of a nature reserve, but of the entire landscape (see also Chapter 15 on p. 186 for a discussion of the effects of habitat fragmentation).

Butterflies are a good example of how and why landscape-scale conservation is necessary, because each one goes through four stages:

egg, caterpillar, chrysalis and sexually active adult. The requirements of each stage are often very different: big old trees for adults to gather over and court and mate; young leaves on middle-aged trees for the caterpillars to feed upon; then old rotten hollows in aged veterans as sites to pupate. Thus, a single population of one butterfly needs a wood whose parts are in all stages of development all at the same time. A reserve is often too small a fragment to provide the full habitat requirements.

The aim of the organisations was to connect reserves and create linking corridors between various protected sites, sometimes through farmland or right across urban areas, to develop a larger, unified, inter-connecting habitat. Such schemes exist still, for example, on the borders of Gwent and Gloucestershire to help preserve the tiny, flower-rich meadows that are scattered in and around the Wye Valley.

Each of the 'big three' organisations has its own showcase landscape-scale conservation project in or around the Fens of eastern England: the National Trust at Wicken Fen, the Wildlife Trusts in the Great Fen Project and the RSPB at Needingworth Quarry. All are completely wonderful projects and do involve extraordinarily long-term commitments and enhanced ambitions by the main voluntary NGOs.

Yet more recently they have been overtaken by another landscape-scale scheme known as 're-wilding'.* It draws to some extent on pioneer work undertaken by Dutch environmentalists at Oosvardersplassen, a polder in the province of Flevoland. These 55 square kilometres of open water, marsh and dry grassland or carr, which make up a reserve about two-thirds the size of the north Norfolk SSSI, are managed not directly by human agency like the latter area, but by a mix of wild deer and primitive breeds of horse and cattle. These hardy creatures function

---

* Incidentally, it is another good example of the same backward-looking and future-averse tone to environmental language that I discussed earlier. By its very nature 're-wilding' implies a return to an original state; to a time when things were once 'wild'. Surely setting nature free upon its own future path should be termed 'wilding'? But such is the irresistible lure of the underlying mental habit, expressed in the root of that Latin past participle of the verb 'to be born', that even this project involves a recovery of what is lost.

in a way that is close to the wild herbivores of Europe's pre-agricultural past. They are left to roam and graze and die at their own whim. The aim is to create natural systems with the least interference.

In 2013 the British environmental campaigner George Monbiot, in his book *Feral* (2013), popularised a second key element of re-wilding: the introduction or reintroduction of large predators. The wolf and European lynx are often the main candidates for any project or theoretical proposal, although the beaver is another keystone animal that is valued for its transformative impacts on the way that riverine landscapes behave.

The overarching goal is to radically change the ethic and methods by which nature is governed. Rather than using established farming or ecological management practices to preserve land or habitats in a state they once enjoyed, Monbiot and his collaborators seek to set nature free to take its own uncharted course. Wildlife will not be steered or controlled by us; it will flourish when we are absent – self-willed, autonomous and wild. That, at least, is the theory.

All these schemes have deep merit and build upon important new research. The real problem is that the endless churn of new, separate, sometimes complementary, but often just competing initiatives creates an intellectual framework that is overly complicated and utterly exhausting to master. Resources are poured into the latest plans, which often lose momentum slowly until a brighter successor sweeps all before it. Then the new scheme sucks all the oxygen out of the room. Meanwhile the former models survive but as co-existing relics, or they find a way to rebrand themselves to fit the latest phase. All that has really changed are the buzzwords, the logos and the branding. The other key consequence is an additional layer of complexity. The underlying essentials, however, often remain pretty much the same.

The result of all this shifting of scenery is that the public has got lost and become bewildered in a forest of 'stuff' – jargon, acronyms, quasi-official terminology and technicalities. And their confusion is partly of our making. Today the public has only minimal grasp of this overly bureaucratised field. So often people are tripped up even by the most basic of terms. I wish I could recall all the various, sometimes hilarious, versions I have heard of the term 'Site of Special Scientific Interest', either as acronym or in full. And that gem has been around since the 1940s. In short, environmentalists need to simplify their world, to speak with Orwellian clarity and to unite, if possible, in a commonly agreed and settled plan.*

If I could wave my magic wand and achieve one outcome then it would be on this very issue. It is a wish in three parts: a round table to harmonise us all and to create the single clear recognisable voice for nature; a blueprint that expresses our shared (and evolving) ambitions for the more than human parts of the country; and a maypole beneath which we can gather to celebrate – in simple song – the nature of our achievements.

For the location of those celebrations I propose the north Norfolk coast.

---

* By Orwellian I do not mean the lingo of control called 'newspeak' that was used by the totalitarian regime in his dystopian novel *Nineteen Eighty-Four*. That, in fact, is closer to what we get already. I mean Orwell's famous dictum on composition: 'Never use a long word when a short one will do, never use a foreign phrase, a scientific word or a jargon word if you can think of an everyday English equivalent.' I was once witness to two environmentalists engrossed in conversation about their shared recognition of the impact and implications of 'Urtica' in a particular field: *Urtica* this and *Urtica* that. It was all very erudite. Turns out that *Urtica dioica* is the Latin name for nettles.

6

WE DON'T LIKE HILL WALKERS IN DERBYSHIRE

Yet my mind was not at rest because nothing was acted, and thoughts ran into me, that words and writings were all nothing, and must die, for action is the life of all, and if thou dost not act, thou dost nothing.

Gerrard Winstanley, seventeenth-century Leveller

The international arts exhibition the Venice Biennale has been running since 1895, and for almost all of its 123 years the organisers have invited officials or governments from various countries to profile the work of their own artists in separate pavilions. Today there are about sixty of these around the city, and the British Council has managed its own national space since the 1930s.

At the 55th Biennale the British conceptual artist Jeremy Deller was asked to curate a personal vision of his country, which he entitled *English Magic*. In the spring of 2013, as you approached the building, with its soft pink-marble facade and the legend in bold capitals above the entrance, GRAN BRETAGNA, visitors were dramatically confronted by the image of a gigantic bird of prey on outstretched wings, its immense yellow claws wrapped around a brilliant scarlet automobile. By the time they had reached the door, the visitors could see that the vehicle was a blood-coloured Range Rover and the bird a British species called the hen harrier.

A bird big enough to carry off an SUV was certainly magical. Deller explained how he wished to create an image suggesting something mythological, and there is about it a hint of those classical sculptures in which Zeus as an eagle swoops away with a young Ganymede. The painting's title, however, speaks peculiarly of Deller's own place and time. It is called *A Good Day for Cyclists* and refers to the artist's passion for riding his bike in London, but it also glances at the recurrent dangers posed to cyclists in the capital by just such four-wheel-drive cars. A raptor that predates those vehicles is clearly doing its bit for safe cycling.

The exhibition was entitled 'English Magic', and Deller intended it to mean also the darker variety, the subtle unseen powers that exert their baleful influence on British society. Implicit within *A Good Day for Cyclists* is a compelling statement about the age-old English class system, the injustice of class privilege and the assumptions of invulnerability that inform the British ruling classes at play. For Deller's beautiful bird was exactly the same as two creatures observed on the evening of 24 October 2007 as they circled a well-known roost site at a spot in Norfolk called Dersingham Bog.

It is part of the royal Sandringham estate in north Norfolk, and for several minutes three eyewitnesses, all ornithologists, enjoyed the flight of these elegant hen harriers before a loud bang rang out, followed by a second gunshot. The two birds plummeted instantaneously to the ground, as one witness reported, 'like a stone'.[1] Then there was a third shot.

One of the people who had been watching, a warden at Dersingham, instantly rang his employers to notify them of the illegal slaughter. That person, in turn, rang the RSPB investigations team and within a matter of minutes police were on their way to Sandringham. In the following weeks there ensued a furore of complaint and public interest, as well as press speculation about who had killed those birds. It transpired that the only people shooting at that time on the royal property were Prince Harry, fifth in line to the British throne, and his friend William van Cutsem. No hen harrier carcasses were ever found. No charges were ever brought.

The notion of loud, declamatory, eye-catching public protest was on my mind as I climbed the slope above Hayfield in north Derbyshire.

I was on a track known as the Snake Path, which was officially opened two years after the first Venice Biennale and was a kind of triumph itself over injustice and social exclusion.

By most standards, however, it was a very modest triumph. It enabled the British public to trek across unproductive grassland and moor to a famous watering hole known as the Snake Inn and then on to the Snake Pass that continued into Sheffield. However, the Peak District and Northern Counties Footpath Society, which had erected the original sign at the start of the track, were not treating the path's establishment lightly. There in bold capitals at the foot of their plaque are the words:

'DEDICATED FOR EVER MAY 29 1897.'

I was on a footpath that wound through one of England's most distinctive upland places. But it is also a track that passes through time.

At a point where I could almost glimpse my first destination on that day, I was lost to politics by the fresh sunlit rain-shower of a skylark's song and then by a reflection about the way that, apart from this glorious songster over my head, the vocalisations of upland birds possess a systemic simplicity: the flat, desultory, piping notes of meadow pipits, the monotonous tick-tock of a distant cuckoo and then the higher, more piercing alarm calls of curlews. They were all companions on this sunny afternoon.

Briefly I stopped at a pool by the path, which was thick with tadpoles. All around that blue eye of water, even in the middle of the day, there was a residual hoar frost in the surviving areas of shadow. It spoke of nights earlier in the month, when the ground was white all over and those silk-throated frogs sang to a cold moon. Now their offspring squirmed and the embryos of their offspring lolled in a thick warm April soup of their own making.

I continued along the trail that passed the lonely squat structure marked on the map as the 'Shooting Cabin', and overlooked the grouse butts running up the slopes of Leygatehead Moor. Then it was just the path over White Brow high above Kinder Reservoir, away to the right, and I began a shallow descent into the sinuous cleft called Nab Brow. And all about me to north and east, as far as the eye could see, was a high, gently enfolded tableland of gritstone country. In sunlight it is a four-toned mosaic of grey rock, fresh-flushed bilberry green, that bitter brown note of flowerless heather and then the softer lion-flank oat of old grass – sweet vernal grass, crested dog's-tooth and pink-tipped bents.

It is powerful country, and from Kinder's wind-cut edge, facing towards you, you know eventually you will be able to look west, over where you now stand, over the head of Manchester and all the way to Wales. I was walking to that place, with its rain-sculpted monoliths of gritstone, but first I had to drop down into William Clough. There, in that intimate water-loud spot, my own route converged with that of an historical party which had also walked from the village of Hayfield on a Sunday afternoon in 1932.

At this part of the walk they too would have splashed their boots where the path crosses and follows the course of the River Kinder, careering down through the narrow, high-banked gully of William Clough. It is the kind of river I have known all my life. For my first eighteen years the rush and babble of such a stream was my nightly companion. It is the quintessential Derbyshire brook: a narrow gurgle of water lined by bare gritstone that is stained brown by algae, and with water the colour of dissolved peat.

The narrow, deep-cut track is not easy for walkers when they are two abreast. How it must have been on that clear bright Sunday, one can only surmise, because there were about 400 of them.* I try to imagine their mood. Apparently, they sang rousing songs as they marched, but at William Clough I guess that all that will have ended. For they were confronted by one of the worst walks I know in the entire Peak District.

There are two interlocking issues. The gradient is steep and one is essentially climbing from the 1,000- to the 2,000-foot contour in less

---

* The organisers said 600–800, the police 200, while journalists for the *Manchester Guardian* and the *Daily Express* reckoned 400–500 and 500 respectively.

than a mile. Then there is the awkward, rock-strewn character of the path, which for a good deal of the time is through the flow or adjacent seepage lines of the River Kinder. For half of it you are virtually walking through water. As you get higher, so the path gets rougher and steeper and, by the time you near the top, hard breath rasps in your lungs and most walkers have sweat-soaked backs and overheated bodies. In that inescapable self-generated cell of discomfort you begin to ponder exactly what motivated those walkers of 1932.

In those days they didn't call themselves walkers. They were 'ramblers', an altogether more politically loaded name, despite its connotations of aimless meandering. That army of 400 that trooped up William Clough did not lack purpose. They were there precisely because it was *not* permitted.

I think the best measure of how subversive walking was assumed to be at that moment in British history is the story of a young policeman from Stalybridge called 'Ginger' Jackson. Ginger was a rambler too, and when he went for his interview, the police officer in charge spotted that on the application he had listed 'hill walking' among his pastimes. Staring hard at Ginger as if he might have met him before, Assistant Chief Constable James Garrow said, 'We don't like hill walkers in Derbyshire. They are not welcome.'[2]

True, the Peak District and Northern Counties Footpath Society had negotiated those important rights of 1897. Yet above William Clough and all along Kinder Edge, where those views over all Manchester are best, it was forbidden territory. There was absolutely no public access to any of the fifteen square miles of Kinder Scout, and of 109,000 upland acres which stretch from Marsden in Yorkshire to Matlock in Derbyshire, ramblers were allowed on 1,212 of them, a fraction over 1 per cent of a landscape stretching for more than forty miles.[3]

There had been a prolonged dialogue to try to secure further rights for people to tramp on such unproductive country. But the concessions were few and the attitude of landowners deeply hostile. Some young working-class men and women, largely from the Manchester area, were not willing to wait any longer, and on the Sunday morning of 24 April 1932 they took direct action.

They were led by a diminutive figure (he was under five feet tall), a twenty-one-year-old engineering worker called Bernard 'Benny' Rothman, brother to four siblings, son of Jewish immigrants of Romanian extraction. Benny's group was rather grandly titled the British Workers' Sports Federation, and they had organised what was called 'a mass trespass'. It got good publicity in the Manchester and the wider Lancastrian press and attracted some distinguished attention. Among the hundreds that walked that day were the composer Sir Michael Tippett, the renowned historian A. J. P. Taylor and a young Salford folk singer called Jimmie Miller, who later changed his name to Ewan MacColl (and later composed 'Dirty Old Town' and 'The First Time Ever I Saw Your Face' among 300 other songs).

Although it received the backing of fifteen Lancashire ramblers' clubs and two from Sheffield, the proposed action didn't win the support of the entire rambling community. Other organisations saw it as unnecessarily provocative, and Rothman later claimed that some thought it would set back access to mountains by forty years. The Manchester Ramblers' Federation, for instance, disowned the protest completely.

Another official body that disapproved of the march was the Derbyshire Constabulary. All the previous week the police had tried to serve Rothman with an injunction restraining him from going on his walk, but the twenty-one-year-old dodged all their efforts by arriving on his bicycle. At Hayfield itself on the Sunday morning the place was swarming with police and the ramblers were forced to set off before the allotted hour.

Yet not before Rothman had climbed onto a sheer ledge in an old derelict quarry – now the National Trust car park for Kinder Scout – and delivered a rousing address to urge on his fellow subversives, whose high spirits the *Manchester Guardian* likened to university students at rag week. Stirred on by their choruses of 'It's a Long Way to Tipperary', the Manchester band hammered up William Clough. On that Sunday afternoon they may have placed a picket to protect a mother meadow pipit on her nest of eggs, but they were less kind to a posse of stick-cradling gamekeepers who were waiting on the hilltop. As the two sides closed on one another a confrontation broke out and in the fracas a part-time keeper called Edward Beever was downed.

According to Rothman the cause of his collapse was a sprained ankle and a blow to his stomach from one of the protesters.[4] According to the gamekeepers it was a boot in his groin that felled poor Beever. Either way, it was little more than the rough stuff dealt out by the keepers themselves. But Beever's injury was enough for the authorities, who had apparently deployed a third of the entire Derbyshire force as a reception committee, to arrest the 'trespassers' on their return to Hayfield. All hell was just about to break loose.

7

THE LEGITIMATE LORD OF THE LANDSCAPE

For whoever may own the land, no man can own the beauty of the landscape; at all events no man can exclusively own it. Beauty is a kind of property which cannot be bought, sold or conveyed in any parchment deed, but it is an inalienable common right; and he who carries the true-seeing eyes in his head, no matter how poor he may otherwise be, is the legitimate lord of the landscape.

G. S. Phillips, *Walks Around Huddersfield* (1848)

It is instructive to ponder the exact historical antecedents that had given such a strongly politicised charge to the brief adrenalin-driven exchange of boots and fists on Kinder Scout. What was it that had set one party of rural labourers to brawling with another group of working men from the city? The two opposed sides were probably not very different in terms of background, education and circumstance. What historic processes had put them on such differing paths?

Most historians identify the starting point for the protest walk about 170 years earlier, and link it to the intensifying enclosures between 1760 and 1844. During those eight decades more than 3,979 acts of parliament delivered what were deemed heath, moorland and barren mountain – 'wasteland' was the classic term – out of common usage and into private hands. (In contrast there had been just eight private enclosure acts in England before 1714.)[1]

The process was concomitant with a revolution in farming practice that had seen productivity soar, largely because of measures pioneered by agriculturalists like Coke of Holkham in Norfolk. Coke had used lime-rich marl to reduce the acidity of his 'hungry soils', and had also introduced what became known as the 'Norfolk Four Course' rotation (in truth, the measures had been first developed in the Low Countries, but innovators like Coke got most of the credit), which involved growing wheat, turnips, barley and clover in successive years. The last crop served both as a nitrogen fixer and as a temporary pasture for grazing livestock, which then manured the ground and further improved overall fertility. The sum of the measures boosted output and massively increased profit. Over his life the famous incumbent at Holkham Hall was able to raise his farm income fourfold from £5,000 to £20,000.[2]

This so-called Agricultural Revolution ran in conjunction with both a huge growth in the national population and the expansion of British industry and British cities. In 1790 four out of every five people in England and Wales had lived in the countryside. By 1830 half were living in towns or cities.[3] Higher productivity entailed in the enclosures helped to underpin these developments, but it also inflicted major social and economic change upon the mass of England's rural population. Its essential effects can best be summarised by the opening lines of Billie Holiday's song 'God Bless The Child' – 'Them that's got shall have/ Them that's not shall lose.'

The enclosure at Fulmodestone Common, Norfolk, about 8 miles south of those National-Trust-owned saltmarshes at Stiffkey, absolutely typified how it worked. There were 556 previously shared acres that were reassigned to private hands with that single act of parliament. Of all the neighbouring landowners, Coke of Holkham got no fewer than 406 acres, to add to the tens of thousands he already possessed, and in the decade from 1806 to 1816 he acquired a total of 1,500 acres in a similar manner. As one eighteenth-century cleric wrote, enclosure 'beggared multitudes'.[4] It was precisely the inequitable redistribution of wealth and resource that would later goad Robert Hunter into his legal practice for the Commons Preservation Society.

The loss of income, fuel, free grazing as well as other important economic resources; the denial of a common space to meet, to re-create and recreate, to court, to make love and to feel free, were all deficits inflicted by enclosure on the common people of rural Britain. On top of that the dispossessed were often subjected to a new kind of privation as the enriched feudal classes corralled their green and pleasant lands unto themselves.

An issue that burned as fiercely as any other for the owners was their presumed and exclusive claim to the consumption of wild creatures present on the newly obtained acres. Essentially their anxiety was about 'game' – pheasants, hares, partridges, grouse, rabbits etc. – and who could eat it and who could hunt it. The attempt to exert control over this wild protein by means of harsh game laws would endure for a century and a half.

In his classic study of the issue, *The Long Affray*, Harry Hopkins suggested that the game laws triggered a social conflict that was nothing less than a civil war, involving hundreds of fatalities and many thousands of casualties. 'War', he wrote, 'is admittedly a large word. But as the larger jigsaw slowly fitted together and the macabre details took shape, it seemed to me that … no other word would do.' It was also, he proposed, a war between 'the two nations that were England'.[5] Yet the sides were not drawn up strictly on the lines of the haves and have-nots.

One of the more bizarre facets of England's poaching wars – as well as its democracy – is that it initially required one to own fifty times more property to have a legal right to shoot a partridge than it did to vote.[6] Originally, only half of 1 per cent of the population was entitled to hold a game licence and, while this changed over the course of the nineteenth century, it ensured that the man who filched a rabbit or pheasant from under the nose of his local laird enjoyed a flow of sympathy and support from a broad-based coalition including many substantial farmers and smaller landowners.

A perfect illustration of the social complexities inherent in Britain's game wars is another story from Sandringham shortly after Prince Edward (later Edward VII) snapped up the estate in 1862. The young prince was an obsessive 'sportsman', and he not only embodied the intensifying Victorian mania for shooting birds; his example also served as catalyst for society's wider excesses. It was not unusual for the guns at Sandringham to kill more than a thousand birds in a single shoot, but it was his heirs who claimed the national record: 3,937 pheasants on one day in 1913. Parts of the estate were eventually little more than a breeding station for hares and gamebirds, to the extent that some tenant farmers could, at times, neither tend nor harvest their crops.

A gentlewoman called Louisa Mary Creswell, who was wife to a banker and daughter to a squire, had the misfortune to take the lease at Appleton Farm on the royal property. Later, from the safe distance of the American West, she described her experience in a book titled *Eighteen Years on Sandringham Estate*. The place was so densely populated with game, she complained, that when she 'drove across the fields the hares would start up at my pony's feet, gathering like a snowball, and run before me like a little pack of hounds'.[7] She was often helpless to protect her crops or to stop the depredations.

She was no rural radical: on the contrary, in politics she was an arch Tory. Eventually she went bankrupt, partly on account of falling agricultural prices but also because of the unsympathetic regime on the royal lands. In 1887, when her book appeared criticising her landlord's methods, the estate's agent took no chances. On the orders of Edward's secretary he bought and destroyed almost all copies of the work. It is an indicator, if nothing else, that Jeremy Deller's artwork at the Venice Biennale tells a right old royal tale.

It would be wrong to suggest that this was an entirely one-sided conflict or that landowners had it all their own way. As the eighteenth-century artist Thomas Bewick suggested, 'To convince the intelligent poor man, that the fowls of the air were created only for the rich, is impossible and will for ever remain so.'[8] The oppressive intentions of the game laws served often to provoke people's sense of injustice. As a result poaching wild creatures remained a rural commonplace, if not an outright duty of country folk. It also became a major industry. One game dealer in London admitted that he had 19,000 suppliers on his books. More than nine-tenths of them operated under the counter. Another reported that in a single season he received 1.2 million partridge and pheasant eggs. When he said that all of them were poached he was not referring to the method of preparation.[9]

This freebooting appropriation of the landowner's game was bound to excite opposition, especially in view of the escalating costs. For the sportsman the sums doled out on the management of pheasant shooting by the lords of Longleat estate in Wiltshire typify the massive rise in expenditure: £264 (1790), £410 (1810), £2,555 (1856).[10]

The response from the landed gentry to their neighbours' poaching was ever more draconian legislation, which the Whig politician Charles James Fox would call a 'mass of insufferable tyranny'.[11] The worst had reached the statute books as early as 1723 and was known as 'the Black Act', which created fifty new capital offences. Merely to appear at night with a blacked-up face or a suitable firearm in the presence of game was a hanging offence. So too was the harbouring of such a person, or the sending of an anonymous letter or even the cutting down of a single tree.

In 1800 the legal right of seizure, without warrant, was extended to the servants of landowners and to their gamekeepers, which effectively made the man who reared his lordship's partridges an officer of the state. The fact that it was working-class gamekeepers on Kinder Scout who physically blocked access to Benny Rothman and his fellow ramblers in 1932 illustrates how enduring was this assumption that keepers were quasi-official agents of law enforcement.

North Derbyshire already had a long history as a royal hunting preserve. In the Middle Ages the Crown had carved out a massive sporting estate running from the Derwent to the Goyt Valley. Kinder Scout was right at its heart. But by the time of the enclosures the region was synonymous with one particular kind of game. Its gritstone plateaux were unsuited to the pheasants and partridges that flourished in the softer rolling pastures and wooded coverts of southern England. The Derbyshire uplands are tough and forbidding, especially during winter.

In the early eighteenth century Daniel Defoe, visiting the county as part of a national tour, referred to the area west of Chesterfield as a 'waste and houling wilderness'. His strongest verdict, however, was reserved for the section that included Kinder. It was, he suggested, 'perhaps the most desolate, wild, and abandoned country in all England'.[12] Desolate and wild it may have been, but red grouse love it.

This endemic British galliform, which can survive in those cold wet latitudes up to 3,000 feet, feeds on little more than the tough fibrous tips of common ling. By burning the vegetation on a roughly ten-year rotation and encouraging a constant growth of fresh heather, game-keepers managed those upland areas almost entirely in the interests of this bird. The privatisation of the moors thus had none of the justifi-cations underpinning the enclosures further south – that of increased agricultural efficiency. The local people had been evicted from the uplands in the interests of upper-class sporting pleasure.

One of the few 'efficiencies' that had accompanied these enclosures was the way the grouse were slaughtered. Originally the sport relied on parties of two to three guns tramping through the heather, armed with flintlocks, and aided by specially trained dogs – setters or pointers – whose uncanny sensitivities to the presence of crouching gamebirds was at the heart of its skill and practice. All that changed with the quicker mechanism of the breech-loaded shotgun, invented in 1847. It gave rise to a sporting format in which shooters didn't go in search of prey, the birds were brought to them. A cordon of flag-waving beaters would drive the grouse, forcing them to fly high over the butts and their armed occupants. Many of the shooters had supporting 'loaders', which enabled them to use more than one gun on each drive.

This type of shooting is said to be technically challenging and immensely exciting, and today it is pretty much the standard format for shooting grouse. It is predicated upon a management regime that delivers in early autumn – 12 August is its famous start date – high, post-breeding surplus stocks of a single gamebird. It goes without saying that it has always been accompanied by intensive slaughter of anything that might reduce the grouse monoculture.* Yet when driven shoots were first introduced, adverse comment was entirely indifferent to the extermination of predatory hen harriers or foxes; what irked some of its critics was the effortlessness of it all.

A commentator in the *Daily Telegraph* (in August 1872) suggested that a *battue* 'at which, without fatigue or danger, some young sybarite destroys or wounds from six to eight hundred head of game in five or six hours is one of the saddest features of our existing civilisation'. (The psychopathology that allows someone even today to slaughter dozens, sometimes scores, and possibly hundreds of living animals during the course of a day's sport, and all in the name of pleasure, is not only beyond challenge, it remains almost entirely unexamined. Why?)

In order that their leisure pursuits shouldn't be witnessed by the envious classes, grouse-moor owners drew upon a helpful strand of legislation additional to the game laws. It concerned the decommissioning of old footpaths. It first acquired force in 1773 with an act that had been intended to rationalise England's transport network under a single piece of legislation. But it also allowed for the stopping-up of existing rights of way. Theoretically a landowner was obliged to provide an alternative route, but only, and most significantly, if two magistrates found it necessary. Unfortunately for any would-be pedestrian, the alignment of interests between the rural squirearchy and provincial justice system was almost total. In his book *The Decline and Fall of the British Aristocracy*, David Cannadine called England's justices of the peace 'a self-perpetuating oligarchy rightly … known as the "rural House of Lords"'. Often the two institutions comprised exactly the

---

* Jeremy Deller's hen harrier on the walls of the Venice Biennale implicitly gestures towards this secondary characteristic of driven-shoot management. For harriers are often considered the enemy-in-chief by grouse-moor owners. The systemic and illegal persecution of this raptor has led to its functional extinction in the English uplands. The red Range Rover, meanwhile, is a perfect motif for the super-rich practitioners of grouse shooting. A car that costs anything up to £125,000 is often the vehicle of choice for folk who think little of spending several thousand pounds for a day's killing on the moors.

same individuals. It meant that the law was no more than a simple expedient to achieve physical exclusion.[13]

In 1815 the system was screwed down tighter with the explicitly named Stopping-Up of Unnecessary Roads Act. 'The motto of the English nation', William Hazlitt wrote, is 'exclusion':

In this consists our happiness and our pride. If you come to a gentleman's park and pleasure-grounds, you see written up, 'Man-traps and steel-guns set here' – as if he had no pleasure in walking in them, except in the idea of keeping other people out … [14] *

John Ruskin despised the owners' perverse trend towards exclusion. 'Of all the small, mean and wicked things a landlord can do', he suggested, 'shutting up his footpath is the nastiest.'[15] According to the land rights historian Harvey Taylor, the Stopping-Up Act reflected nothing more than a 'cynical manipulation of legal forms' by the legislating and land-owning classes.[16] What made it particularly shoddy was the underlying wish by a privileged minority to reserve for itself the entire spiritual, aesthetic and moral possibilities of fresh air and panoramic scenery.

The expanding populations of urban Lancashire were among those that felt the unfairness of this territorial exclusion. Between 1801 and 1861 Manchester and Salford grew from 90,000 to 400,000 inhabitants. It is often claimed that a third of the English population lives within fifty miles of the Peak District (16 million people). Many were even closer. Just as one can see the full spread of Manchester from the heights of Kinder Scout, so is it possible to view that high plateau from the city's terraced backstreets. No wonder it became almost the defining landscape of the entire region. Unfortunately, while the grouse were welcome on Kinder, Mancunian labourers such as Benny Rothman were not.

---

* Man-traps were steel-jawed, often toothed, spring-loaded devices with the power to catch and hold a human leg. 'Steel-guns' were loaded and concealed firearms triggered by a wire that blasted indiscriminate shot at any would-be intruder. They killed and maimed the innocent, the naturalist and the stray child as often as they stopped the grim-faced poacher.

Some began to rail against that situation. In the grimy substrate and smoke-filled air of the urban rows there sprouted exotic new blooms with names such as the Mount Zion Baptist Band of Hope Rambling Club of Nelson, or the Colne and District Temperance Cycling and Rambling Club, or the Huddersfield Co-operative Holidays Association Rambling Club.[17] The simple act of placing one foot in front of the other was seldom just about walking.

Rambling was entwined with all manner of moral, intellectual and recreational (in both of its senses) goals. 'A rambler made is a man improved' was the logo of one of Sheffield's most proactive groups. Bert Ward, the person who coined it, spoke of the 'trinity of legs, eyes and mind' as a glance at the spiritual implications of rambling.*[18]

In *Mary Barton* (1848), her novel about industrial life in Victorian Manchester, Elizabeth Gaskell had earlier celebrated the cultural achievements of the working and walking classes. There was a breed of person in that city, she wrote;

> whose existence will probably be doubted by many, who yet may claim kindred with all the noble names that science recognises. I said in 'Manchester', but they are scattered all over the manufacturing districts of Lancashire. In the neighbourhood of Oldham there are weavers … who throw the shuttle with unceasing sound, though Newton's 'Principia' lies open on the loom. Mathematical problems are received with interest, and studied with absorbing attention by many a broad-spoken, common-looking factory-hand. It is perhaps less astonishing that the more popularly interesting branches of natural history have their warm and devoted followers among this class. There are botanists … who know the

---

* It speaks volumes of the sense of moral mission to be found in mid-twentieth-century ramblers that when this impressive, if somewhat cantankerous old man was given the title deeds to 54 acres on the summit of Losehill, across the valley from Kinder, Ward instantly gave them to the National Trust. Just before he died, at a ceremony to confer an honorary MA, the citation read: 'No man, in the last half century, could have done more, by precept and example, to foster the spirit of rambling.'

name and habitat of every plant within a day's walk from their dwellings; who steal the holiday of a day or two when any particular plant should be in flower … There are entomologists, who may be seen with a rude-looking net, ready to catch any winged insect, or a kind of dredge, with which they rake the green and slimy pools; practical, shrewd, hard-working men, who pore over every new specimen with real scientific delight. Nor is it the common and more obvious divisions of Entomology and Botany that alone attract these earnest seekers after knowledge. Perhaps it may be owing to the great annual town-holiday of Whitsun-week so often falling in May or June that the two great beautiful families of *Ephemeridae* [mayflies] and *Phyrganidae* [caddisflies] have been so much and so closely studied by Manchester workmen, while they have in great measure escaped general observation.[19]

As well as moral and intellectual self-advancement, walking was muddled up with politics almost from the start, especially working-class politics. A figure like Tom Stephenson (1893–1987) – author, editor, walker, mountaineer, administrator, lifelong access campaigner and co-founder of the long-distance footpath the Pennine Way – exemplified the links. His mother had worked in a cotton mill from the age of nine. A young socialist and conscientious objector in the First World War, Stephenson was heavily involved in the Labour Party by the 1930s and the editor of *Hiker and Camper*, a magazine published by the TUC. As Stephenson noted in his own book *Forbidden Land*, the events on Kinder in April 1932 were almost pure politics. In fact, some felt the 'trespassers' of 1932 'were more concerned with the class struggle than with the struggle for access to mountains and moorlands'.[20]

Yet more important than any possible divisions among ramblers was a fundamental, shared proposition, which was succinctly expressed by G. S. Phillips, a Yorkshireman and prominent campaigner for rights of access. In one of his books he wrote: 'Whoever may own the land, no man can own the beauty of the landscape.' Anyone who could see and appreciate its magnificence, Phillips added, was 'legitimate lord of the landscape'.[21] It was a direct challenge to the moral position of many landowners who, according to Canon Rawnsley, were 'apt to look upon a piece of property in land much as one looks at the possession of a piece of china or a consignment of cotton'.[22]

When the gamekeeper Edmund Beever caught it in the balls around 4 p.m. on the upper slopes of Kinder Scout, it was these two opposing existential positions on land and landownership that played out in a brief rainstorm of sticks, fists and boots. Within hours of the collision the state authorities had decided there could be no possibility of triumphalist celebrations in the cafés of Hayfield or, later that evening, in the pubs of Manchester. The grand finale to this so-called Mass Trespass would take place at the Derby Assizes and, afterwards, in the grey-walled cells of Leicester jail.

The trial and prosecution of six of the 'offenders', all aged between nineteen and twenty-three and including Rothman himself, purported to be a routine act of justice in the aftermath of a public disturbance. Rothman, for example, was charged with riotous assembly, assault and incitement to riot. In retrospect, however, the court case looks exactly what it was: an orchestrated piece of establishment revenge and an overly harsh punishment intended to act as a deterrent to others.*

Just in case the legal processes did not quite square with the expectations of the state, the courtroom's twelve good men and true were somehow contrived to include two brigadier-generals, three colonels, two majors, three captains and two aldermen. Apropos of very little except perhaps the assumed anti-Semitism of that establishment-packed jury, the judge pointed out in session that half the rambling defendants were Jewish. One of the trespass organisers was eventually acquitted on a technicality, but the other five received sentences of between two and six months. It was a sledgehammer to crack a nut, and the public spotted it.

---

* One can perhaps appreciate the underlying concerns that propelled the court case and its verdicts when you see the *Daily Mail* headline at the time of the Mass Trespass. It read 'The Crimson Ramblers': 'Our hikers by the ten thousand shoulder their packs and fare forth to discover the beauties of Nature. But the Communists are determined that they shall tramp our footpaths … musing only on the iniquities of the capitalist system.' Jailing trespassers was thus a way of halting the spread of Marxist agitation across England's gritstone moors.[23]

The affairs on that Sunday afternoon and their aftermath, rather than scotching agitation for ramblers' access, triggered an immediate increase in public attention for the issue. Those ramblers' organisations that had previously opposed the trespass swung instinctively behind their imprisoned fellows. Two months after it had occurred there was a rally in Winnats Pass, just to the south-east of the Kinder plateau, involving 10,000 people. Follow-up events of similar stamp occurred all over England, while the press railed against the severity of the sentences for the Kinder five. The Mass Trespass had been firmly set on its journey out of the realms of simple fact and towards its legendary status.

Yet therein lies a curious irony, which Tom Stephenson highlighted. What transpired that Sunday, in and of itself, was actually a minor affair. The Kinder event was neither the first nor the last rally of its kind. The turnout that day was not particularly large. The level of physical confrontation was small, and probably nothing more than the sorts of scuffles that had accompanied the unrecorded eviction of trespassers by gamekeepers – or vice versa – all over northern England for decades. Even the rambling community acknowledged that very little genuinely took place. The would-be offenders on that Sunday didn't really know Kinder Scout and were not entirely familiar with the places where they were *not* permitted to walk. As a consequence, Stephenson suggested that 'there never was a mass trespass'.[24]

He also questioned its historical impact. For him it contributed 'little, if anything' to 'the access to mountains campaign'.[25] Technically Stephenson may have been right. By 1932, at least twelve separate draft laws had already been submitted to the House of Commons seeking public entitlement to walk on mountains and other unproductive lands.* They were all blocked or thrown out, and when an eighteenth, the Access to Mountains bill, reached the statute books in 1939 it had been so mauled during its passage that it was little more than 'a monstrous unrecognisable changeling'. It was repealed ten years later.[26] One further

---

* The first had been proposed by James Bryce in 1884 and was by no means the work of a socialist agitator. Bryce was a Liberal statesman, future ambassador to the USA and eventually Viscount of Dechmount. He and his brother Annan resubmitted the bill eight times in variant forms until 1909.

law, three other bills and a new millennium all came and went, before the CROW Act (Countryside and Rights of Way Act) was finally passed by Tony Blair's New Labour government in 2000. With that law, full public access to the countryside was truly delivered, but it had taken 116 years and twenty-three different pieces of legislation before Parliament.[27]

This timeline suggests that Rothman's merry march on Kinder had small influence on those processes, and yet one cannot help noticing that the first national park to be declared in Britain (1950) – the Peak District National Park – had that myth enshrouded plateau at its heart. The country's first long-distance footpath, the Pennine Way (1965), championed so persistently by Tom Stephenson, begins in the long shadow of Kinder Scout. At the fiftieth (1982, when a new access bill was also submitted), sixtieth (1992), seventieth (2002) and seventy-fifth (2007) anniversaries of the Mass Trespass there were major gatherings at Hayfield. Now its birthday is celebrated annually. It has been so embroidered through endless retellings that my guess is the Mass Trespass will never be forgotten as long as hill walking remains a popular pastime. And Kinder will be for ever a landscape associated with environmental politics.

Perhaps it doesn't matter now what took place or whether the events on that day were trivial. What is important is that it *is* remembered. We should think of it less as a collection of verifiable details and more as a myth. 'And the question we should ask of a myth', suggests the cleric Richard Holloway, 'is not whether it is true or false, … but whether it is living or dead, whether it still carries existential meaning for us in our time.'[28] The Mass Trespass has come to summarise the entire 150-year social conflict entailed in access to the countryside. For many people it is the *only* story they now know or recall about the issue.*

---

* As David Hey notes in his excellent *A History of the Peak District Moors*, perhaps the ultimate expression of its mythic status is that modern websites regularly suggest that the Ramblers' Association (RA) was founded in 1935 as a result of the Mass Trespass. In fact the formerly named Federation of Rambling Clubs was established in 1905 and in 1932 it actually opposed the events on Kinder as a stunt! (see p. 184).

In some ways its relevance and importance has not decreased with time. It has become more powerfully symbolic of divisions in this country between those who hold and control land and those who do not. In the 1970s the richest 1 per cent in Britain held more than half of all the personally owned land, and today just 40,000 families control almost three-quarters of Britain's entire 60 million acres.[29]

The disproportionate dominance of the few has only intensified in the last decade. Between 2005 and 2011 the average size of landholdings had risen by 12 per cent. George Monbiot speculated whether this was the fastest consolidation of land ownership since the Highland Clearances.[30]

By contrast, the rest of us, the 16.8 million households that make up the UK population, possess just 4 per cent of the country, equivalent to 2.4 million acres and about the same size of area as that owned or managed by the Forestry Commission.

In its capacity to capture our imaginative encounter with these issues we should perhaps think of that Rothman-led crusade up the slopes of Kinder Scout as a piece of activist art, in much the same way that we view Jeremy Deller's powerfully mythological hen harrier at the Venice Biennale. Technically that latter piece was only briefly installed and has long since been painted over but, like the Mass Trespass, it lives still in people's memories.

Jeremy Deller's *A Good Day For Cyclists* and the myth of the Mass Trespass are alike in another sense. Ultimately they redound to the same fundamental questions that were triggered by the enclosures from the moment they were first enacted. The killing of hen harriers, as some mysterious person(s) did so publicly on the Sandringham estate in October 2007, flows from the same kinds of assumption about land ownership as does the blocking up of a footpath. In both cases the fact of possession is viewed in absolute terms. What dwells upon the land, whether it be beauty or bird, remains the exclusive goods of him or her who holds the title deeds.

The development of environmental values has frequently entailed a challenge to that legal posture. It has demanded to know what entitlements remain to those of us who hold no such legal claim. It asserts the reclamation of common rights. It proposes that there are elements in our relationship with land that are immaterial but universally applicable. And no faction can corral those intangible parts exclusively to itself. These include the right to enjoy the beauty of a hen harrier, or the pain of possession as one battles up the path in William Clough.

The long historical campaign for the right to roam was the restatement of a human need for intimacy – mental and physical – with nature. In this sense the Mass Trespass on Kinder Scout was indisputably part of Britain's journey towards an environmental ethic, every bit as much as the foundation of the National Trust, or the establishment of our national parks.

8

THINGS ARE GOING TO BE DIFFERENT AFTER THE WAR

America, our Dominions, and most advanced European countries have long since adopted the principle that the State should take responsibility for the preservation of some part of its native wild life for the benefit of future generations. It has proved that the only way to do this effectively is to supplement the preservation laws by the provision of national parks or reserves to act as breeding reservoirs … This country alone has left this task to chance and the initiative of private individuals and societies.

RSPB committee chaired by Geoffrey Dent, 1940

It is remarkable to reflect that in December 1950 Kinder Scout and a further 530 square miles of Derbyshire, east Cheshire, north Stafford-shire and the southern edge of Yorkshire's West Riding were all designated part of the Peak District National Park. It was only five years since the end of the war, and it was only eighteen years since people had been arrested and imprisoned for merely walking on the moors above Hayfield.

What had happened to bring about a complete volte-face in local affairs? No one could now say with Assistant Chief Constable Garrow that Derbyshire didn't like hill walkers. The Peak District was soon to be among Britain's top visitor attractions. Today there are 22 million day visits a year, more than to any other national park save Mount Fuji in Japan.[1]

Kinder's summit must still be among the most walked parts of the entire park, and its popularity says something utterly different to the other notable hotspots. Dove Dale, like Kinder, is among the park's best-known and best-loved places. The car park near Ilam, where the River Manifold meets the Dove and about the most popular venue of all, is overflowing with picnickers every bank holiday. Just upstream the village of Hartington has bustling crowds almost every weekend. However, if you walk for just fifteen minutes down the valley from the latter there can be almost no one.

Go at Whitsun and, by the time you enter the limestone cleft of Wolfscote Dale, you can have the whole place to yourself, except for the mesmerising mayfly swarms running in flux above the line of the river. These shoals of millions glint like mica as they catch the sun dapple and cause the fish to rise. Then suddenly, the whole shimmer turns around and surges back, an invertebrate stream flowing headlong against the water's current.

Kinder edge, by contrast, is several miles and at least a 1,000-foot climb from the nearest car park. Yet the Saturday traffic is relentless, and particularly along that curving line between Sandy Heys and Kinder Low. It doesn't matter from where the walkers come – Ladybower and the Snake Inn, or the National Trust car park at Hayfield, or up from Edale via Jacob's Ladder. Kinder is their point of convergence, and people pass in both directions all the time. In fact, the erosion of the path is a serious issue. The trail down through William Clough is now a deep gully of loose gravel. But, in a sense, the worn trails over Kinder are our collective, renewed signature on the purpose and importance of national parks.

The process by which the British government slowly arrived at this undertaking, and then founded an accompanying post-war network of state nature reserves, is tangled and complex. It is also spread over several decades. It is a story that builds through the incremental pressure exerted by specialist committees, expressing themselves in formal bureaucratic prose. Notable among them were the Addison Report (1931), the Nature Reserves Investigations Committee (1942), the Scott Report (1942; technically it was the Report of the Scott Committee on Land Utilisation in Rural Areas), the Huxley Report (1947), and the Hobhouse Report (1947).

No single part of the process was decisive. The unfolding story, therefore, reads like a narrative measured in the minutes of meetings and highlighted by the bullet points of memoranda. In truth, it is rather dull. There are remarkably few events and absolutely no dramas.* It is probably another reason why the Mass Trespass is remembered, while so much of the surrounding tale has been lost. Nor are there many dominant personalities, but one or two names stand out.

John Dower resembles Charles Rothschild both in the multiplicity of his talent and the brevity of his life. Born in 1900, he was an archi-tect and town planner by profession, but by vocation he was a fell walker and ardent campaigner for the right to roam. As much as anything, however, it was his marriage that determined his decisive career as a civil servant working for the establishment of national parks.

In 1929 Dower had wed Pauline Trevelyan, daughter of the Liberal politician and later Labour minister, Charles Trevelyan. Her uncle was George Macaulay Trevelyan, historian, passionate outdoorsman and National Trust devotee. In 1908 her father had brought before the House of Commons a private member's bill that would have given right of access to the UK uplands. Like all such early measures this one failed, but ramblers' rights and national parks were the table talk of the Trevelyans' and Dowers' domestic world.

In 1936 John Dower had been appointed secretary to what was called the Standing Committee on National Parks. This had been founded largely by a new organisation entitled the Council for the Preservation of Rural England. The committee was made up of an amalgam of interested voluntary groups all in favour of the establish-ment of English regions administered in the interests of walkers and wildlife. However, it was Dower's dynamic role as their secretary that

---

* The history of environmentalism in the interwar and post-war periods may be short on action and long on bureaucratic detail, but it has been meticulously documented by the indefatigable John Sheail. His various books and papers, especially *Nature in Trust* and *Nature Conservation in Britain*, are indispensable to an understanding of the times.

gave weight to its work. He wrote several key pamphlets that were widely disseminated. These efforts came close to success, but government austerity in the aftermath of the 1930s depression and then the brewing sense of international crisis thwarted plans for national parks.

At the outbreak of war Dower enlisted as a soldier, but was soon invalided out as a result of the tuberculosis that would later kill him. He was eventually well enough to resume work on national parks, as a civil servant in the Ministry of Works and Buildings, which had been tasked by government to supply a lead on post-war reconstruction. Part of it involved Dower researching and publishing a document that would eventually bear his name. The Dower Report of 1945 played a decisive role in Kinder Scout's inclusion in Britain's first national park just five years later. It was a blueprint that would lead eventually to fourteen other parks. Dower, alas, would never live to see any of them. He died in 1947, aged forty-seven. (Pauline Dower, his widow, would later become a founder member of the National Parks Commission and, later still, its deputy chair, while his son Michael Dower would run the Peak National Park.)

The other dominant personality during the period is perhaps *the* towering figure of all British environmental history. Edward Max Nicholson, known always as Max, lived almost as long as the century in which he played so decisive a role. Born in 1904, he died aged ninety-eight in the week that the cuckoos start to sing on Kinder: 26 April 2003. By the age of thirty-five and before the Second World War had even begun Max had already turned in a lifetime of achievements.

His first book, *Birds in England*, was published when he was just twenty-two. Within three years he had written three more and edited two others.[2] While at Oxford he founded both the university's exploration club and then a project entitled the Oxford Bird Census, which grew eventually into the British Trust for Ornithology, now one of the nation's leading institutions in the field of environmental research. Nicholson was its secretary and then its chairman.

Afterwards came several years in an influential and progressive think-tank, Political and Economic Planning, which had been founded in response to a paper Nicholson had written and published in 1931 entitled 'A National Plan for Britain'. Max was PEP's first director. In turn, this brought invitations to join the Civil Service, where he took up war work in the Ministry of Transport. The role would later lead to his attendance at the Yalta and Potsdam Conferences.[*3]

If Dower's work was decisive in the creation of national parks, then Nicholson should be credited as midwife-in-chief at the birth of the Nature Conservancy, the government agency tasked with identifying, gazetting and administering Britain's areas of greatest wildlife importance. Max would eventually serve as its second director general, but his post-war influence in bringing about its creation flowed from his role as head of the office to the Labour government's Lord President and Deputy Prime Minister, Herbert Morrison.

There is yet a third figure that should be identified as perhaps the presiding genius in the establishment of state-sponsored conservation. Even in the middle of Hayfield there is a special memorial to that important catalytic party. If you come off Kinder Scout, past the Sportsman Inn, where the spotted flycatchers still dart and tack in the sycamores above the river, you finally come into the village. There is a shortcut to the memorial via the cricket ground. Out of the dust-and-sunshine quietness overhead, the jackdaw calls rebound off the slate roofs, which are the precise shade of the birds' own wings. Their richly echoic *chak chak* notes mimic the clump and tempo of your own

---

[*] I met Max once in 1995 at a British Ornithologists' Union conference in Dartington, Devon. At ninety-one he was then the grand old man of British nature, but still trim and stylish in a three-piece suit and as sharp as a tack. We got to speak as I helped him with his bags to the railway station (an attack of polio in his twenties had left him with a permanent limp). His most moving words were his response to an enquiry: who of all the extraordinary friends, colleagues and work associates he'd known over the years did he miss most? Max had known all the environmental figures of the age, at home and abroad: Phylis Barclay-Smith, General Sir Alan Brooke, John Dower, James Fisher, Richard Fitter, Bernard Grzimek, Julian Huxley, Guy Mountfort, Derek Ratcliffe, Miriam Rothschild, Sir Peter Scott, Professor Sir Arthur Tansley, Roger Tory Peterson. His response was instant: Bernard Tucker. He was a friend from Oxford days, fellow founder of the BTO, legendary editor of *British Birds*, who had died in 1950. Max had missed him for half a lifetime.

boots as you pass the whitewashed gritstone walls, which serve as a very Derbyshire version of a batsman's sightscreen.

Just beyond the Hayfield cricket ground, by the River Kinder, between the church and the Royal Hotel, where the mallards gather and the sounds of tumbling waters mingle with traffic noise, there you'll find the memorial itself. On four sides of the column, in block capitals, are the words:

PATRIOTISM, HONOUR, SACRIFICE, FREEDOM

It largely commemorates the carnage between 1914 and 1919, but there at the foot of the main cross is an additional tablet. It reads,

Also in grateful memory of those who gave their lives in the Great War 1939–1945

The pillar is now encircled by large carmine-blossomed rose bushes, which are lined on the near side with lavender. When I saw them last I noticed how the stalks of the latter trembled and flexed with the comings and goings of common carder bees. Around the punctuated quiet of the memorial was the warm swell of bumble drone, so that even the seismic rift of warfare was folded back into the everyday at Hayfield.

The Second World War had a decisive impact on our entire relations with nature and the countryside. The elemental clash of forces and values over those six years of conflict liberated people to talk about how they wanted to live and what they were fighting for. As one historian noted, the most frequently repeated political declaration among the ordinary ranks during the early 1940s was, 'Things are going to be different after the war.'[4]

'A land fit for heroes' had been the constant rubric of peacetime politics a generation earlier, except that after 1918 very little of that promise was truly translated into action. With the advent of a second global conflagration people were determined that such misery had to yield a silver lining. Almost from the very outset there was strategic planning for peace. Max Nicholson had even been part of a Post-War Aims Group in the month before any fighting had actually occurred.

Later he would offer a more cynical reflection on why war had been so decisive for the foundation of state-based nature conservation.*

It is an ironic commentary on the workings of the British system of government that it should have been possible under heavy German bombing, and subject to petrol rationing, black-out and absence on military service of so many able-bodied observers, at last to carry through, within a mere couple of years, a survey and review [of the country's best sites for wildlife], which had clearly been urgently needed since the previous century. This was thanks to the wartime suspension of ... the normal British mechanisms for ensuring inaction.[5]

It was not just the temporary cessation of good old British dither that brought change. The nation willed it. Life under war conditions had entailed the almost total supervision of every aspect of soldiers' and civilians' lives. Conscription and rationing affected equally, and without favour, the country house and the tenant's cottage. In the absence of so many men at the front, women had been elevated and were soon comfortable with traditional masculine roles. All this inspired a deep-rooted desire for greater equality, as well as for a proper share in national prosperity and a real stake in the country.

The parliamentary election of July 1945 did not merely replace one party with another. 'The result', noted one historian, 'was the most decisive verdict in favour of radical change that the British electorate had ever delivered.' The people, he continued, had 'passed a vote of no confidence in the past and proclaimed a quiet, determined wish for a social revolution.'[6]

---

* Nicholson's full sense of government ineptitude was captured forcefully in his book, entitled *The System* (1967). This indictment of British culture, high and low, was said to be the reason why this extraordinarily talented man never received his just deserts, although he was made CVO and CB for his war work.

In specifically rural affairs there were strong practical reasons why a massive shake-up was imminent. The relentless bombing of towns and cities during the Blitz had inflicted damage the length and breadth of the country. This required a programme of reconstruction not just of key industries but also of much of the civil housing stock. Yet the German Luftwaffe had brought opportunity as well as devastation. Many of the damaged houses were the deplorable old slums from the Victorian age. As part of the reconstruction there was scope for new improved housing and planned settlements in peaceful rural settings. Town and country could be made equally attractive and part of a single wholesome blended community.

Another unlikely instrument to decisively re-shape land policy was the German U-boat. For six years the nation's encirclement by enemy submarines had placed extraordinary pressures on the Allied merchant fleet. (It was the effort to counter these effects that had in turn placed demands on Nicholson's organisational genius, when he was the Head of Allocation of Tonnage.) The losses to British shipping had affected the country's capacity even simply to feed itself. A prolonged depression had settled over UK agriculture since the last decades of the nineteenth century, and in 1939 Britain produced only a third of its food requirements.[7] The U-boats' impact on imports demanded immediate, radical overhaul of both agriculture and rural planning, and by 1944 the country was growing almost two-thirds of food consumed domestically. The British had genuinely dug for victory.

Despite the many good reasons why the events of 1939–45 had catalysed the British political classes to take up the official reins of rural management, one cannot help but be impressed and even shocked by the way in which the environmental developments ran in parallel with the sombre chronology of war. One of the most influential occasions was a gathering of like-minded activists that entitled itself the Conference on Nature Preservation in Post-War Reconstruction. It held its first meeting in June 1941. It is hard to imagine a less auspicious moment for advancing the cause of birds and bumblebees.

In the weeks before the environmentalists assembled, Adolf Hitler had diverted his all-conquering army south to crush Yugoslavia and snatch Greece. Within just forty-two days Belgrade had been utterly destroyed and the Nazi flag set fluttering over the Parthenon, while Germans troops had even captured the Allied-held island of Crete. This was despite British naval supremacy and a defending garrison of 42,000 Greek, British, Australian and New Zealand troops.* The invaders had enjoyed command of the skies, however, and they had simply dropped their paratroopers by transport plane.

With these Mediterranean conquests settled by the end of May, the Führer felt free to indulge fully his psychopathic loathing of the Soviet Union. 'Operation Barbarossa' required seventeen Panzer and thirteen motorised divisions with their 3,350 tanks – a total of 3.2 million men – in what would be the most intense and brutally destructive conflict between two nations in history. In the days before the invasion began on Midsummer's Eve 1941, Hitler suffered sleepless nights in feverish anticipation of the victory he assumed.

As the world rose towards that watershed, the delegates of the RSPB and the Society for the Promotion of Nature Reserves settled down to talk wildlife and national parks. The secretary to the Conference on Nature Preservation in Post-War Reconstruction was none other than Herbert Smith, that same self-effacing servant who had kept the SPNC afloat in its years of quietude following the death of Charles Rothschild. The conference deliberations were summarised in a 1941 memorandum that eventually caught the attention of the Paymaster General, Sir William Jowitt, one of Churchill's cross-party war cabinet.

It is strange for us now to contemplate the parallel strands of history, but it seems stranger still to imagine those figures like Jowitt, or even Churchill, dealing with the destruction of Yugoslavia, the fall of Greece,

---

* One of the officers captured on Crete was Lieutenant George Waterston, who would become the RSPB's man in Scotland and would later dream up his own campaign, entitled Operation Osprey. Prior to the German airborne invasion he'd kept a diary of his Cretan bird observations. The last entry read: 'Little bird watching was accomplished during May due to the exigencies of war service; this was unfortunate as many summer visitors and passage migrants were on the move during that time.' See Derek Niemann's enchanting memoir of POW ornithology, *Birds in a Cage*, p. 29.

Crete, the siege of Tobruk, the invasion of Russia, Pearl Harbor, Japanese entry into the war, and all the while fielding questions on landscape amenity and the creation of bird sanctuaries. Yet, in a sense, they were all of a piece. Creating space for birds or wild flowers and halting Axis tyranny were two parts of the same civilised future for which people felt they were striving.

Although national parks and state-administered nature reserves were conceived in the same wartime ferment and brought to life through the same piece of legislation, the two environmental institutions enjoyed quite separate trajectories. (The development of the Nature Conservancy and National Nature Reserves is treated under the next landscape, Upper Teesdale.)

Environmentalists have long called this severance of landscape conservation from nature protection – for which one could substitute the words *natural beauty* and *other species* – the 'Great Divide'. It is a schism that they ascribe to this particular historical moment. In truth, the divisions pre-existed any kind of state concern for the environment.

One need only recall the broadly separate histories, methods and intentions of the National Trust or CPRE as opposed to the RSPB or the Wildlife Trusts, to understand that the Great Divide is systemic in British environmental history (see the footnote in Chapter 5 on p. 69). Do we cherish nature's manifest beauties measured by some arbitrary aesthetic code? Or do we value and protect wildlife diversity for its own sake? The integration of the two approaches should have been straightforward and was achieved in many other countries, but not in Britain. As the historian Michael Winter argues, the division was intellectually flawed and 'a debilitating feature of the British arrangements'.[8]

Men like John Dower agreed. He had envisioned the two designations – national parks and nature reserves – as equal entities administered by a single body, and this bifurcation in their management was entirely contrary to his wishes.[9]

Unfortunately, Dower's own report of 1945 was not the last word. Instead it inspired the creation of yet another new forum, the National

Parks Committee. It included Dower among its members, but the group delivered its findings in a report named after its own chair, Sir Arthur Hobhouse. It was this document that finally gave a green light to legislation, which was passed in 1949 and named the National Parks and Access to Countryside Act.

For all its shortcomings, the creation of the national parks, like so many of the other achievements of Attlee's premiership, is the sort of accomplishment that it is difficult to envisage in our own time. We have certainly built on that post-war foundation, adding new parks every decade or so; but for a later government to have begun the creative process from scratch is now hard to imagine, and more so with every passing administration.

As a state institution, national parks were certainly long overdue. James Bryce, the MP who had introduced the 1884 Access to Mountains bill, is credited as the first to have used the words 'national park' in Parliament (1877).[10] He would later suggest that they were the best idea the Americans had ever had.[11] Yet it had taken English politicians seventy-seven years and the largest war in history to follow that lead. When they arrived, national parks were a remarkable achievement. The setting aside of large tracts of country to safeguard natural beauty and to serve as amenity areas for all citizens was an indisputable part of the radical programme, articulated by Tommy in his combat khaki, that things were going to be different after the war.

Perhaps it was an attempt to underscore how different things would be that the National Parks Commission decided that the first park should include Kinder Scout, with all its dark remembering moors.* One might have imagined that the Lake District, given its seminal role in the entire British relationship to nature, would have possessed deeper, sharper symbolism. But Wordsworth's beloved hills and lakes had

---

* The administrative body for national parks has been a victim of the same kind of nomenclatural confusion that has beset all environmental history. In fact the name changes begin to seem almost conspiratorial. In 1968 it was re-christened the Countryside Commission for England and Wales, and then the Countryside Agency in 1999, after it had merged – groan! – with the Rural Development Commission.

enjoyed a long tradition of free access. What made the Peak District such an apt and inspired first choice was its equally long record of exclusion. Soon public footpaths were entwined not just with this local geography, but with the entire texture of the British landscape. In England and Wales alone there are 129,723 miles of path of various grades, according to that scrupulous auditor of our landscape, Marion Shoard.[12]

The gradual opening up of Kinder and its neighbouring gritstone places was complemented by the establishment of nine more national parks: the Lake District (1951; 885 square miles); Snowdonia (1951; 840 square miles); Dartmoor (1951; 368 square miles); the Pembrokeshire Coast (1952; 240 square miles); the North York Moors (1952; 554 square miles); the Yorkshire Dales (1952; 683 square miles); Exmoor (1954; 268 square miles); Northumberland (1956; 405 square miles); and the Brecon Beacons (1957; 519 square miles). In total they amounted to 5,300 square miles and 5.5 per cent of the total UK landscape. There should have been a round dozen, had the Norfolk/Suffolk Broads and South Downs been added as many hoped. But both these places were rejected in the original assessment because of landowner opposition. It was not until 1989 that the Broads (117 square miles) became a semi-official national park, with full status in 2015, while the South Downs (628 square miles) were at last added in 2011.*

The original ten were all largely within that portion of the country north or west of a line between the Severn and the Humber. They were underlaid by the older, harder formations of upland Britain: the ancient schists, gneisses, the granite masses, volcanic rocks and older limestones. They were often distinguished by those sweeping, even

---

* Today there are 15 parks in total. An English addition, the New Forest (150 square miles) was made in 2005, while two large Scottish landscapes, Cairngorm (1,748 square miles) and Loch Lomond and the Trossachs (720 square miles) contribute to a present grand total of 8,848 square miles and 9.45 per cent of the UK landmass. Wales, however, has the highest relative area, with three parks that represent 19.9 per cent of the Principality. Two of the English parks have increased their size since being first designated. The Yorkshire Dales have acquired 158 miles[2] and Lake District a further 27 square miles.

feminine, contours left by the brutal and bulldozing impacts of glaciation. Our national parks are thus rich in features associated with ancient ice: U-shaped valleys, moraines, corries, drumlins, eskers, erratics, cwms. The youngest in the geological sequence are the fossil-rich shales and sandstones beneath the North Yorkshire Moors, which were laid down in the Jurassic, 200 million years ago. The oldest – in Snowdonia and the Lake District – are the Cambrian massifs of oceanic or volcanic origin, when Britain was part of a great continent that drifted inexorably north from the Equator.

It is odd to reflect on those ancient southern climes wherein our national parks were made, because these same British places are now thought of as northern, rain-soaked and impoverished. With thin soils of high acidity and low agricultural value, they are predominantly areas of rushy pasture, open moor or bog, and offer little other than poor grazing to hardy stock, especially sheep. As a result, the population centres of the national parks are few. Nevertheless, they are there.*

Unlike the equivalent parks in, say, sub-Saharan Africa or even continental USA, they were not devoid of people. On the contrary, they had been humanised and owned and farmed for millennia. That, in a way, was part of the whole point of the British national parks. They preserved something of which its citizens had been proud since the time of Shakespeare: a sense that this island had been shaped and made beautiful by a perpetual collaboration between its human inhabitants and the ground on which they dwelt. Britain was not one thing or another – land or people: its loveliness embodied a fusion of the two. It was this idealised notion of partnership between farm and fell, plough and partridge, culture and nature, that inspired Octavia Hill and Canon Rawnsley alike.

This harmony had perhaps been best encapsulated by Ralph Vaughan Williams's piece *The Lark Ascending*. The dark, soaring strains of its solo violin may have presaged the melancholy of war – it was

---

* The total population for the original ten parks in 1981 was 243,300 at a density of 42.6 per square mile, compared with the average of 660 per square mile for the UK as a whole.

written in early 1914 – but also it seems to carry aloft the spiritual connections to place of an entire people. It is a sublime piece of musical nostalgia and patriotism and even now remains the most popular choice on the BBC's *Desert Island Discs*, as well as the nation's favourite classical melody.

It is worth recalling that its inspiration is a bird vocalisation from a species that is the most agricultural in Britain. As Max Nicholson himself noted, skylarks not only dislike woods: they are seldom to be found even close to a tree. The skylark is the quintessential inhabitant of ploughland or pasture, and our agricultural presence in Britain made its own abundance possible. Prior to the echo of a Neolithic axe upon our post-glacial wildwoods, there may have been no such thing as a singing skylark in this country.

George Meredith's poem of the same name, which had first unlocked Vaughan Williams's responses, enlarged upon the shared ecology of bird and Britons. Take this single sentence:

> The woods and brooks, the sheep and kine,
> He is, the hills, the human line,
> The meadows green, the fallows brown,
> The dreams of labour in the town;
> He sings the sap, the quickened veins;
> The wedding song of sun and rains
> He is, the dance of children, thanks
> Of sowers, shout of primrose-banks,
> And eye of violets while they breathe;
> All these the circling song will wreathe,
> And you shall hear the herb and tree,
> The better heart of men shall see,
> Shall feel celestially, as long
> As you crave nothing save the song.

Essential to that national ideal of landscape beauty was human presence. Yet there are genuine ecological underpinnings for the notion that Britons and British nature had been good for one another. The great twentieth-century ecologist Colin Tubbs suggested that biodiversity in his own Hampshire reached its peak, not in the early Holocene when the first people were hunter-gatherers, but in the middle of the eighteenth century and after several millennia of continuous farming.[13] Tubbs's assessment of his agricultural home county probably holds true for the country as a whole.

It was this sense of intrinsic mutual benefit between farming and wildlife that lured all the environmentalists involved in the post-war developments to assume that nothing would change any time soon. One such figure was Sir Arthur Tansley (1871–1955).* In *Our Heritage of Wild Nature* (1945), his short book laying out the need for state conservation, Tansley regretted the wartime ploughing of heath and fenland, but suggested that the loss was not serious. And 'it is scarcely probable', he added, 'that the extension of agriculture will go much further, for the limits ... must have been reached in most places.' Not that he feared it in any case. For Tansley, the expansion of farming, as the British had dug for victory, had increased the beauty of the countryside.[14]

By 1945 his claim was already untrue, but we have to forgive him, for it is only now, and in retrospect, that we can see and measure the scale of his error. Flower-rich meadows, beloved by Tansley and central to the very idea and substance of British landscape beauty, are a perfect index of the changes.

Meadows were omnipresent in Tansley's day. Fields of rich herb, created by human interaction with the land, and mown in late summer for hay as winter fodder, had sometimes been used in this manner since Neolithic times. In the 1920s there were still 4.2 million acres threaded

---

* As a student and during his early career as an academic botanist, Tansley worked with Professor Oliver, the very man responsible for Blakeney Point's purchase by the National Trust. Tansley was also the founding editor of the *Journal of Ecology*, founder president of the British Ecological Society and pioneer of his discipline as a tool of environmental understanding. Derek Ratcliffe described him as the 'foremost thinker of those who launched the post-war conservation movement'. If Max Nicholson supplied the organisational groundwork and then possessed the political nous to create the Nature Conservancy, then Tansley was the brains in the outfit. He was also an early convert to psychotherapy and during the 1920s had studied under Freud in Vienna.

into the very fabric of England and Wales. In summer around 300 species of vascular plant had accommodated themselves to meadow in a multicoloured patchwork that turned yellow or magenta or mauve, depending on the dominant bloom – yellow rattle, orchid, harebell, scabious – and its month of flowering. There can be fifty species of vascular plant in a single square metre.

> I know a bank where the wild thyme blows,
> where oxslips and the nodding violet grows,
> Quite over-canopied with luscious woodbine,
> with sweet musk-roses, and with eglantine;

Oberon and Shakespeare knew and loved meadows – their luxuriance, their simple innocence, but also their eroticism and their power to set us dreaming.* Three hundred years later, Edward Thomas, chancing upon men mowing a meadow, was moved by the scene's ancientness and its aura of deep continuity. 'All was old', he wrote in his poem 'Haymaking':

> This morning time, with a great age untold,
> Older than Clare and Cobbett, Morland and Crome,
> Than, at the field's far edge, the farmer's home,
> A white house crouched at the foot of a great tree.
> Under the heavens that know not what years be
> The men, the beasts, the trees, the implements
> Uttered even what they will in times far hence –
> All of us gone out of the reach of change –
> Immortal in a picture of an old grange.

Alas, after Thomas's poetic vision of 1915 there would be far fewer meadow 'times far hence' than he imagined. Within thirty years

---

* Or at least, Oberon and Shakespeare loved flower-rich glades because their particular choice of plants includes a blend of woodland (oxslip, woodbine and eglantine) and open grassland (thyme and violet) species. The dreaming innocence and sensuality of such places are, however, not in dispute.

two-fifths of them would have been destroyed. By 1960 another 1.75 million acres had gone. In 1984 just 3 per cent remained. Today it is 1 per cent.[15]

What was taking nature out of the fields and from under our very noses? It was certainly not the thing that Tansley feared. And what really worried him were the same issues that had aroused Patrick Abercrombie and his friend Clough Williams-Ellis. It was the enterprise that they had called the 'octopus': the insidious piecemeal expansion of development – airports, industry, public works, roads, new housing estates and suburban sprawl. There were some grounds for caution: roughly 750,000 acres, about 2 per cent of England and Wales, had been built over between the wars.[16]

All those involved in the post-war management of the British countryside thought that the chaos of unregulated development had finally been brought to an inspired conclusion through a law that had preceded the National Parks and Access to Countryside Act by just two years. This earlier legislation was called the Town and Country Planning Act. It was not an original title. There had been another of the same name in 1932 (there were also three subsequent acts in 1949, 1962 and 1971). But the 1947 version was a sweeping and transformative statute.

It decimated planning authorities to just 145 beefed-up borough or county councils and established the guiding principle that ownership of land did not confer a right of development. That decision was vested in the elected council or authority, and everyone must apply to it for planning consent. Its other great provision was to encircle cities and towns with what we cherish today as the Green Belt, a preserved perimeter of farmland whose boundaries were almost impermeable to fresh development.

It heaped up much higher the powers of local authorities, giving them control at last over the planning process. Yet there was a funda-mental downside. The newly invigorated local politicians, many of them landowners themselves, had no intention of ceding control of the coun-tryside to the new-fangled authorities in charge of national parks. From the very outset, therefore, the National Parks Commission, the body to govern and administer the parks, was a feeble thing with 'no executive, administrative, landowning or land managing function'. In the first twenty-five years of operations, its achievements, according to Ann and Malcolm MacEwen in their meticulous history of national parks, were 'pitiful'. A long-time campaigner for parks called the same administrative body 'window-dressing for sub-standard goods'.[17]*

It was too feeble to affect, let alone to stop, the culprit that was really stealing flowers from a million meadows. And that thief was not industry or housing, but farming. Marion Shoard has called the years between 1945 and 1980 the Third Agricultural Revolution. Indicative of their real impact on nature is the name given them by Oliver Rackham: 'the locust years'. It is the failure to perceive, let alone anticipate, the developments in the post-war dispensation that explains the paradox of so many and so much of our national parks: landscape beauty almost devoid of biodiversity.

The Peak District has many such barren places. The best example I can point to is the stretch of field between Chelmorton and Sheldon, about sixteen miles south-east of Kinder Scout. Take that long country lane, with its suggestive pattern of dry-stone walls turning away from the walker's vision at right angles to the road. Over centuries farmers cleared their pastures of the bone-white rocks, arranging them in a rhythmic geometry of limestone. It looks beautiful. Indeed, it is. As landscape it is quintessential, chocolate-box Derbyshire.

But it is also now a monoculture of rye grass, reticulated by walls and devoid of the orchids or the primroses or any of the living filigree that makes a meadow. Its regimented uniformity now supplies habitat

---

* The authority may have been largely toothless and incapable of halting the changes that subsequently ripped through these so-called bastions of natural beauty, but at least it existed. In Scotland, where a parallel process was pursued under the chairmanship of Sir Douglas Ramsay, his committee reported in 1945 and 1947 and argued that national parks in that country should resemble those of the USA: areas controlled for the people by the nation. If necessary, they should be purchased compulsorily. Scottish landowners thought otherwise and killed them off at birth. The enfeebled English model was deemed acceptable only as recently as 2002 (the Trossachs and Loch Lomond) and 2003 (Cairngorms). See Ann and Malcolm MacEwen's classic work *National Parks: Conservation or Cosmetics?* (1982).

for almost none of the breeding birds that would once have flourished in such country: grey partridge, lapwing, curlew, yellow wagtail, wheatear, skylark and meadow pipit.

Kinder itself, for all its symbolic importance and its status as a Site of Special Scientific Interest and a National Nature Reserve, has a comparable emptiness. The National Trust, which has owned the estate since 1982, has regular information boards along the trails, proudly displaying the icon of upland Derbyshire, the red grouse.* Yet during my last five visits I have never actually seen one.

Ironically, part of the problem on Kinder is attributable to the 'octopus'. Manchester and the other industrial towns of Lancashire and Cheshire exported more than just militant ramblers. Acid rain seeded by centuries of factory smoke inexorably poured down and degraded the vegetation, until large areas of the upper slopes have shocking open sores of rotted peat. In the words of one commentator, it is among 'the most degraded and eroded upland areas in Europe'.[18]

Nor is farming exonerated from the fall of Kinder. Like so much of upland Britain it has been relentlessly overgrazed and overstocked with sheep far beyond its true carrying capacity. The estate's herd rose from 17,000 in 1914 to 60,000 by the mid-1970s, largely in a quest for headage payments from the European Common Market. Farmers, in short, were not harvesting wool and meat, but government subsidy.[19] The knock-on consequence of all those extra grinding ovine molars on Kinder is the spread of bracken, which suppresses most of the other upland vegetation. It is now sprayed with Asulox herbicide from helicopters.

In many places the sheep have grazed the heather and grasses down to the very quick. A £2.5 million restoration project between 2011 and 2016 involved an impressive array of commercial and conservation

---

* The NT's actual purchase of Kinder is a telling episode in the history of both. As one of the Trust's biographers noted, its chair and director general broke every rule in the book to obtain the site. That ruthless speed and efficiency delivered what one of its council called 'the most important open space acquisition ever to confront it,' a remark that is surely one more subliminal nod to the mythic significance of the Mass Trespass. [Waterson, 1994, pp. 229–33.]

forces, which have banished all those ruinous sheep flocks, installed 25,000 gully-blocks to halt run-off, while treating the exposed substrate with a mix of lime (to neutralise the effects of acid rain) and thousands of bags of heather seed. The regenerated areas have then been plugged with tens of thousands of cotton-grass plants.

All these landscape remedies have been carried to the summit beneath the hammering rotors of helicopters. The shuddering din of the aircraft is not uncommon on Kinder. Strangest of all, perhaps, as you stand there contemplating the wreckage of this place, is to reflect how the brutal war-zone drone of the machines, which rise up out of the Kinder valley like some monstrous dragonfly predator on blade-wings, violating the wind-buffeted silences and casting alien shadows on its gritstone monoliths, will be the remaking of the Kinder landscape fit for heroes and trespassers alike.

9

PLUTO'S DARK-BLUE DAZE

On my drive up to the car park on Cow Green I stopped briefly in Langdon Beck, but the weather seemed too brutal and the river too swollen with run-off even to get out. Instead I sat and watched a scrap of black plastic – the defining foliage of the oil age – that had somehow escaped the farmer's control. It had snagged across eight tines of a barbed wire fence.

While its iron-claw grip anchored that sheet down, the gusts wanted to take it, and I was mesmerised by the physics of their contest. Minute corrugations in the fabric relentlessly rippled across its surface so that it resembled molten lava freshly setting, or perhaps the black motile liquid from which it was originally made. With each lull the sheet's ragged edge slumped under gravity. Then battle resumed and the plastic bellied out and heaved, and I noticed how its upwelling dark shape momentarily resembled the wider contours of Cronkley Fell immediately beyond. It was strange to reflect how that rippling crag was made from the same kind of elemental arguments, but over a period of 295 million years.

From the Cow Green car park there were just two small receding eyes of snow somewhere on the high slopes of Great Dun Fell. At 2,782 feet it is the second highest hill in the entire Pennines, and the average May temperature is the same as London's in January. Then the cloud mass rolled steadily down from those northern English vertebrae and the snow eyes were obliterated and the light fell.

I braced myself for the walk while the wind snuffled at the car's undersides. I could feel the whole vehicle rocking with quiet violence on its axles, but I had not thought through the angle at which I had parked, so when I finally opened the door it was snatched from me and there was a hideous crunch as it whanged against the hinges. Then I got out and my hat flew off fifty feet before coming to Earth. I raced after it, having almost to fight for each in-breath against the pull of the wind.

I retrieved the cap and set off along the track by the spot where the gentians are seen. I found it hard to conjure anything so rare or so colourful in this landscape. In fact, it was hard to imagine any plant, of any description, in flower today; in this vile weather, when there were just the leached sand tones of dead grass and the leached russet of dead rush and the long dark cloud brood passing to the east.

Cow Green Reservoir was on my right as I headed towards the dam head. The westerlies scoured the down slopes and jack-knifed off the water, sending clean white mares' tails across the surface. The rain never stopped until I got back to the car two hours later and with each gust it clattered at the surface of my waterproof. I dragged the hood down but the wind found a way to squeeze in and prise it off my head so that rain could sleet full in my face and coat my spectacles in blobs of water. When I arrived at the vehicle, all down one side, sleeve and trousers, was slathered cold and wet onto bare skin.

In the blur I picked out this handful of details: the way the elements had hollowed out the wooden fence posts until only the hardest lignin cores remained. Yet each post top had its own headful of grey lichen, and between the skeletal uprights were strands of barbed wire, buckled and snapped with rust. In my notebook I wrote:

There were few flowers but probably dried remnants of last year's bog asphodel and sundew without their fly-trap stems. Withered and desiccated lichen and drab heather, but no fresh green anywhere: only winter recoil. Spring was not here. The single sign of recent human was an apple core crushed to the path. Cow Green was entirely free of vertebrate life, aside from two curlews blown slantwise and silent across the cloud race. And me.

You realise that, while this has been a site of constant human traffic – the old adits of the lead mines and the reservoir's 1,700-foot concrete dam were proof of that – the elements test everything to destruction. Cow Green admits of nothing that is not weighted down. And you are always aware of wind: either its imposing, even brutal presence or, occasionally, its momentary lull. It affects the grand – the clouds over the Pennines – and the trivial – stray wool strands wittering at snags in the wooden posts. Like a tongue in a tooth cavity it is incessant and erosive. All is shaped and made fit to meet it, gravity and mass holding everything to the place – stone, water, tree, plant – until it is entirely true. Temporarily.

A few weeks later, as I head for Cow Green at dawn, the sun is at my back, the whole landscape cleanly engraved by low-angled soft light. Below and immediately above Middleton-in-Teesdale is that stock northern blend of cattle and sheep pasture segmented by drystone walls or stout wind-slanted thorn hedges. The River Tees flows by the town and at intervals bends close to the road as I climb west, all shallow blue shimmer and white-flecked stone. Then it is lost to view in the valley; the cattle fall away; so too the ash and the sycamores towering over the fields, while the lime-washed white cottages grow more distant from their neighbours. I pass the High Force Inn, where botanists have stayed since the 1840s, and just after the turning for Force Garth Quarry I drive out on to the upper reaches of the dale and the grandeur of it all seizes me.

Even as I absorb the panorama, a lapwing in full display blusters like a wind-slewed cloth just in front of the car, and even through the glass and engine drone I can pick out the ecstatic sweet ache of its song. A pair of pied wagtails flushes up from the road edge and the cold dawn glow fringes all their feathers, so that the two birds look momentarily as if they had just been freshly minted from bright light.

But nothing equals the impact of the marsh marigolds. In the roadside fields, which weeks ago had been the pastel shades of snow-burnt grass, they are spread in such profusion that they embody the ideal of the colour yellow. I'm heading for Widdybank and Cow Green, but the flowers immediately unravel my programme. I fling the car door wide open. Within a minute the knees of my jeans are swollen with ground water (despite a plastic sheet I roll out to lie on), but there is also the joy of photography: it forces you to get on eye-level terms with flowers.

Our friend Polly Monroe (partner of Richard Mabey) calls the same species by their old Norfolk name – 'molly blobs' – which evokes the way that the stems and leaves of her local plants rise up with robust, water-filled, lily-like fleshiness. Here in Upper Teesdale, marsh marigolds are wind-sculpted creepers. I find a patch that has grown just high enough to meet my wide-angle lens, and behind their crisp detail is the blurred lustre of the yellow pool; beyond, a whitewashed gable end to a farm and, blurrier still, the Whin Sill plateaux of Cronkley and Widdybank Fells. The smothering of flowers reminds me of what has been lost with the destruction of 4 million acres of herb-rich meadow, of which this is such a singular, gold-glimmering example.

I have never seen its like before, and I am pitched into an elevated state of mind, so that when I arrive, a few moments later, at a flower-lined trickle just by Langdon Beck, it feels nothing to stop again. Weeks ago this very spot was a foam-flecked torrent, and the sound of angry water had been obliterated by the insane skitter of black plastic snagged in barbed wire.

Now I am straight across the brook and flat on my front before bird's-eye primroses. I saw the basal leaves last time – star-like rosettes of pale waxy green, prostrate to the ground – but here the plants are a spring song of exquisite colour. The petals are gently notched in their outer fringes so that a central yellow eye, formed by the cluster of pollen-bearing stamens, is encircled with five hearts of deepest pink. Almost without end they quiver in the breeze, and it is more than an hour before I align everything to my satisfaction: the blood pulse of my own hands, the detail of the flowers, a lull in the wind and then May sunshine coming and going between white cloud. As I lie to attend to this scarce resident of Upper Teesdale, I can listen to the sky songs of its most abundant bird neighbours – the lapwings and snipe, whose displays are fletched higher and higher by the morning's warmth and sunlight.

That hour with the primroses reflects how the whole day goes – a 7-mile distracted meander right around Widdybank Fell, which occupies me until seven in the evening, entirely alone, through scenes of overwhelming beauty punctuated with moments of absolute joy: the five-bar gates mottled white and grey and crusted along their upper beams by intricate gardens of fruticose lichens; the weathered slabs of Whin Sill, so empathetically curved to the human rear you would swear they were hand-cut stone benches (yet the upper planes of the dolerite are entirely smothered in a lichen cartography. My favourite, which I photograph over and over and later select as screen saver for my computer, is a Rothko-like blend of desert sand with islands of black-flecked ginger or grey).

I have my lunch sitting on such a stone with the white rush of Cauldron Snout boiling down beside me and my senses immersed in its force-drenched music; and despite its power a dipper, nesting in the crag above where I sit, manages to pierce the heart of all the water noise with song.

Around teatime a short-eared owl, wafting like some kind of finned sea creature from the depths, performs a slow-savoured display that makes it seem larger than it truly is. I notice also as it passes over the outcrops of sugar limestone, which are the colour of an Aegean shoreline, how the whole of the owl's underwing acquires its own calcareous glow. Then it swims away with the breeze and across the predominant rust-infused straw of Widdybank's wider vegetation, and in direct sunshine the bird is oat-white like freshly setting steel.

This is all preparatory to the gentians. In a sense it has taken more than 300 million years to create the conditions for this flower. The decisive element is the Whin Sill itself, which began as lava from deep within our planet's core around 295 million years ago. On its journey through the crust it met strata of carboniferous limestone, sand- and mudstones, which had been laid down around 33 million years earlier when this part of England lay near the Equator.

The magma extruded through faults in the older sedimentary rocks and, as it rose, so it cooked the adjacent limestone layers to a coarse crystalline marble. When the latter weathers it acquires the consistency of fine sand or, according to geologists, of white sugar granules; hence the name: 'sugar limestone'. The surface outcrops of it are found only on Cronkley and Widdybanks Fells, and it is these that in large measure give rise to the botanical significance of Upper Teesdale.

The special nature of the flora was noted by the late seventeenth century, when the pioneer botanist John Ray published records of shrubby cinquefoil, which grows in Upper Teesdale and in only one other English location, the Lake District. By the early nineteenth century botanists had found most of the famous Teesdale plants, including alpine bartsia, alpine bistort, alpine cinquefoil, alpine meadow-rue, alpine penny-cress, bearberry, bird's-eye primrose, bog orchid, hair sedge, hoary rock-rose, hoary whitlow grass, holly fern, another fern called kobresia, mountain avens, Scottish asphodel, sea plantain and three-flowered rush.

On paper the most special of all is a tiny tufted, glabrous perennial called Teesdale sandwort, *Minuartia stricta*. Yet the five-millimetre flower is entirely insignificant. Were it not for the fact that the species grows on just two isolated patches here at Widdybank, and nowhere else closer to these islands than Norway, it would be hard to be aroused.

Not so the gentians. And I find them eventually in good numbers. I know instantly, exactly, what they are. Here's one. Quite soon they surround me. I am routinely amused by the way in which a naturalist sets off with a long-brewed sense of longing for some rare organism – a bird or a flower – which she or he dreams of seeing; and then the ever-so-casual manner in which anticipation confronts reality. There is no drum roll. No climax. Not even fumbling excitement. You just pass quickly, efficiently almost, from one existential state to another.

With the gentians there may be no dramatic transformatory moment, but there is indubitably the life-lasting star-like beauty of them. It is not hard to see why they are the ultimate botanical symbol for Upper Teesdale. Of her own Californian gentians, the writer and pioneer feminist Mary Austin, a woman seldom lost for the *mot juste*, could only pile the one hue upon itself as if the meaning of the word might intensify with repetition: 'blue–blue–eye-blue, perhaps'.[1] D. H. Lawrence saw gentians in Bavaria and wrote in his inimitable style of a blue so blue that, like the Whin Sill itself, it seemed sourced from the Earth's inner core:

> flattened under the sweep of white day
> torch-flower of the blue-smoking darkness, Pluto's dark-blue daze,
> black lamps from the halls of Dis, burning dark blue.* [2]

It is a colour so much more striking than that of the sky, or of the sea – as blue as the Earth itself when seen from space. The gentians are all-seeing eyes of happiness in a brown and wind-troubled place, and I fall to my knees to meet them.

---

* Given the poem's reference to a plant with autumn blooms, it is likely that the inspiration for Lawrence's 'Bavarian Gentians' is a species called willow gentian, *Gentiana asclepiadea*, whose peak flowering month is September. It is regularly seen in gardens, a point also made in the poem. This particular species has a more trumpet-like flower shape but, if anything, the depth of colour in willow gentian is less than in its relative in Upper Teesdale. I am deeply grateful to botanist Bob Gibbons for helping to unravel its probable identity.

10

ONE OF NATURE CONSERVATION'S BIGGEST DISASTERS

As John Sheail has pointed out, 'there was nothing inevitable about the decisions, nor ... the circumstances that caused the Nature Conservancy to be established in 1949.'[1] Nor were its immediate prospects at birth very rosy. Only two years after it had been created, the Attlee government was pondering how to kill it off to make financial savings.[2] That the Nature Conservancy survived at all to declare Widdybank Fell a SSSI and give legal protection to those spring gentians was almost a matter of pure luck.

Yet one of the happier circumstances at its birth was the presence of Herbert Morrison in the office of the Lord President of the Council. Morrison was not only in charge of scientific research for the whole government, he was also actually convinced of its importance: 'It was my belief', he wrote later, 'that science and the scientist had a real contribution to make to the well-being of our country in peace and war.'[3] More than that, Morrison believed in the merits and judgements of his chief adviser, and that post, luckiest of all for the Nature Conservancy, was filled by Max Nicholson.

Nicholson and Morrison's mutual insistence that government required a biological service rooted in science would have far-reaching repercussions. Although, as we have already noted, the Nature Conservancy and national parks were born of the same post-war conception, the twins were almost immediately split asunder at birth. To many the enforced separation, the 'Great Divide' as it is known, has been characterised as a disaster for the environment in the long term, but in one small way it was a blessing.

Ironically, a key problem for national parks was the long years of campaigning by their advocates, individuals like John Dower and even Benny Rothman. The persistent clamour for the right to roam had allowed ample time, according to Ann and John MacEwen, for opposition to 'develop among farmers, landowners and local authorities and within factions of government'.[4] It was the collective antagonism of these sections to both militant trespassers and upper-class ramblers that enabled the disparate land-controlling forces to neuter the National Parks Authority at the outset. As we have seen, the national parks fell under the suspicious control of the Ministry of Town and Country Planning.

The Nature Conservancy, by contrast, as steered by Morrison and Nicholson, was conceived as a junior partner to the other scientific advisory bodies of government, the Agricultural Research Council and the Medical Research Council. It was duly given its own royal charter and brought under the aegis of the Privy Council, where it was billed as a bright young enterprise, staffed by new men in white coats, who would speak wise and scrupulously objective truth unto power. Or, as the charter said, 'provide scientific advice on the conservation and *control* of the natural flora and fauna of Great Britain' [my italics].[5]

The perceptual disentanglement of conservation's cause from that of national parks meant that there was no such premeditated resistance to the fledgling Nature Conservancy. On the contrary, the insistence on its working as a branch of science silenced most of its critics. Typically, when its future was being contemplated at the Treasury, one member of the economics team noted that if 'the scientists say the job ought to be done, then we should not oppose it'.[6]

That remark, incidentally, speaks volumes on just how different an age it was compared to our own. Science, especially government-authorised science, had not sullied itself by allowing a brand of high-protein cattle feed to include the infected brains of sheep, as in the case of BSE. Nor had a man in a white coat proposed that a herbicide and carcinogen was as safe to drink as his cup of tea. Science was virtuous and knight-like, clad in the light-filled vestments of reason. Fourteen years after the Nature Conservancy had been founded, the Prime Minister Harold Wilson could still call upon science as the primary agent in his nation's self-renewal. The new Britain, he suggested, would be 'forged in the white heat of this [scientific] revolution'.

Once the Nature Conservancy had survived the early debate on financial viability, it sailed into the post-war age with a sense that its time and scientific mission had come. And that optimism was reinforced when, in 1952, Max Nicholson pooled all his immense professional resources in the services of nature and became the Conservancy's second director general. His programme, like that of his predecessor Cyril Diver, relied on a blueprint that was almost as old as he was.

It was a scheme devised in embryo by Charles Rothschild and his fellow founders of the Society for the Promotion of Nature Reserves. While the SPNR had largely proved ineffectual and played only a secondary role in the development of the Wildlife Trusts, its pioneering effort to draw up an authoritative list of Britain's best wildlife sites, based on objective principles rather than some hazy and entirely subjective notions of landscape beauty, was groundbreaking. It was exactly the approach that informed the Nature Conservancy's earliest efforts.

They entailed a county-by-county search for the nation's finest wildlife areas, which eventually blossomed into a massively ambitious cadastral project to grade the entire British landscape. In the process the Nature Conservancy slowly developed an overlapping system of habitat classification and protection, the basis of which was known as a Site of Special Scientific Interest.*

---

* The work would only reach full fruition in 1977 with the publication of the massive, two-volume *A Nature Conservation Review*. The project had been formally initiated in 1965 and, as one wag noted in the *New Scientist*, it had taken eight times longer to assemble than the *Domesday Book*. Although technically spanning efforts over twelve years, in truth the book was a synthesis of the cumulative knowledge and evolving methods of the Nature Conservancy (by that date it was actually called the Nature Conservancy Council) since its foundation. It offers a full breakdown of all Britain's best 735 sites which, in an ideal world, would have formed a single system of National Nature Reserves. That they got more than halfway there (the current NNR total is 394) is perhaps achievement enough.

This cumbersome and even contentious label is invariably shortened to the acronym SSSI, while in conversation it is proverbial as a 'triple-S I'. Peter Marren has observed that 'Here "Scientific" really means "nature conservation" in an adjectival sense.' He adds: 'Every now and then someone suggests changing the name, but nothing has ever come of it for fear of adding to the confusion.'[7] Whatever its shortcomings – and one commentator has spoken of its connotation of 'elitism, obscurity and officiousness' – the concepts behind it are still central to all UK conservation.[8]

SSSI status is a way of denoting that a place retains many or all its semi-natural or natural features. While a site could be designated on the basis of geophysical elements, more usually it is as a consequence of its communities of plants and animals. So the Widdybank meadows, smothered in marsh marigolds, edged by bird's-eye primrose and full of nesting lapwings, snipe and redshanks, would qualify. The same fields, drained, re-sown and reduced to a monoculture of rye grass, would not.

Sometimes, however, even a site as wonderful as those Widdybank meadows might not automatically be designated. This is because SSSIs were seen as a network of *representative* examples of the country's best habitats. If there happened to be a great deal of a particular land form in an area, then only the best parts would be chosen. That principle still applies in some regions, such as northern Scotland, where there are large areas of the same wildlife-rich habitats. Yet in southern England, where so much of the landscape has been fundamentally simplified by agricultural improvement, every scrap of high-quality countryside is almost by definition of SSSI status. (In fact the protection resulting from an early designation is often the only reason that it has been spared at all.)

Running in overlap with the SSSI label was a second designation, known as the National Nature Reserve (NNR). In essence such a site was considered among the very best places for wildlife in Britain – the indispensable minimum that would serve as a sample suite of Britain's natural heritage. Indeed, a very large number of the 284 sites that appeared on the Rothschild-inspired list of 1916 eventually became NNRs.

It is important to emphasise that NNRs and SSSIs were not mutually exclusive categories. In fact, NNRs were almost automatically of SSSI standard.* Equally, national parks contain places that are of both conservation categories. For example, Kinder Scout is both an NNR and an SSSI and, of course, part of the Peak District National Park.

While the classification overlapped, there was a broad distinction in the Nature Conservancy's attitude towards the two kinds of land area. While it wished to ensure proper management of SSSIs, these places were numerous, spread right across the entire country and invariably in private ownership. No organisation, let alone a cash-strapped fledgling, could have hoped to exercise direct control over them all. But from its inception the Nature Conservancy did have a 'shopping list' for National Nature Reserves. Either it sought outright purchase of such sites or, at minimum, a lease or management agreement with the owners that guaranteed proper maintenance of its wildlife value.

Among the first places that the Nature Conservancy ever acquired is an area visible from Widdybank Fell. It is noteworthy that even in its very infancy the organisation had flagged this part of the Pennines as one of its earliest desiderata. The Moor House NNR is a vast, 10,000-acre expanse of high-quality mire and peat moorland, which includes that snow-pocked cold-catching hill Great Dun Fell. Its eastern boundary also runs onto the flank of Widdybank. It was bought in the very year that Max Nicholson became director general: 1952.

Although the ideas that underpinned the work of the Nature Conservancy may have been maturing for decades, the speed at which it carried through its tasks in the early years is hugely impressive. By 1965, and a year before Max Nicholson stepped down as director general, there were 113 NNRs. The pace slowed somewhat thereafter, and in the year, 1971, that Cow Green Reservoir was finished and parts of Widdybank Fell were irretrievably flooded and destroyed, the figure stood at 130 reserves, covering a grand total of 270,000 acres.

---

* Technically some minor parts of an NNR might *not* be of SSSI quality, but their inclusion is deemed admissible on the basis that the lower-grade land is integral to the site's proper management.

To administer them and carry out its other works, the Nature Conservancy had a payroll of 630 employees, almost half of whom were scientists. Of SSSIs, in the quarter of a century since its foundation, those staff had managed to identify and schedule an astonishing 3,737,181 acres on mainland Britain spread over 3,209 sites.*

When Max Nicholson came to reflect in his book *The Environmental Revolution* on how things stood at the end of the sixties, he subtitled it *A Guide for the New Masters of the World*. He probably had every right to feel smug. Today, almost seventy years after the founding of the Nature Conservancy (with all its later confusing and splintered avatars), we take for granted the idea that the state incorporates nature into the very fabric of government. The language and terminology of environmentalism – even if the substance of real concern is often missing – are institutional parts of the nation's cultural conversation.

Yet we should reflect that it had taken almost exactly the same length of time – seventy years – *before* a British government had followed the lead of its American counterpart. It had taken seventy years for the state to place any legal or symbolic value on land in the name of its native non-human inhabitants. Charles Rothschild never lived to see that happen. Neither did John Dower.

Before the war there was not a single acre held in trust for nature by the state for the right of the public to have communion with it. All efforts prior to that time had been piecemeal and privately conducted.

---

* The current figures for both NNRs and SSSIs break down as follows. There are 394 National Nature Reserves in Britain: England (224), Northern Ireland (47), Scotland (47), Wales (76). The area covered by NNRs in England and Scotland alone is 470,000 acres, and with its mere 47 sites Scotland accounts for marginally more than half the total. Glen Affric NNR alone, for example, runs to almost 36,000 acres. There are now about 7,000 SSSIs in the entire United Kingdom (in Northern Ireland they are known as Areas of Special Scientific Interest, ASSI) and on mainland Britain they account for more than 5,608,014 acres and as a percentage of their respective country's land area, the figures are England 8 per cent, Scotland 12.7 per cent and Wales 12 per cent. Once again, the size of some of the Scottish sites is impressive. The Cairngorm SSSI is about 72,000 acres.

True, there was a quasi-official quality to the National Trust's purchases but, as we have seen, time after time, the organisation had chosen architecture, Chippendale chairs and the grand prospect of the stately home before biodiversity.

The process initiated in 1949, the systematic mapping and grading of almost every square inch of this country, is probably unequalled, in terms of its sophisticated methodology and accumulated knowledge capital, in any other nation on the planet. Much of that probably has to do with the relatively small size of Britain, but in its day the founding achievements of the Nature Conservancy were truly revolutionary. When Max Nicholson paused to sum up his half-century of labours in the name of nature he must have believed that he was on the brink of a new kind of planning utopia, a world in which we could rationally, sustainably, sensitively organise our affairs so that wildlife would have a place at the decision-making table in perpetuity.

That was what he hoped. That was what he thought he had set in place during his time at the helm of the Nature Conservancy. Unfortunately, it didn't work out that way. Just a decade after Max died came the *State of Nature* report, with its news of systemic losses across thousands of species in Britain. How can we square his radical vision of the future and the scale of his achievements with the implications of the savage environmental declines that are outlined in the 2013 report?

They were actually built into the processes that Max worked tirelessly to implement. They were ingrained in the very way that the SSSIs functioned. While that designation introduced formal procedures and was applied according to carefully considered criteria, once a landscape had been given SSSI status, it did not guarantee protection. The Nature Conservancy forwarded all the information to the local planning authority as land was notified. What it ensured was that the same authority whose powers had been enhanced through the Town and Country Planning Act of 1947, would notify the Nature Conservancy if there were an application for proposed developments that had a bearing upon the wildlife conditions at the site. Theoretically the Conservancy could then object and have the planning application modified or rejected.

What it did not have influence over, however, were changes in agricultural practice or forestry. Neither the farmer nor the forester was obliged to seek planning permission for changes in the ways they worked. When faced with a landowner's plans to drain and plough an SSSI meadow or grub out an NNR's ancient woodland and replace it with a single-age conifer plantation, the Nature Conservancy was in pretty much the same position with regard to these operations as the National Park Authority when faced with similar proposals. It was powerless.

In its first thirty years of operation the SSSI was a designation that lacked the meaningful content of official sanction. It bestowed upon a site the recognition of high environmental quality. It expressed a wish that the landowner might take account of that status. It empowered the Nature Conservancy scientist to go and offer friendly persuasion or helpful advice but, at the end of the day, the farmer could ignore any amount of moral encouragement and could do precisely as he or she wished.

Ted Smith, the pioneer environmentalist, co-founder of the Lincolnshire Wildlife Trust among many other achievements, spoke of the 'frustrating ineffectiveness of the original SSSI provision'. Far worse, however, was what he called 'the scandal of an agricultural policy which not only took little or no account of nature conservation … but which actually rewarded people for destroying part of the country's natural heritage'.[9] This often took the form of grant payments by the Ministry of Agriculture to underpin drainage or clearance. All this was in the name of improvement, so that, in effect, separate branches of government were in direct opposition to one another.

The full consequences of those contradictions are considered in detail under the next landscape, the south Lincolnshire Fens. Here, two examples of radically different scales will have to suffice. The flower-rich, butterfly-blessed chalk downlands of southern England, celebrated in the works of Thomas Hardy, W. H. Hudson and many other writers, were one of the great environmental treasures of our nation. In Wiltshire, however, during the early 1960s, no fewer than 15 of the 27 SSSIs, designated for their outstanding communities of plants and insects, were converted to intensive arable.[10] Marion Shoard has pointed out that it destroyed not only the environmental value of such downs. The plough also obliterated 250 of 640 scheduled ancient monuments in the county.[11] All it left, according to Shoard, was 'a vast barley prairie, whose monotony is relieved only by barbed wire fences and oil stores'.[12]

In Ted Smith's Lincolnshire the tragedy of Waddingham Common brought into precise focus all the frustration and contradictions implicit in the 1949 legislation. Located fifteen miles due north of Lincoln, Waddingham was a 'delightful' 22-acre expanse of flower-rich grassland and a surviving relict from pre-enclosure times. In 1951 the Lincolnshire Naturalists' Trust had listed the common as one of the main locations in the county deserving of SSSI status. (Of the total 21 sites identified by Smith and his colleagues, no fewer than a third were destroyed completely or severely damaged after they had been designated.) This was mainly on account of what Smith called a 'fascinating assemblage of calcicole and calcifuge plants' including common butterwort, fragrant orchid, bog pimpernel and grass-of-Parnassus.[13]

It turned out, unfortunately, that Waddingham was not a 'common' in the truest sense. In 1963 a large landowner, Mr J. Owen Day, claimed to have acquired the freehold from a vendor whose name he would never divulge. Worse still was the fact that he viewed his latest acquisition as an 'eyesore infested with vermin', and he had given notice of an intention to drain and plough it. The Lincolnshire Naturalists' Trust immediately notified the Nature Conservancy and Ministry of Agriculture. While the latter expressed a hope that Waddingham could be spared, it also confirmed a prior legal obligation to underwrite Owen Day's drainage costs, with a grant of £12 per acre (the equivalent total today would be roughly £5,000).

In a last-ditch effort to salvage something from oblivion, Smith and colleagues, including the regional chair of the National Farmers' Union, attempted to persuade the owner to allow them to lease the richest 6–7 acres as a remnant of Waddingham's floristic value. Owen Day counter-proposed with the offer of a single acre. In December 1963, he drained and ploughed the whole lot.* More than four decades later Ted Smith described how he passed Waddingham and was able to recognise the area only by a hedge along its old approach track; the common itself had been entirely obliterated. 'It is as though it had never been,' he wrote.[14]

In its day Waddingham had been a minor cause célèbre. The Lincolnshire Naturalists' Trust's campaign to save the site had gained the attention of the national press and inspired support from many people in the environmental movement and beyond. The local MP Marcus Kimball had been sufficiently moved to introduce a private member's bill in the House of Commons to ensure that at least landowners had to give six months' notice of their intention to destroy an SSSI. For all its modesty and deference to what Ted Smith called the 'agricultural juggernaut at the peak of its power', this legislative caveat was refused parliamentary time by the government.[15]

Yet even as that bill was being killed off and Waddingham obliterated, a new controversy was struggling to be born. It would become the largest and most significant environmental drama of the post-war era. It involved many of the same dramatis personae: outraged naturalists, indignant politicians and adamant agents of modernisation.

It would draw into its orbit and heighten awareness of all the same issues. It would challenge the Nature Conservancy, both its willingness to defend the cause of nature and its capacity to do so. Most of all, however, it would ask of the highest decision-makers in this country how much they valued the nation's finest wildlife areas. In the words of a leading protagonist, 'one of nature conservation's biggest disasters in Britain' would happen on Widdybank Fell in Upper Teesdale.

---

* In 1974 the same farmer applied for a separate grant to drain and plough another 100-acre SSSI of wet heath at nearby Manton. However, the Nature Conservancy Council, following the stand-off at Waddingham Common, refused to de-notify the SSSI to allow Owen Day to have his way. Because of the NCC's refusal to back down on the issue, MAFF was obliged in this instance to refuse the farmer his drainage grant. Owen Day ploughed up the entire site regardless.

The Chaotic Conditions
of a Public Inquiry

The first and only time I have ever seen Billingham was when I was seventeen. It was 14 August 1977 and we'd driven overnight from Cley in Norfolk all the way to County Durham with the intention of being there at dawn. True to its custom, around 5.10 a.m. the sun rose up out of its North Sea bed and filled Cowpen Marsh by the River Tees with the softest summer light. Creased and grimy from hours on the car's back seat, even we were not unresponsive to the manner of the day's holy renewal; the way that the sun suffused the pool before us and turned it into a coral-coloured mirror.

All the birds over the lagoon, including the eighteenth British record of Bonaparte's gull that we had travelled to see, were bathed in that rose light. And as each white bird landed on the surface, its breast seemed dipped in a deeper version of the same delicious hue. The gulls, the pool, the marsh, ourselves – everything belonging to that dawn world was touched by the same exquisitely innocent shade.

So too the things just beyond the nature reserve: the railway lines, the repeatedly passing trains, the steel gantries over the tracks, the bristling networks of power lines and lamp posts, the massive squat chemical-holding tanks, the gleaming steel structures, the smokestacks, their funnels of vapour and the entire built complex that enveloped and gave unity to its heterogeneous parts. For this was Billingham, home to Imperial Chemical Industries, the largest industrial company and, at one time, the largest manufacturer of any kind in Britain. Even dressed in the rosy light of dawn, Billingham looked a vision from a dreadful future: an intricate man-made zone of technology and chemicals that Aldous Huxley visited in the twenties and in which he found the perfect inspiration for his dystopian novel, *Brave New World*.

In the early 1960s Billingham also represented power, influence and opportunity, especially to a community deeply sensitive to a regional history of poverty and unemployment. At that time 30,000 men and women, a tenth of the entire Teesside workforce, were employed by ICI. Since the twenties Billingham had been at the forefront in manufacturing ammonia, a key ingredient of explosives and armaments. In the post-war period it was the major source of artificial nitrate fertilisers and, almost more than any other single innovation, these products led to the Third Agricultural Revolution. Eventually British farmers could not get enough of them, by the end of the century using 1.5–2 million tons of nitrates.[1]*

In a highly competitive market Billingham's research chemists had developed a new technique called the naphtha steam reforming process, that promised economic viability and jobs into the future for ICI. The company had thus decided to build three of the world's largest ammonia plants, producing 3,000 tons of the chemical a day. A pressing issue set in train by this decision, however, was that of water. The company needed lots more of it.

The Tees Valley and Cleveland Water Board was the institution tasked with meeting those needs but, as recently as the autumn of 1963, ICI had requested no additional allocation. At a stroke the naphtha steam reforming process boosted requirements by an additional 113,000 cubic metres a day. Combined with expanded demand made by other companies, such as Shell, the water board was suddenly confronted with a major problem. Its total output from existing sources

---

* What now amounts to a virtual fertiliser addiction is not without cost. Such fertilisers drove in part the loss of millions of acres of flower-rich countryside, such as Waddingham Common. It also unleashed an estimated 300,000 tons of nitrates into Britain's rivers and lakes, where it has to be stripped at considerable expense from drinking water.

was 292,000 cubic metres. It now required at least 450,000 cubic metres a day. Its engineers were tasked with making up the shortfall. And fast.

The best solution lay in what was called a river-regulating reservoir, which gathers the flow in the wet months and then releases it in the drier seasons to ensure year-round security of supply downstream. The new site had to be cheap to build. It had to be geologically sound with no leakage. It had to be accessible. And it had to be ready by 1970. The place that best met the criteria was in Upper Teesdale, but the Nature Conservancy had already recognised the extraordinary wildlife importance of the whole area, surrounded much of it with SSSI designations and converted a major part of it into the Moor House National Nature Reserve.

Technically the application to build there breached the terms of the SSSI and the attendant planning regulations. Official permission would thus be needed. The Tees Valley and Cleveland Water Board had already run foul of this issue in 1956 in a previous dispute. This time they were playing by the book. So in August 1964 its engineer Julius Kennard went to meet Max Nicholson at the Conservancy headquarters in Belgrave Square to show him no fewer than seventeen sites they had identified as potentially suitable locations. Kennard then visited Upper Teesdale to scout out the options and returned in October to talk with Max again about a narrower field of choices.

There were three places that eventually became central fixtures in the gathering crisis. One was just below the large village of Middleton-in-Teesdale, ten miles downstream from Widdybank Fell. This would submerge no land of environmental importance and convert it into the largest reservoir of the three – 338,000 cubic metres – more than twice the size of the other two options. Unfortunately it would have taken in land from thirty-nine smallholdings, a little over 2 square miles (or 1,285 acres), which provided grazing for 250 dairy cows, 700 other cattle, 1,000 sheep, 100 pigs and 2,500 poultry. Drowning farms was an emotive business and, in the event, the National Farmers' Union opposed it tooth and nail. So too, eventually, did ICI and the water board.[2]

Another site was actually located within the Moor House NNR and became known as Upper Cow Green. However, it had demerits for ICI and the water board because it held less water (135,000 cubic metres as opposed to 157,000 cubic metres at Cow Green), yet involved a dam structure three times longer (1550 m as opposed to 525 m), which would have taken more time to build and involved greater expense, a maximum additional £4 million. (It should be noted that the price tag as well as the figures on its capacity fluctuated according to whether they came from an advocate or opponent of this option.)[3]

Kennard also went to Belgravia with a third alternative in his briefcase. Initially there seemed little reason to suppose that the environmentalists would not accept it. After all, relations between the two men were highly cordial. Nicholson said he would have to get his colleagues to do their own on-site visit, but he tried to reassure him that he wanted to come to a quiet arrangement that avoided 'the chaotic conditions of a public inquiry'.[4] So when Cow Green came up as one of Kennard's most favoured sites, Nicholson said he would try to gauge the reactions of his colleagues. Then in a letter three days later he added that 'the Cow Green site … would be most unlikely to be objected to by the Nature Conservancy'.[5]* Not only that, Nicholson thought that his organisation could even support the water board in their efforts to face down local opposition that would inevitably follow once the Cow Green proposal had been announced.

For once Max had lost his sureness of foot in matters of bureaucratic finesse. What Kennard and his colleagues took as the first glimmer of a green light was ill-advised reassurance by the director general of the Nature Conservancy based on ignorance. In fairness to him, his organisation possessed no detailed maps of the botanical importance of Upper Teesdale. None of the three colleagues whom he had consulted

---

* This brief quotation and much of the rest of the letter appear in the late Professor Roy Gregory's minutely detailed account of the whole Cow Green controversy, which was published in *The Price of Amenity* (1971) and then subsequently in *The Politics of Physical Resources* (1975). They are indispensable to understanding the issues and the technical procedures surrounding the case. Much of this part of the chapter relies heavily on his fastidious research.

had objected when the fatal two words had been uttered and, in truth they probably had almost no idea where or what 'Cow Green' was.

Worst, in many ways, was the fact that Moor House NNR ran down to the very boundary of the valley that Kennard deemed best for his reservoir. But the actual area of Widdybank Fell that was referred to by the words 'Cow Green' was not in the NNR, although it was included in the SSSI. That it had not been recognised by formal inclusion in the reserve boundary suggested that it might not matter to lose it.

However, as a matter of routine Nicholson then sent one of his staff to take a look at Kennard's reservoir scheme. From the point of view of nature conservation the man he chose was the best there was. From the perspective of the Tees Valley and Cleveland Water Board or their ICI clients, Derek Ratcliffe would have been their worst nightmare.

Ratcliffe died in 2005 just short of his seventy-sixth birthday, by which time he was a giant for anyone deeply interested in nature and the environment. Among his eight publications, his monographs *The Peregrine* (1980) and *The Raven* (1997) had been models of their kind. He was one of the few modern British naturalists who could genuinely lay claim to the label 'explorer'. His early work in the late 1950s and early sixties crisscrossing the Scottish Highlands, covering thousands of miles on foot, took him to places that few if any had ever visited. His thoroughness was legendary. Before he wrote his book on the peregrine, he was personally monitoring 500 nest locations, and very often descended cliff faces using ropes and climbing tackle to inspect active sites in person. He was also a gifted mountaineer.

What was perhaps most notable about this shy and silence-loving Cumbrian was his all-round gifts as a naturalist. In 2015 a form of ecological biography was assembled that reflected his range of achievements as ornithologist, plant ecologist, conservationist, author, photographer and champion of all things wild. Much about his character can be gleaned even from its title, *Nature's Conscience*. Yet what is most illuminating about Ratcliffe's many-sidedness is that over 570 pages it required a team of thirty experts to tell the tale.

By 1965 not only was he an authority on upland vegetation, he was also a specialist in what are known rather dismissively as 'the lower plants' – ferns, mosses, lichens and liverworts. Even botanists are often at sea in these difficult groups, confining themselves to plants with flowers. Many mosses are only separable with a powerful microscope. But Derek 'did' it all, and in each separate sub-branch of natural history he was welcomed by the experts as an equal. One of the editors of *Nature's Conscience*, Des Thompson, himself an eminent environmentalist and lifelong friend to Ratcliffe, proposed in his obituary of the man that he was the greatest British naturalist since Charles Darwin. In the intervening decade no other name has suggested itself.*

A botanical survey of the parts of Widdybank that would be drowned by any reservoir could hardly be conducted in winter. So it was well into 1965 before Ratcliffe brought all his expertise to bear on the proposed Cow Green area. His findings were devastating for any future smooth relations between the Nature Conservancy and the Tees Valley and Cleveland Water Board. The 'loss of even twenty acres', Ratcliffe reported, 'would be a very serious matter, for each part of this highly diversified complex of species was almost totally dissimilar from the rest'.[6]

Unfortunately, spurred on partly by Max's premature encouragement, the water board had already announced in December that they intended to build a reservoir in Upper Teesdale. Although no specific site had

---

* This sketch glances at Ratcliffe's achievements but omits what may well be his two major contributions to conservation. He drafted and edited almost singlehandedly the influential *A Nature Conservation Review* (1977). He also alerted the world to the pernicious impacts on predatory birds of organochlorine pesticides such as DDT. It was specifically his work on peregrines from the late 1940s onwards that revealed how this so-called wonder chemical caused eggshell thinning in the raptors and led them often to break their own eggs in the nest. As a consequence, the peregrine, one of the world's most widespread and successful predators along with ourselves and the red fox, was considered at risk of global extinction. Ratcliffe's paper on the issue demonstrating a causal link in 1970 was cited as one of 100 most important ever published in any British ecological journal. Against massive opposition from commercial and agricultural interests, Ratcliffe's hard facts won the day and led to an international ban. Many of the world's storks, pelicans and peregrines owe their lives to this quiet and quietly remarkable man.

been agreed, at a board meeting in January they had pondered with incredulity that a bunch of nature cranks would even dare to object to such important industrial development. One member, however, urged patience and pointed out – in language perfect to the occasion – that opposition was annoying, but so was a flea and it could be tackled with a single puff of insecticide. In February the consulting engineers completed their survey and in May they delivered their report. The findings were clear: Cow Green it had to be.

In July the Nature Conservancy issued its response to that decision: Cow Green only in the teeth of their official opposition. The two sides were now destined for conflict and, in Max's now miserably prescient words, 'the chaotic conditions of a public inquiry'. Then a spanner was thrown into the works. It turned out that part of the site on which reservoir construction was planned was common land. This discovery introduced major unforeseen complexities in law, and ICI and the water board were advised not to seek approval via the relevant parts of the planning law, but to proceed through a private bill in parliament.

It meant that the most significant environmental clash that had ever occurred in this country was about to take place at the very heart of the nation's decision-making processes – in Westminster.

12

IRREPARABLE HARM TO A UNIQUE PLACE

Whilst we are not unmindful of the claim of industry in an expanding economy we cannot believe that the values of our society are so crudely materialistic that we shall consciously permit the destruction of such a splendid heritage for what can be, at best, only a short-term solution of the problem of industrial water.

Letter signed by fourteen botanists in *The Times*, 4 February 1965

The decision to fight the proposed reservoir at Cow Green was a major trial not only of the environmental legislation: it also tested the very mettle of the Nature Conservancy and all that it stood for. The campaign was also symptomatic of a larger and wider social development. Cow Green triggered one of the first major public outcries in a green cause and it was, in a sense, a measure of the age.

When the private member's bill finally came before the House of Commons in January 1966, the Beatles were at number one ('We Can Work It Out'), the Who at number sixteen ('My Generation'). London was about to swing (the phrase was first used in *Time* magazine in April 1966), just as a tanker called the *Torrey Canyon* was heading inexorably towards its destiny on Pollard's Rock off the Scilly Isles. Long before that fated vessel ran aground and spewed 32 million gallons of crude oil into the sea in March 1967, the forces of environmentalism were up in arms.

News of the proposals for Cow Green provoked passionate resolve among a group of specialists not hitherto associated with protest movements. The academic and august Botanical Society of the British Isles, deploying language more typical of the student rally or the street barricade, had formed a Defence Committee in early 1965 and fired off a letter to *The Times* signed by fourteen of its most illustrious members.

By the end of the furore the opponents of Cow Green reservoir included virtually the entire green community of the day. In addition to the BSBI, the campaigners had rallied to their cause the British Ecological Society, the Council for Nature, the Council for the Preservation of Rural England, the Lake District Naturalists' Trust, the Northumberland and Durham Naturalists' Trust and the Yorkshire Naturalists' Trust, the Commons, Open Spaces and Footpaths Preservation Society, the Linnean Society, the Ramblers' Association, the Society for the Promotion of Nature Reserves, the National Parks Commission and even less centrally connected bodies such as the Countrywide Holidays Association, the Cyclists' Touring Club, the Youth Hostels Association and the Holiday Fellowship. The outdoors and recreational establishment of all Britain were now brothers in arms for Cow Green. Thereafter all of them would be engaged in much protest. Yet here, now, was the first.

There was also celebrity support in the dapper form and polished public-school vowels of Peter Scott, then at the height of his fame as founder of the Wildfowl Trust and the World Wildlife Fund.* He was the David Attenborough of his day, the establishment presenter of a highly popular BBC wildlife television series called *Look*. He even turned up to give evidence at the House of Commons, but Scott was not the main advocate for his team. Another BSBI member, a specialist on chalk grassland called J. E. Lousley, was an amateur

---

* As is the way with conservation organisations both of Scott's NGOs changed their names. The Wildfowl Trust became the Wildfowl and Wetlands Trust, while the World Wildlife Fund (a name, incidentally coined by Max Nicholson) became the Worldwide Fund for Nature. Strangely, it kept the acronym WWF.

botanist but a professional banker. He and J. C. Gardiner, another flower-hunting city friend and a financial adviser to the businessman Charles Clore, helped to organise funds that were placed at the disposal of the Upper Teesdale Defence Committee. They allowed the environmentalists to commission the services of the Labour MP Samuel Silkin QC.

Ultimately it was Silkin's task to present the strength of his colleagues' arguments and undermine those presented by the expert witnesses called by ICI and the water board. The primary forum for this occurred once the bill had come before an MPs' select committee, by which date it had also been scrutinised by various departments of government.

In theory a private member's bill was judged to be entirely separate and unattached to the main business of the incumbent administration. Yet it was expected that the objectives to which the bill would give legal entitlement would bear upon the interests of various branches of government. Thus, at least five of these – Education and Science, Economic Affairs, Land and Natural Resources, Housing and Local Government and the Board of Trade – had eventually made their views known. Convention required that they speak with a single voice, so prior to the select committee sitting they had reconciled their various opinions. In the end, only the Department of Science and Education expressed any reservations about the water board's case for a reservoir at Cow Green. It was not a good start for the botanists.

Then it was the job of the select committee, comprising four MPs, two Labour and two Conservatives, under its Labour chair Clifford Kenyon, to hear the detailed arguments of the two parties. Over twelve days of hearings from 4 to 27 May, they listened to often complex and occasionally arcane expert testimony that was sufficient to fill 700 typescript pages. Ultimately this whole debate boiled down to what seem like simpler choices about money, jobs, industry and hi-tech chemical exports, set against some form of unspecified but higher human value centred on the importance accorded to Widdybank Fell by the botanists and their supporters.

In a sense, even without the benefits of hindsight, one could have predicted that the fight for a flowering fell was a lost cause. Professor Roy Gregory in his brilliant summation of the dispute called it a case of David versus Goliath. Unfortunately, it was one of those many instances where the metaphor was invoked to indicate how the little guy couldn't win. The Upper Teesdale Defence Committee was pitched against ICI: not just the nation's biggest industrial company, but in many ways *the* hi-tech essence of Business Britain plc. What government would dare to oppose a national symbol?

Yet the arguments deployed by the botanists are still important, because they shed light not only on that historical moment and the context in which Cow Green was, as Gregory suggests,'an international *cause célèbre*'.[1] The events of 1964–7 also illustrate the challenges that have almost always confronted environmentalists. That problem could be summarised as how to place nature's needs before or on a level with those of people.

As one of his lordships announced as he was called to weigh the issues at hand, 'In my own simple way I am asking whether I should decide between flowers on the one hand and people on the other – people and their prosperity, Britain and its industrial prosperity.'[2] *Flowers* versus *Britain's industrial prosperity*: the very rhetoric illuminated the scale of the task before the defence committee.

Their tactics at Westminster in 1966 included a two-part strategy. One part involved a constructive alternative to the proposals of the water board that would seek to meet the latter's needs but without damaging an irreplaceable botanical site. The second and more difficult part of their case was to articulate exactly what was at stake if parts of Widdybank were submerged.

On the practical issue of replacement sites for Cow Green, the environmentalists were divided and, over the course of two hearings, first by the MPs and then again in front of a panel of peers, they shifted their position. Initially they had proposed that the most tolerable option was at Upper Cow Green, since a reservoir there would submerge far less significant habitat, of which there was much more elsewhere in the Moor House NNR and in the Upper Teesdale area generally. If there had to be such a thing, then better it be there than elsewhere.

However, this option was rejected by the water board on the grounds that a reservoir at Upper Cow Green would involve costly delay. It required a dam three times longer than at lower Cow Green, and the site would not be operational until 1972. There was a risk, in the event of a drought, of lost industrial output for twenty-four months. Also there were additional costs for the larger construction, which were calculated at £12 million in loan charges over a sixty-year period.[3]

When the bill cleared the Commons select committee with a majority of three to one (Paul Hawkins, a Conservative MP for south-east Norfolk, withheld his consent), the environmentalists shifted their argument. Of the three main options in Upper Teesdale, they suggested that neither Cow Green nor Upper Cow Green were suitable, not just because of the irretrievable loss of important habitats. They were inappropriate sites because they would not truly meet the region's long-term needs. The inevitable requirements for more water in a not-too-distant future would recur, and only Middleton would genuinely meet these medium-term demands. If development took place at Cow Green it would merely be a case of that site today, but Middleton tomorrow. Better, therefore, to build at the much larger site, albeit on productive farmland, and then investigate how to achieve longer-term sustainable water supplies in a strategic manner.

In the final analysis these alternative schemes cut no ice with either the water board or, ultimately, with the majority of politicians. On 28 July 1966 the bill came back before the House of Commons and was further debated because of a blocking amendment moved by another Conservative, Marcus Kimball, the same Gainsborough MP who had sought a strengthening of the SSSI legislation a year earlier, after the loss of Waddingham Common. On Upper Teesdale he proposed that:

This house declines to consider a Bill which would involve irreparable harm to a unique area of international scientific importance, fails to have regard to the proper long-term planning for water requirements of the area, and is contrary to the declared advice of the Nature Conservancy and the National Parks Commission.[4]

Of the 200 MPs present at the debate, the bill received the support of 112, with 82 against.*

On 8 November 1966 the pattern was repeated in the Lords, once the bill had completed its second unopposed reading. It then faced their lordships' own scrutiny in an enlarged select committee. While they ultimately gave their own assent to the reservoir's construction they wished to suggest how difficult the decision had been by publishing a report on how and why they had so concluded. There remained finally a third reading in the House of Lords, an event that was largely a formality, given that there was by convention no division.

Regardless of the nicety of the judgements they claimed were so difficult to reach, all of the Westminster decision-makers were susceptible to the issues that were central to society at that time and to the arguments that touched upon mainstream values. These were about productivity and the priority needs of an important business enterprise and a major employer: namely Imperial Chemical Industries. After all the furore, the cost and the tortuously slow deliberations, the Tees Valley and Cleveland Water Bill received its royal assent on 22 March 1967.

A few days later, almost as confirmation of the human gift for error in matters environmental, the Fleet Air Arm dropped forty-two 1,000 lb bombs on a stricken *Torrey Canyon*. When these failed to ignite the vast winding plumes of black sludge, they switched to dropping drums of aviation fuel to set the oil alight.

Hindsight has allowed us to see a number of striking ironies in the aftermath of the controversies at Upper Teesdale. One of the most

---

* The party politics of the vote were as follows. Those for the reservoir construction included 100 Labour and 12 Conservative. Opposing Cow Green were 44 Conservatives, 29 Labour and 9 Liberals (of the total 12 Liberal MPs in the house). I'm not sure there is much to glean from the political complexion of conservation, except to note that the government of the day was Labour and both the various departments and the select committee had all approved the private bill. It was likely therefore that Labour MPs would fall in behind the 'official' position of their administration.

telling concerns the manner in which a bunch of botanists had tried to tell a water board its business. For all the accusations they might have faced, those unworldly naturalists – 'selfish eccentrics' was a phrase suggested by Roy Gregory – had identified a gaping cavity in the planning procedures for supply of industrial water. What was required, they had argued, was a rigorous, strategic vision of the whole way in which such resources were managed. And how right they would be proved.

What had been projected as a burning necessity to the Imperial Chemical Industries of 1971, when Cow Green reservoir was finally finished, was shown to be a touch less essential just ten years later. That was once Kielder Reservoir had been built, fifty miles away to the north in the Upper Tyne valley of Northumberland. This vast structure, with the largest water capacity of any reservoir in England, buried in its depths twice as much farmland as would have been lost in any Middleton reservoir. Part of the infrastructure developed at the new mega-site was the Kielder Transfer Scheme, which delivers water to the Tees and Wear Rivers to make up any shortfall in their respective capacities. Kielder was opened in 1981. It meant that Widdybank Fell, with its more than 12,000 years of remarkable post-Ice-Age flora, was lost to supply a single industrial enterprise for merely a decade.

The second great irony of Cow Green was the way in which the advocates of business and industrial water, for all the cynicism and self-interest of which they were accused by their opponents, exposed a fallacy at the heart of the environmental case. The green lobby might have protested of Widdybank's central scientific significance, and contended that damage to any part would impair a place of incalculable research potential. Alas for these arguments, and as the QC for the water board was able to show, if it was so important, why had sections of the site not even been included in the Moor House National Nature Reserve? Many of the botanists who paraded before the select committees to attest to its irreplaceable scientific importance were shown to have only the very shakiest knowledge of Cow Green itself. The truth was many of them had hardly ever been to the place.

One final consequence came after the bill's successful passage with a gesture of compromise offered by its ultimate beneficiaries. ICI made a payment of £100,000 to the Nature Conservancy to fund a detailed study of the area that would be drowned by the rising waters. It was these monies that really delivered the work which captured the full scientific significance of the area. It was the ultimate exquisite irony in the whole affair: a company profiting partly from the manufacture of fertilisers, which themselves were helping to obliterate England's botanical heritage, was now supporting research into the floristic importance of a place it had specifically campaigned to spoil. And what those studies proved beyond cavil was the need to keep Widdybank inviolate.

A question arising from the aftermath of the whole case is why exactly the Nature Conservancy and the botanists had vested so much import-ance in science. The endless refrain of Widdybank's champions was the loss to science inflicted by a reservoir. In summarising his own objections to Cow Green, the eminent geographer Sir Dudley Stamp had written that the 'reservoir as planned would submerge some unique habitats: if it were moved but a short distance away, those habitats would be preserved for study'.[5] Even the MP Marcus Kimball had succumbed to the same rhetoric, referring in his blocking motion to the site's 'international scientific importance'. Why had this specific appeal been at the heart of all their arguments?

The answer has two key parts. One has to do with the original expectations that were placed on the Nature Conservancy at its creation. As we have seen, what had helped to ensure its safe delivery during the rocky post-war birthing period was an assumption that it would investigate how to get more out of Britain's natural resources. This may now look at odds with its work to salvage natural places and wild species from human development, but that was how many people, especially in government, viewed its raison d'être. In its founding charter, words that I italicised earlier, the Conservancy's remit included the provision of 'scientific advice on the ... *control* of the natural flora and fauna of Great Britain'.

That notion of ecology as a pragmatic study of natural processes had a long pedigree. As far back as 1912, Professor Oliver, the man instrumental in securing Blakeney Point, was motivated not merely to protect aesthetically pleasing coastal vegetation. He hoped also that Norfolk's famous shingle spit would be a testing zone where ecologists could unravel the economic and agricultural benefits of such habitats.[6] In his own book, Arthur Tansley had written: 'Ecology ... is not only a fascinating study in itself ... it lies at the foundation of all the industries which depend on the management and use of vegetation.'[7] These ideas were still very much alive.

As Bill Adams pointed out in a superb analysis of the relationship between science and environmentalism (*Future Nature*, 1996), Max Nicholson referred to nature reserves in a 1957 report as 'outdoor laboratories' where ecological processes could be investigated. Adams further describes how a reviewer of Nicholson's report 'wrote disparagingly that "ecological research is evidently to be merely the handmaiden of conservation, and conservation to be virtually equated with preservation".' What this critic wanted from the Nature Conservancy was not less science, but more, and by science he meant research that produced utilitarian benefits.[8]

Another botanist prominent in the 1960s, Professor W. T. Williams, had been asked to comment on the Nature Conservancy's activities. Reserves were essential, he contended, for research, but too little attention had been focused hitherto on how to raise agricultural productivity on these marginal lands.[9] So when botanists played the science card in respect of Cow Green they were hoping to appeal precisely to these pragmatic leanings in the decision-makers of Westminster.

There is an implicit irony in this use of science as a means of buttressing their case. For it was the green lobby generally and even the very individuals working at Widdybank, such as Derek Ratcliffe, who were helping to undermine science's exalted status. Even as the Upper Teesdale reservoir was being bulldozed and concreted into place, Ratcliffe was working on what the author of *The Peregrine* (1967), J. A. Baker, would call the 'filthy, insidious pollen of farm chemicals'.[10] A particularly filthy pollen that was devastating birds of prey across the entire western world was dichlorodiphenyltrichloroethane. Better known as DDT, it was firmly in Ratcliffe's sights, and his work would eventually help bring about its international withdrawal.*

The second reason why science was invoked so regularly and with such emphasis in the Cow Green controversy requires that we look more closely at what exactly was at stake with the partial destruction of the site. This sheds light on all efforts to place value upon non-human nature, and the specific challenge faced by environmentalists when countering the stock utilitarian arguments that underpin mainstream capitalist values.

In 1971 the reservoir's deep waters submerged, along with hundreds of other acres, a tenth of one of the richest botanical sites in England. In all about 22 acres of sugar limestone were destroyed. In specific terms it caused the loss of all Teesdale's tall bog sedge *Carex magellanica* (virtually at its southern limit in this country), 40 per cent of the rare spring or heath sedge *Carex ericetorum*, 40 per cent of alpine rush *Juncus alpinoarticulatus* (also at its southern limit), and a tenth of the Teesdale violet *Viola rupestris*, which is confined in Britain to Durham and two adjacent counties.[†] What was compromised was the site's integrity.

---

* In the year that the Tees Valley and Cleveland Water Bill was passed, science as an ethical index of western society was taking further hits. The United States Air Force had done much to change perceptions with another product of science, through its annual destruction of 1.5 million acres of crops and rainforest in Vietnam. It had achieved this by spraying chemicals from the air. One of the most efficient herbicides, which had been euphemised as 'Agent Orange', as if it were a bottled substitute for sunshine or a health drink, contained high levels of the carcinogenic compound dioxin. In all 18 million gallons of herbicide were dumped on the Vietnamese environment. By the war's end, the people in the south of that country had three times the levels of dioxin compared with the citizens of their ally, the USA. As Cow Green was being built, British society learnt of the consequences of yet another wonder chemical, a drug called Thalidomide that caused birth defects in thousands of newborn babies. Although the earliest cases were more than a decade old – my mother was offered it before I was born in 1959 – government compensation to British victims was paid only in 1968.

[†] One of the last-ditch efforts made by botanists, and almost certainly subsidised by the ICI grant, was the physical removal and transplant of some of the rarest individual plants in the lead-up to Cow Green's submergence. How successful these eleventh-hour relocations were has never been properly established. Yet many highly localised organisms are confined in range precisely because they are dependent upon tiny nuances in their physical settings. Re-location often breaks these invisible threads of connection.

The word 'unique' in an environmental context is a dangerous term. Few sites are truly unique. A community of plants and animals is not like Picasso's *Les Demoiselles d'Avignon* or even Stonehenge. Nature seldom does singularity. The glamour of the 'unique' or the 'rarity', however, excites us. The public can respond to it, and environmentalists often fall into the trap of using it to express the meaning and value of a place. Rare species are trumpeted as a shorthand substitute for ecological complexities.

At Teesdale there are many highly scarce plants. The spring gentian is just one of them. So too the hoary rock-rose *Helianthemum oelandicum*, which has a handful of outposts in Wales, western Ireland and near the Cumbrian Lakes, but Teesdale is its most northerly station. Another is a beautiful pink-bloomed cushion-forming plant called thrift *Armeria maritima*. This is actually abundant on many British coasts, but it is highly unusual inland in England (although it is fairly common on Scottish roadsides).

What is indisputably special about Upper Teesdale is not the presence of any single plant, rare or common: it is the whole community – the different flowers, rushes, sedges, etc. that are each, in turn, often limited in British distribution, but occur together on Widdybank and Cronkley Fells. It is the convergence of all that is rarest of all, and which speaks most tellingly of its past history.

Until 18,000 years ago much of northern England had been covered in ice that was more than a mile and half thick in places. As the Earth warmed and the glaciers retreated, so they exposed buried soils where plants could finally re-colonise. Trees came later and covered Upper Teesdale as they did most of Britain, but never so completely that they shaded out the first post-glacial vegetation. Eventually humans obliterated most of that post-glacial world in almost every part of these islands. Ironically, it was their specific clearance of trees in Upper Teesdale that helped to retain the ancient and original flora at Widdybank.

Irrespective of the forces and circumstances that enabled its survival, this suite of flowers persisted, through thousands of springs and summers, as it had nowhere else. No fewer than twenty-four of the seventy-five exceptional plant species found in Upper Teesdale are now typical inhabitants of the Alps or the Arctic. Its botanical community is thus a tiny isolated relict of that post-glacial world. To see it, to be among it, is to get as close as we ever shall to that time, those conditions. It is as pristine a part of England as it is possible to see. Cow Green reservoir violated all that.

The Canadian ecologist John Livingston, in his extended essay entitled *The Fallacy of Nature Conservation*, pointed out that as a species, despite our millennia-long preoccupation with civilised art and with the contemplation of beauty, we have not developed a way of valuing something he calls *life process*.

> The nearest thing we seem to have is the appreciation of form in music or poetry or dance – form, as opposed to specific content. This, as a kind of process, we understand and appreciate aesthetically. But we have not developed an aesthetic of life process. This is because our culture is essentially abiotic.[11]

In short, according to Livingston, what humans value most is what is made by us, but dead. However, his analysis contains a major omission. Gardens. Of all people the British are attached to the traditions of gardening. The whole approach to environmentalism in this country is sometimes construed as a form of gardening, with its associated fetish for perpetual meddling. I would qualify Livingston's argument to say that we have no aesthetic appreciation of *wild* life process.

What unfolds every year on the banks of Widdybank Fell is beautiful, not merely as a visual display but as an interconnected and seasonal vegetative unfolding that has been ongoing for more than 10,000 years.

Yet our legislators had no way – and, in large measure, still have no way – to appreciate it or to attribute meaning to it.

The living community at Widdybank constituted one part of the loss. The second part is more difficult to quantify, but it is entailed in the very language used to describe those final physical characteristics. In essence it was a cultural payment. When the land and its inhabitants were drowned we washed away with them some of their imaginative possibilities, their historical richness, their symbolic power, their creative opportunities as well as their scientific and even spiritual potential. We lost some of the things that *we* bring to that place and which are latent in the landscape.

Of course, we didn't lose it in its entirety. We lost part of it: specifically, the twenty-two acres of sugar limestone that were drowned. You can still go there and *almost* completely immerse yourself in its post-glacial world, especially if you avert your eyes from Cow Green reservoir.

But to return to the central issue, those two parts – the physical place and our reactions – are totally separate entities but they are entirely, inextricably, fused together. Environmentalism is always binary in nature. You cannot have the sum of human responses without the totality of its natural counterpart. And conservation seeks to safeguard the potentialities of both: the other species for themselves so that they might persist on our shared planet; but also the spectrum of our own internal engagements, which those other life forms inspire – responses that are imaginative, creative, cultural, intellectual, spiritual. It is a point conservationists often fail to convey, or even to grasp themselves. Environmental loss is not just out there in the real world. It is lost from within us too.

The central point to emphasise, however, is that it is complicated. How do you summarise all that in a language that people can readily assimilate and appreciate? Don't you need a shorthand form to express the intellectual and moral content of environmental values, but also to encapsulate what we understand about the physical ecosystem itself? And isn't it even more pressing that your case be simple and direct, especially when your opponents are talking the brass tacks of money and jobs and loss of export markets?

Science, therefore, for those defenders of Upper Teesdale, was a kind of summary expression for all this. Yet there is a second set of implications entailed in the word 'science' that made it so appealing to the ecologists. For it was a way of suggesting that the values to which they appealed were somehow outside of themselves. By invoking the goddess of knowledge, like a *dea ex machina*, they were summoning alongside her radiant presence elevated and objective truths that were above the hurly-burly of human debate. Of course, they were not objective; they were entirely subjective choices. As Bill Adams has asserted in *Future Nature*, 'science does not make meanings: people do.'[12] But when they raised themselves to their fullest height and squared up toe-to-toe with the agents of industry, David to Goliath, the defenders of Cow Green thought that science was the most effective slingshot they had.

Thirdly and finally, science was a way of capturing a whole other set of ideas. Citing the work of the American historian of science Donna Haraway, Bill Adams points out that 'Science is still the most significant source of myths about nature.'[13] By this he means the endless revenue of stories about life around us that is generated by science and scientific processes. In the minds of Cow Green's champions it implied what was best about the place, but also what was best about us.

It was a way of compressing the extraordinary richness that humans represent – including our compassion for nature itself, a trait so far discovered in no other species – which is passed on from generation to generation as a treasure trove of cultural riches. Much of that inheritable legacy is precisely because of science: the capacity to cure leprosy, to eliminate the guinea worm, to fly across an ocean, to send men to the Moon, to give a name to a blue flower, to find value within it.

Was that insistence upon science enough? Did the Teesdale Defence Committee fail posterity? All we can say is that *they* thought it the best means to get across their arguments. If anything, it reveals how extraordinarily difficult it is to explain what an environmental ethic entails. And if they failed, haven't we failed? Have we come up with a better way of making the case?*

*

---

* It is worth recalling Peter Marren's words on that venerable official name for an environmentally significant place – the Site of Special Scientific Interest. Scientific, in this context, he argued, 'really means "nature conservation" in an adjectival sense'. For what it is worth, I believe we do need to replace science and scientific, to rebuild an understanding that when wild places are lost the deficit is to the whole of ourselves, and not just to one human community or to a single portion within us. Equally, what is gained through intimacy with non-human nature nourishes all parts of who we are. For are those places not also sites of importance for artistic inspiration, for human health, for mental well-being, for spiritual restoration? We need a wording that encompasses all. Special Places for All Nature would be my alternative (SPAN). 'All' Nature because it would ask us to remember that we are not separate, we are an indivisible part, of what is special. It spans us too.

I swing into the car park at Cow Green and I am surprised to find that there is even one other vehicle present. It is getting late. As I close my door I'm somehow expecting more resistance, and I fling it to with what is instantly revealed as unnecessary force. For the whole valley is under an immense hush, and the clang of steel sounds like gunshot in all its stillness.

The sun's descent over the line of the Pennines intensifies the sounds of this place, like the choral voices of the curlews that stretch long frail lines of music across the heavens. Somewhere in the gloaming I can also pick out a distressed lapwing, a mother perhaps, fussed and warning her near-fledged chicks of some imaginary danger looming in the half-light. I imagine them there, huddled together, as a weird and comical microcosm of the place. A mother with a ridiculously swollen chest where two chicks nestle, creating the vision of a bird with six legs. As I start down the track towards Cauldron Snout and the reservoir dam, the hills on the opposite side of the water are draining of colour. The distant heather forms monochrome patterns intensified by the repeated folds of the terrain. A skylark is somewhere above the water and is invisible in the gloom, but it drizzles down its zany granular song and I think of all the skylarks over the whole Pennines, in fact over all upland Britain as far as Cape Wrath or even the Atlantic shores of Cille Pheadair, with its shell-and-sand soils smothered in wild flowers in South Uist, where the Atlantic pounds ashore beyond the dunes and where there is a cemetery I know – Cladh Hallan – and where skylarks make their music too. In all those places larks rise and sing. From there to here the birds will spray it down upon us, until evening dissolves into night. This skylark connects me now to those other birds and to those other places. It is one of their gifts to us: they help us transcend time and place.

As I walk I think of those men in Westminster in 1967* and their decision to build the reservoir. Can we or should we blame them?

---

* They were mainly men. In the House of Commons just 22 of the intake at the 1966 election were women, representing 4.1 per cent of all MPs.

Across the political spectrum, the majority felt that it was in the national interest to do as they did.

We should recall equally that there were powerful and prescient voices of opposition. William Strang, a crossbench peer, was singled out by Roy Gregory for the eloquence of his case. Strang likened Cow Green to the worst excesses of a more ecologically indifferent age, but with one difference: we knew better. Yet here we were, repeating their destructiveness.

> For what was done to the countryside in the first Industrial Revolution, in those days of laissez-faire, the blame, for the desecration of the landscape, could be cast upon the greedy capitalist. We are now horrified at what he did. But what is the position today, in these days of planning? Are we not in this new Industrial Revolution doing the same thing all over again, but with a difference – the difference being that it is now the government itself, and industry and the trade unions, who are all at one in giving priority to the claims of industry? As a result of this, what we now face, unless a halt is called somewhere, is the continuing irreparable spoliation of the dwindling countryside and the desecration of the already heavily damaged coast.[14]

I think the question we can answer is the one posed in the opening chapter of this book. There I asked, how could a people who appear to love nature more almost than any nationality – to which that Lords debate in 1967 bears witness – have still destroyed so much of their richest countryside in so short a time?

The crisis of Cow Green and the building of the reservoir help to explain away that apparent paradox. For if there was ever a place that should have been beyond the reach of development and industrial intrusion then it was here amid all this skylark song, where a post-glacial flora had persisted for who knows how long? Perhaps 12,000, and maybe even 18,000, years. And if this place was not beyond the cut and thrust that bargains wild nature for material benefit, then which of our places was safe?

The answer was nowhere. So it has proved. In the intervening decades since Widdybank was flooded, industry, agriculture and development have taken precedence time after time after time after time. Insignificant and piecemeal they may have been in their individual demands – Waddingham Common, the downlands of Wiltshire, those twenty-two acres on Widdybank Fell – but the sum of those small impacts is expressed through the *State of Nature* report's overarching point that 60 per cent of species measured have declined and 31 have declined seriously. It is the slow, inexorable, incremental subtractions that modern humanity makes, which explain how we lost 44 million birds from our avifauna between 1966 and 2008. It is precisely how you lose 99 per cent of all flower-rich meadows. At every turn in the road we chose ourselves.

If we should ever once have opted for nature, then Cow Green was the place and the moment to have made an exception. That we did not and could not do that is the measure of all our losses to the British environment. Perhaps there should be a plaque that reads: 'Cow Green Reservoir: British Nature was Lost Here 1964–71.'

Just before I reach the dam it is almost dark, and I am suddenly surprised to find that I am not alone. Two figures, the owners, I surmise, of that other vehicle in Cow Green car park, emerge into view and we fall into benighted conversation. What it is to be out when everyone else is at home. And what a place it is to take peace. And how regularly we visit. And listen to the skylark! Then I ask them what they think of the reservoir. Did they know that it was the cause of a major controversy in the sixties? No, they knew nothing about that, they say. But they exclaim how much they love it and how it completes the beauty of the place.

13

FACTORY FLOWERS

Towns hunker down
In the owl-measured spaces between,
Pray to Guthlac, patron saint
of imagined terrors

Matt Merritt, 'At Gedney Hill'

As you drive along the A17 northwest from Kings Lynn to Sleaford you can't miss the place: the Famous Farm Café at Gedney. It's a massive complex on both sides of the road, and I'm here to see an area renowned not for wildlife and biodiversity, but for the primary use to which we have put our countryside for the last 6,500 years. The Famous Farm Café is surrounded by farmland supreme.

The firebrand rural campaigner of the early nineteenth century, William Cobbett, once wrote of Holbeach, a town two miles down the road from where I sit, that it 'lies in the midst of some of the richest land in the world'.[1] In the course of writing this book I repeatedly asked farmers and landowners where the best agricultural country was in these islands. 'Around Boston' was the commonest response. Holbeach is just fifteen miles from Boston. Both places, like Gedney, are part of the same district of South Holland. That name alone conjures the extraordinary topography of these parts. It's a region where two crops a year from the same ground are commonplace, and where an acre of grade-one arable land changes hands for nothing less than £10,000.

The consequence for wildlife, on the other hand, is starkly revealed on any map of environmentally important sites. There is a great sweep of country whose boundaries create an enlarged and roughly parallel replica of The Wash's own semi-circular shoreline. It's a district that includes parts of Norfolk west and south of the River Nar, a bloc of north Cambridgeshire as far south as Ely, and a substantial swathe of Lincolnshire south and east of a line between Gibraltar Point (on the coast) and Grantham. It has fewer SSSIs than any other part of terrestrial Britain.*

Driving across its famously corrugated roads, whose undulations are the product of perpetual land shrinkage, one is confronted by an unrelieved plain reticulated by a network of dykes and made dramatic and, occasionally, sublime by the vaster skies overhead. No country in England has larger skies than fenland. Such is the lack of relief or land contour that the region offers little sense of perspective. All is flattened out and compressed to a single linear horizon. Among the few things to give scale or indicate distance are the electricity pylons, which march as man-made monsters across the flats. To these today one can add wind turbines.

Cobbett noted that

> The whole country was as level as the table on which I am now writing. The horizon like the sea in a dead calm: you see the morning sun come up just as at sea; and see it go down over the rim … Everything grows well here: earth without a stone so big as a pin's head.[2]

The A17 runs right through its heartland, and in the last thirty-eight years I've driven that whole stretch about 400 times between the two geographical fixtures of my life, Derbyshire and Norfolk. Despite its flatness and apparent hedge-free openness, where all is visible at all times, this stretch of countryside strikes me as one of the most baffling and unfathomable in England. I have long intuited, however, that the Famous Farm Café at Gedney holds a key to its landscape character.

---

* It does include the Ouse Washes, which is one of the great sites for wetland birds in Norfolk. It is part of the 1 per cent of the Fens that has survived in a relatively natural state.

It's a huge open compound west of Gedney roundabout, bounded to the north and south by dark leggy cypresses and dominated by several factory-like premises. The café alone seats 500, according to one of the huge noticeboards prominent throughout the site. Many signs are garish pink or fluorescent yellow with multi-coloured block capitals, announcing:

FARM STEAK PIE
CHIPS PEAS GRAVY

or

FULL
ENGLISH
BREAKFASTS
ROAST
LUNCHES
LOGS
£2.80 BAG

and, more obliquely:

D-DAY 1944 HELP YOUR LOCAL HEROES & VETERANS

The first impression it gives is not of anywhere English, but perhaps somewhere in the American Midwest, a feeling compounded in part by the dead level un-Englishness of the place. Another transatlantic note, functioning in summer, is the sound of 1940s and 1950s music – Dean Martin, Frank Sinatra – blasted from a tannoy above the traffic roar on the A17. Then there is the motel on the road's south side with its proud display of military hardware: a decommissioned fighter jet cordoned off with red-and-white traffic cones, or the armoured personnel carriers, one in conventional army green and another in desert khaki complete with tank tracks, or, next to it, in the same car-park area, the huge field gun whose barrel, I notice, is the length of a Transit van and caravan combined, and is aimed north-east.

The last looks so new and ready for combat that you could imagine it scorching holes in one of the several Union Jacks or the flags of St George and St David that flutter opposite. Its firepower would obliterate the roadside bungalow beyond, around which establishment is a display of old tractor technologies. Last time I counted, in a curving line upon its immaculately manicured lawns, there were about twenty-five ancient farm machines as well as a toy wooden windmill at least ten foot tall. I've never quite worked out if the impromptu tractor museum is part of the café's wider gallimaufry, or an entirely separate, rival demonstration.

Crossing the A17 is seldom easy. The traffic is relentless. As a consequence the Famous Farm Café buzzes with trade. As they announce on one poster, they have 'Enough Staff to Serve 50 Meals Every 5 Minutes'. Today, however, a Friday morning in March, the place is quiet. I nurse a mug of tea surrounded by empty tables and take stock of the counter area.

Heaped high on a stand in front is a preliminary pyramid of toy pandas with cowboy hats. On the wall immediately beyond are piled displays of white-bread rolls or scones and, over these, a panorama of more yellow or pink posters for the FARM HAM FEAST, FARM ROAST LUNCHES, or BIG FARM HOT DOGS (with onions) only £1, FARM BURGER WITH CHIPS, BIG FARM BURGER £1.60, FARM BURGER WITH SIDE SALAD £1, FARM STEAK AND KIDNEY PIE and the FARM HAM FEAST.

Near where I'm seated and throughout the cafe's many cavernous sub-chambers is a comparable visual hotchpotch covering the wall surfaces. It comprises about 150 paintings in cheap gilt frames. Almost all evoke an entirely separate, much older, pastoral world with few connections to the scenes outside, or to the products proclaimed over the café counter. Proud ploughmen urge on huge, high-chested beasts across a field where gulls dance in their wake; ladies in bonnets are riding up top on the stagecoach with the whip-wielding driver beside them, patient sheepdogs quiet in cobbled yards where geese cackle and hens forage for spilt grain. There are prize sheep and lambs with dry-cleaned fleeces. Milkmaids in fancy bonnets. Big-limbed farmhands hump sacks of wheat, while others stack the straw around a freshly risen hayrick. In one image the heavy horses pause, flanks gleaming at the brow of the headland, just before they turn to draw down the plough blade deep into the loam.

The imaginary jingle of the horses' brasses, mist-bloomed in the cold autumn air, has to compete with the zany electronic *bloop* noise of the adjacent slot machine (offering the possibilities of 'Extreme Gaming'). Its incessant lights fire neon at the painting's late-morning glow and, out of that far scene, the horses, with muzzles firing bolts of smoke-breath, look across tables covered with plastic cloths of floral design, where generous sprigs of plastic blossoms – roses, irises, gladioli, daffodils – have been placed at each. And all are now in perpetual false bloom.

At Gedney church just a mile down the road I found a similar synthesis of the archly modern and the completely utilitarian, but here in a setting of the ancient past. For the village of Gedney, or Gadenai as it was spelt in the Domesday Book, pre-dates the Norman Conquest, and its beautiful church of St Mary Magdalene is at least 700 years old. Such is the imposing height of its tower – fifty-six feet at the parapet – that it is often known as the Cathedral of the Fens. One might imagine that the graveyard here would be one fenland spot where a more tender reconciliation could be permitted between its occupants and their natural surroundings.

Yet I notice how many of the spaces between the headstones, especially at the rear of the church, have been treated with a broad-spectrum herbicide. Groundsel has raised a few sickly spikes among the carpet of dead vegetation, but the grave plots themselves are kept entirely free of living greenery, not only by chemicals but also by pebbles in a matrix of glass shards, or by reddish chippings that look like minced house brick. An aura of exacting tidiness prevails, and from any distance the scene has a chromatic range moving only from the dead grey of the graves' raised kerbs to the dun grey of the bare dry soil. The ensemble has the look of a photograph in old sepia. Somehow its constituent parts remind me of the early stages on a building plot, or a bombed-out war zone.

On one whole side of the churchyard even the headstones have been uprooted and moved to the boundary wall. Now in haphazard line, looking uncertain of their new purpose, they stand on the edge of the space they once dominated. The individual whereabouts of the graves' occupants have been lost and homogenised under a monoculture of rye-grass. In turn, it has been freed from the contamination even of daisies. And all done, one assumes, so that a contractor's ride-on cutter can work the graveyard sward more conveniently. Only the newest headstones survive on the other side of the church, and their marble surfaces have the brilliance and bold lettering – even perhaps the short-lived relevance – of magazine pages.

Until half a century ago St Mary Magdalene's had a long-established vegetable motif for the dead in a line of ancient yews that once flanked the path to the church door. Apparently they had become too unruly, and have now been replaced with leylandii cypress. There is, however, a single surviving relict of the older traditional churchyard species: a small yew pruned to a flat-topped blob that looks as unnatural and as out of place as the surrounding hydrangeas and yuccas.

One nicely ironic touch is a board announcing 'The Unkempt Churchyard'.* There is indeed a residual growth of bramble in one corner, but I notice that all the oldest vines of ivy in the trees have been severed at their bases. While they climb still and twist to the canopy, their entire serpent's length of evergreen vegetation is now dead and brown. Perhaps the most striking and least scripted expression of life is a stain of green algae that has colonised one part of the board itself.

As I walk around the church I am reminded of a scene I witnessed several years earlier on the Outer Hebrides. It was in a tiny cemetery by the shallow waters of Loch Hallan, north of Cille Pheadair and west of Dalagrogán Iar. The machair fields landward of the dunes in

---

* It corresponded to a publication of the same name on sale inside the church that describes the wildlife riches of the churchyard. One surprising part of its contents was a reference by the author to 'some letters of complaint about the way the churchyard was maintained'. The implication, presumably, was that it was far too unkempt.

this part of South Uist were truly extraordinary. In high summer they were brilliant yellow from dense sheets of birds'-foot trefoil and buttercup, but plugged intermittently by greater twayblade orchids or the shockingly dense purple of northern marsh orchids. It was gloriously verdant, yet it rose from a substrate of gritty white-shell sand that showed through where the plants thinned, or where the wind had scooped it out and exposed bunkers of bare ground. Its whiteness meant that it all seemed intensely bright and sharp, and the whole place was chiselled out further by the downward-shining songs of skylarks.

The cemetery itself was, in truth, no more than an enclosed area of this wild-flower-smothered machair. In all Britain I have never seen a more beautiful setting for the human dead, where the whole ground was shining yellow with flowers. Regardless of this inadvertent honouring of the departed, someone armed with a petrol strimmer had completely decimated all this display around many headstones and reduced the golden carpet to a bare close-shorn grass sward. At intervals across the ritual destruction were black marble receptacles sprouting plastic flowers in pink and blue.

It struck me that even on this Atlantic shoreline where, as far as I am able to judge, there is a more harmonious reconciliation between nature and people than anywhere else in Britain, the presence of our own dead demands a ritual display of human control and order.

Perhaps affairs at Gedney are an expression of the same deep-seated impulse. Yet I should also add that there are glimpses of something wilder and freer in the interstices between the blanket expressions of rigorous domination. Near the church door was a rosette of feathers on the path, where a feral pigeon had been slaughtered and dismantled by a fugitive sparrowhawk. There was a thrush somewhere overhead that introduced a highly individual motif into the customary bell-like phrases of the species' song. It was a wonderfully elongated *brrrrrrew-brrrrrrrew* sequence that somehow seemed silvered with extra filigree so that it bounced off the church walls with added resonance. Perhaps because of their context, such things tug at the heartstrings with added force.

In truth, I struggle to get real purchase either on my feelings about the detail, or on the underlying attitudes that have informed and shaped the collective relationship to this spot. Somehow Gedney churchyard, like the Famous Farm Café, seems emblematic of the whole. And I go out in further search of it, driving in a wide circuit, down the A17 as far as the bridge over the River Welland at Fosdyke, then back via the settlements of Moulton, Whaplode, Holbeach, Gedney, before returning to walk for a couple of days near the latter village.

A striking feature of the built environment in these places is that there is so often little sense of continuity between one part and the next. Each row of houses, sometimes each individual building, and particularly the bungalows, is distinct in style or construction materials from any neighbour's. Very few places have a patina of age, or their gardens a sense of well-worn traditional management.

I eventually conclude that this haphazard quality to the built environment is entwined with the very richness and singularity of the fenland soils. As Cobbett noted, there is barely a pebble here the size of a pinhead. So there is no local stone with which to build and, thus, no regional, organically evolved style of building to which locals aspire. And since this is pre-eminently a place for crops, relentlessly renewed, year on year, even season by season, and horizon to horizon, there is almost nothing lasting in nature to work with or against, except the skies and their overwhelming sense of space. South Holland is in a state of perpetually reinstated newness.

Perhaps a place that has no fixtures or traditions can offer other kinds of freedom. The very levelness of the landscape, providing no restraint upon any external prospects, may likewise give scope to its occupants' interior visions. One wonders if living in South Holland allows the setting aside of customary limits and norms. Perhaps each is at liberty to cut adrift from his neighbours. An owner might thus adorn his garden with a 10-foot windmill, or twenty-five tractors; or a fighter jet and pink hoardings bidding you 'HELP YOUR LOCAL HEROES & VETERANS'. Certainly South Holland seems somehow more deregulated and disjointed than almost any other place I know in Britain.

It is surely this that helps to explain the supreme miscellany of the Famous Farm Café, where the slot-machine and the Suffolk Punch keep time; where the BIG FARM BURGER and the faithful sheepdog lie down together.

If there is an underlying principle that shapes this place then it is utility. There is perhaps a form of nostalgia for an older, slower, more arduous and organic agricultural age, where men worked and sweated with horses, or where hollyhocks and foxgloves grew at cottage doors. Occasionally, in quieter corners, there is still a hope of some unkempt and wilder dispensation. In the end, however, it always seems easiest to opt for the practical and the monoculture.

Many domestic gardens look like interiors, and are managed as if nature has to be and can be controlled like the constituents of a living room. If the lawns could be vacuumed and preserved dust-free, I imagine that they would be. In fact, I am amazed that plastic grass has not yet taken root here.

Like the sward in Gedney churchyard, lawns are shorn to the very quick and usually purified of all possible contamination – daisies, dandelions etc. Just south of Holbeach St John, two days later, I watched one diligent soul cutting a garden lawn that must have extended for ten acres. The giant ride-on mower was probably the price of an average four-wheel-drive car. At Holbeach Drove there was a twenty-acre paddock with a levelness that looked engineered, devoid of everything except its allocated vegetative cover – a two-inch GI's haircut of rye grass.

At premises that routinely have names such as 'Foxgloves', or 'Hollyhocks', or 'The Willows', I found flowers in the beds that are mostly non-native. Exotic dwarf conifers, many with variegated leaves, or ornamental heathers are particularly popular. I discover later that there are, in fact, specialist nurseries for both near by.

The dominant hedge species in Moulton, Whaplode, Holbeach and Gedney is leylandii cypress, the same tree as that which bounds the Famous Farm Café and is in the churchyard of St Mary Magdalene. A sterile cross between two American trees, the Monterey cypress and Nootka cypress, leylandii may have been developed in Wales but is not a native species, as is claimed sometimes. It supports almost no British insect life, and I am struck how even the green parts – whenever prunings are cut and left – fail to decompose through the actions of either fungi or bacteria. In short, it seems almost completely immune to the natural processes of decay.*

In many ways the species seems a symbol of the entire area, and not just a leitmotif for South Holland but as the default green wall of choice for all of fenland. Holbeach Drove, just south of Gedney, is one of the few places in Britain where I've seen leylandii hedges through the middle of a golf course. The impregnable solidity of its foliage, along with its quick-growing nature – it can rise 3–4 feet in a 12-month period – confers privacy in a matter of a few years. It offers similar opportunities to breezeblock or gravel: stable construction materials that are cheap and practical. I have seen some hedges here that run for hundreds of yards, like towering palisades, around entire farm boundaries.

Then I reach Gedney Fen and come upon the daffodils. It is called Gedney Fen but there is no water except that sunk within its deep dykes. What strikes you, however, are the level expanses of soil – soil drilled and sprouting regimented lines of yellow-headed crops into the middle distance. They are daffodils, but not as you are accustomed to see them, or to think of them.

The flowers have an ineradicable place in the British cultural lexicon. They are the ultimate botanical emblems of Wales: *Cenhinen Pedr*, as they are known, 'St Peter's leeks'. Most importantly they are David's flowers, that rise to bloom on his patron saint's day of 1 March. Remoter still in history, they were *affodilus* (medieval Latin), from *asphodelus* (Greek), the plants that grew on the meadows of the underworld. Our ancestors also knew daffodils as wild blooms, especially in south-west England where they were called 'giggaries', 'lady's ruffles' or – my

---

* Conifers such as cypress support far fewer invertebrates than deciduous trees. I cannot find figures for leylandii cypress, but fir and larch have only 16 and 17 associated insects respectively. Oak and willow, for comparison, have 284 and 266 respectively.[3]

favourite – 'daffydowndillies' or 'king's spears', 'lenty lilies', 'fairy bells', 'gracie days' and 'goose leeks'.[4]

For Wordsworth they were the Lake District's flowers of joy, dancing and laughing. Now they are the archly modern supermarket symbol of Easter or Mother's Day. In all these avatars they have been the floral embodiment of spring, and render the season portable, so that its colour and sense of renewed hope can be plucked and carried indoors. The gold of daffodils is as bright and life-affirming as the thick impasto yellow of Van Gogh's sunflowers, and they are, in a way, the British sunflowers.

Here, however, in this field in South Holland, they mean something very different, and I am mesmerised by the ordering of them. Daffodils collocated in such dead straight lines that they look to be ranked like soldiers on parade. There is nothing alongside or among the regime – in fact, there is nothing at all until the field margin but soil in linear patterns, used as an industrial aggregate in which to manufacture other industrial products.

Here, I come to realise, is a place, below birdless skies, of insectless vegetation, amid a soundscape of man-made engines, where the boundary has angles of such precision and the soil has designs of such regularity that they seem to have been fashioned by computer technology. In truth, they probably have. Tim Dee says in his book *Four Fields*, 'Fields offer the most articulate description and vivid enactment of our life here on Earth, of how we live both within the grain of the world and against it. Every field is at once totally functional and the expression of an enormous idea.'[5] Here is a field that announces the end of nature.

I realise now that in similar fields not far from this place I have seen the same monoculture at various stages of development, but stretching for 40 and even 100 acres at a time. Often the only vertebrate life on such totalitarian ground was a solitary crow that flew away the second I stopped. En masse their daffodil yellow, which should have been so expressive of life, had a quality of being utterly decontaminated of life, as if the colour came from rot-resistant paint or sheet plastic. There were so many of them, so uniformly sown and of such engineered height that they were like the plastic blooms on the tables at the Famous Farm Café or those aligned along the graves at Gedney church. In truth, they are more disconcerting. They are a paradox. Living factory flowers.

14

THE GREATEST ACHIEVEMENT OF OUR ANCESTORS

In his book *Trees and Woodland in the British Landscape*, in the section entitled 'Destruction of Wildwood', the landscape historian Oliver Rackham described the conversion of tens of millions of acres of prehistoric wildwood into farmland as 'the greatest achievement of our ancestors'.[1] If this is true, then at Gedney Fen these daffodil fields represent a double accomplishment. For our forebears here contended for thousands of years not merely with wildwood, but wildwood and wild water. There is an irony in this long interpenetration of people and place, because the very flatness of Gedney – sea-like and undifferentiated and now relentlessly renewed by the operations of agriculture – resists the very idea of a past.

The plainness and single-planed character of it seem without story. It is almost as if we require topography and contour, as well as sustained and traditional cultural engagements with a place, to enable us to see and imagine its historical shaping. When they appear to be absent, or when all is renewed all of the time, we find it hard to conjure an older picture. So, for me, Gedney feels like a place without history. In fact, the village and its hinterland bear a heavier impress of human impact and have been more radically transformed than any other part of Britain. In this sense, they are our ultimate landscape story.

The wetland known as the Fens, of which Gedney is a part, once covered 1,500 square miles from the outskirts of Cambridge in the south, as far as Peterborough in the west, and almost to Lincoln and

Boston to the north. In Roman times it was an immense semi-circular expanse of mire, mere and low-lying marsh, with the maritime bay known as The Wash at its heart. Four major river systems of eastern England – the Witham, Welland, Nene and Great Ouse – still drain in a sequential arc, west to east, into The Wash. Much of it is at sea level or below; much of it was even under the sea.

Where I now stand at Gedney Fen was once on the coast. Today, as the whimbrel flies, that shoreline is over 5 miles to the north. If you drive to it and walk along the embankment near Gedney Drove End, at low tide you can only make out the sea as a pencil line of grey beyond a broad hem of saltmarsh. Further still, over that frail crease of water and under the massive skies of The Wash, are the low crumbling cliffs of Hunstanton, where my journey and this book began. Although they are much further off, those Norfolk cliffs are more readily apparent than the North Sea.

In the Fens this separation of land from water was slow and incremental, but even by Roman times the human estate had been expanded by earthworks and dyke systems. One regional sea harvest treasured in Rome was the supply of oysters from an area known as the Boston Deeps. I imagine them on their banquet couches, discussing imperial politics, relishing the mucilaginous salt savour of the Wash.[2]

As one sails along fenland roads today, perched high above the unfolding geometry of fields, where there is often so little sense of water, let alone of wetland, it is almost impossible to recover the idea that the Fens were once one of the great freshwater ecosystems in all Europe, comparable with the Danube Delta. It is odd in a way that we still call it the Fens at all, because the waters are mere ghosts, invoked in place names or in cartographic references to features that have long been banished. There is now very little fen in Gedney Fen.

The first post-Roman communities celebrated for taming the area were the Saxon monks. The archetype of this religious colonisation was Guthlac, an eighth-century saint, founder of the abbey at Crowland, whose ruins stand fifteen miles to the south-west of Gedney Fen. It was not only a grant, made by King Ethelbald of the Mercians offering Guthlac as much land as he saw fit to enclose, that lured the saint to his watery cell. The inhospitable character of the Fens was a physical whetstone on which he might keep bright his spiritual armoury, a moral wasteland to test the very faith of the committed Christian. In language reminiscent of that used for Beowulf's swamp-haunting adversary Grendel, Guthlac's biographer recalled the demons that the saint had to confront at Crowland. They came 'with such immoderate noises and immense horror', wrote Felix of Crowland, binding and carrying Guthlac'to the black fen, and threw and sank him in the muddy waters'.[3]

Such demons were, of course, simply a metaphor, a way of characterising the amorphous and ineluctable powers of brute nature to repossess humanity's works and to sink them back into swamp. One wonders, in fact, if it is a modern version of these selfsame demons that impels the regime at Gedney's unkempt churchyard, or haunts the man with his strimmer at that cemetery near Loch Hallan in South Uist. Turn our backs, these people seem to be saying with their grass-cutting machines, and it will devour us all.

Not only did Saint Guthlac prevail against his own demons, he also adapted to the peculiarly treacherous ecology of the Fens. One classic indicator of the specialised bounties open to locals was a charter that described how Crowland's monks were in receipt of 60,000 eels as the annual dues from twenty fishermen. And to the Fens' extraordinary harvests of fish or fowl could be added a third. Freedom.[4]

By AD 1000 successive Viking invasions had made south Lincolnshire a magnet for Saxon resistance. At the end of the first millennium the county was home to more freeborn Englishmen than any other. When southern conquerors then stormed the defences in 1066, both the treachery and bounty of the Fens acquired renewed political significance. The Isle of Ely at the region's heart was the site of a final stand by Saxon thanes under the banner of Hereward the Wake. His guerrilla campaign against the Normans is perhaps more legend than verifiable chronicle, while Hereward himself is more shadow than historical figure, yet it seems indisputable that some form of autonomous English presence was made possible by the unnavigable swamps in the Fens, whose channels and dry paths were unknown to William's Frenchmen.

This role in history as a reservoir of political defiance was recurrent. The Fens featured in the rebellions of 1139–42 in the reign of King Stephen, and again when the barons held out against King John. This association with a form of English stubbornness and independence of mind has intriguing support in the fact that the Fens were the location for the Pilgrim Fathers' first aborted exodus – from Boston in 1607. Some of the first parliamentarians to raise a flag of defiance against Charles I were also neighbours to fenland. Even today there seems a strain of suspicion and vehemently maintained privacy among the isolated farmhouses of the area.

One wonders, indeed, if it is the long-inherited tradition of independence that informs the very disjointed quality of fenland's built environment. Each person's castle is their own to do with as he or she pleases, regardless of the neighbours. Near Gedney it has other consequences. During my walk south to Gedney Hill I lost count of the variety of warning and alarm systems deployed on premises with their totem images of snarling dogs and vigilant all-seeing eagles. Fenlanders still seem to feel themselves at odds, if only with the immensity of those Lincolnshire skies.

The eminent historian of its rural economy, Joan Thirsk, noted that before the late eighteenth century most descriptions of the Fens had been written by outsiders. Home-grown champions were few, and their positive accounts were 'so much at variance [that] they were either ignored or dismissed as exaggerations'.[5] Eventually the repetitions of visitors hardened into myth. Lord Macaulay, for example, wrote infamously: 'In that dreary region, covered by vast flights of wild-fowl, a half-savage population, known by the name of Breedlings, then led an amphibious life, sometimes wading, and sometimes rowing from one islet of firm ground to another.'[6] Most notorious among their means of locomotion were their stilts that allowed fen folk to stay dry as they strode through the marsh. A later name, which carries all the weight of disapproval in its aqueous pronunciation, was 'splodgers'.

For those like Macaulay, grounded in the moral certainties of English terra firma, it was the ambiguity of water which was the source of all that vice. Uncontainable, slippery and elusive, the Fens' very liquidity rendered the people and place subversive from the outset. Joan Thirsk described how

> observers reacted … with repulsion, pity or contempt. They depicted the fens as a swamp … their inhabitants as a population sub-human in its lawlessness, poverty, and squalor. Piety and profits demanded, it was felt, the reclamation of both. That attitude – the attitude of the white settler to the agricultural crudities and social irregularities of an African tribe – need cause no surprise.[7]

In his *History of the University of Cambridge*, the seventeenth-century scholar Henry Fuller added to the general charge of water's vice a specific indictment of promiscuity. 'The River Ouse,' he wrote, 'formerly lazily loitering in its idle intercourses with other rivers, is now sent the nearest way (through a passage cut by admirable art) to do its errand to the German Ocean [the North Sea].' What the water needed was the benefits of good, honest hard toil.

It is indisputable that throughout the Middle Ages the Fens were susceptible to terrible floods. The inundations – in 1236, 1254, 1257, 1287, 1467, 1571, 1607, 1613 and 1637 – were occasionally general, but more often affected specific districts. The flood of 1613, for example, had a devastating impact upon the lands around Terrington St Clement, to the south and east of Gedney Fen. One eyewitness account read:

> In their distress the people of Terrington fled to the church for refuge; some to hay-stacks; some to the baulks in the houses, till they were near famished; poor women leaving their children swimming in their beds, till good people adventuring their lives, went up to the breast in the waters to fetch them out at the windows; whereof Mr Browne the minister did fetch divers to the church upon his back; And had it not pleased God to move the hearts of the mayor and aldermen of King's Lynn with compassion, who sent beer and victual hither by boat, many had perished …[8]

It is also instructive to examine how fenlanders viewed their own watery adaptations. In many ways, they were accustomed to such periodic calamities, often merely moving upstairs when the lower levels of a property were overtopped. They also understood that flood brought profit as well as ruin: nutrient-rich silts replenished the fen meadows that were famous for their seasonal grazing. The local shepherds had further learnt to keep an acute weather eye on the tide and wind, so that they could pre-empt the risk of inundation and move their flocks to higher ground.

The places that were dismissed by outsiders as treacherous swamp beyond human control were also the fenmen's commons, where they could gather turves for fuel, reeds for thatch, fodder for livestock, sedge and flags that might be woven into livestock collars or stuffed into cushions and rests for use in chambers, beds and churches. Once the waters receded, the seasonal meadows were grazing for cattle, sheep or the region's famous flocks of semi-wild geese. Driven to markets as far away as London, the fowl were a central part of the fenland economy. They were managed daily by gozzards (goose-herds), who encouraged them to breed in wicker pens and harvested the plumage from the living birds as a source of writing quills. Geese were sometimes lodged in the house with its human occupants and 'even in their bed chambers'.[9]*

Another key avian resource was the wild duck flocks of the marshes. In *The Ornithology* of 1678 John Ray and Francis Willughby give a powerful account of the 'great concourse of men and boats' gathered in summertime at various meres, such as Deeping Fen, about nineteen miles west of Gedney. Huge walls of netting were suspended from poles, when the birds were moulting and known as 'flappers' for the desperate thrashing of their wings on the water's surface. One imagines the churning turmoil of spray as the duck were inexorably steered into net tunnels, where they were caught and despatched. Ray and Willughby wrote of an occasion at Deeping when 4,000 mallard were bagged on a single drive.[10]

---

* One wonders if it was this practice that gave rise to the line in the nursery rhyme 'Goosey Goosey Gander' about a bird in my lady's chamber.

The Fens' unfettered waters further abounded in fish, especially pike, roach, perch and, foremost of all, eels, which had even given a name to the region's main city. Ely, from *Elge* or *Eleg*, 'eel island'.[11] Another intriguingly fishy place that spoke of wild abundance was the village just west of Gedney Fen called Whaplode. This odd name, appropriately enough, comes from that strange, ugly, snake-skinned, freshwater relative of the cod called the burbot *Lota lota*.*

Because so many sources of fenland profit involved harvests of wild animals or plants, rather than crops sown and cultivated, it was commonplace to misrepresent fenlanders as primitive hunter-gatherers 'brutalized by the struggle to maintain life'. However, as Joan Thirsk pointed out, the people making those assumptions were 'the deceivers and the deceived'.[13] She further noted that the 'best advertised exports' of South Holland district, of which Deeping and Gedney Fens formed parts, were precisely those same wild fish or fowl, which they traded in the markets of London and elsewhere.[14] In Tudor times the inhabitants of some of the wildest areas north of Deeping Fen 'paid most of their taxes out of profits from fishing, fowling and hay cutting.[15]

The exploitation of so many wild products reflected the fact that the fenlanders' economy was pleated into the natural, fluctuating abundances of the wetland environment, with its admixture of flooded inconvenience and seasonal plenty. And their ecological adaptations made for not only sustainable lives, but also social contentment. As late as the eighteenth century, the writer on English agriculture, Arthur Young, described how the semi-aquatic residents of the Isle of Axholme near the Yorkshire–Lincolnshire border were 'very poor in respect of money, and very rich in respect of happiness'.[16]

What ultimately threatened and ended this lifestyle was not deluge or famine, but drainage and enclosure. The conversion of the Fens to

---

* In the Fens and elsewhere the burbot was better known by a variety of local names (coney fish, barbolt, ling, eelpout). In the case of Whaplode, however, which means roughly 'burbot stream', the first syllable derives from an earlier alternate name, the *quap* or *quab*, whose root was a verb meaning 'to quiver, flop, palpitate or throb' (describing presumably the burbot's rather eel-like action), whence also the word 'quagmire'.[12]

ploughland, such as the daffodil fields at Gedney, was carried out piecemeal over centuries, but by the seventeenth century, as techniques improved, the pace of change quickened. The schemes were frequently initiated by local landowners, often with the support of businessmen, known as 'adventurers' or 'undertakers', who had no stake in local affairs or existing conditions. Their involvement was often to the detriment of the poorer residents, whose long-established common rights were disrupted or terminated entirely by land privatisation.

Regardless of the commoners' opposition, and despite a reclamation process that was slow, expensive and complicated – even the drainage of a single area often required multiple initiatives and repeat failures – the eventual success is clear from the statistics. Today, just a solitary 1 per cent of the original Fens remains.

The most famous of all drainage projects, the one which has come to stand as an emblem for the entire process, was initiated south of Downham Market and west of Ely in an area once called the Great Level (now better known as the Bedford Level). A syndicate of financial backers had gathered under the banner of a local grandee, Francis Russell, the 4th Earl of Bedford, who already held 20,000 acres to the south-east of Crowland Abbey. He, in turn, commissioned an engineer from the Netherlands, Sir Cornelius Vermuyden, an appointment which reflected the Europe-wide celebrity of the Dutch in matters of agricultural improvement.

Vermuyden had already been knighted for earlier works in the wetlands on the Yorkshire–Lincolnshire border south of the Humber estuary, where he had attempted to reclaim a 70,000-acre block. The project was typical for its combination of ambitious excavation and embankment, for its wholesale redirection of existing rivers, but also for its mixture of success and failure. Vermuyden left the area with huge profits, but also a trail of disgruntled investors and a history of intense opposition to his works and especially his use of foreign labour.

On the Great Level of Cambridgeshire, the Dutchman was to pursue his grandest ambitions as a changer of the English countryside. His involvement spanned two distinct periods and would extend beyond the life of the man who first commissioned him. It was the son and heir of Frances Russell, the 5th earl and 1st Duke of Bedford, who, more than thirty years later, would witness the fulfilment of the entire project. In their way Vermuyden's achievements rival the mighty modern engineering feats that can be seen on the Firth of Forth, or spanning the Thames at Dartford.

The Dutchman's two phases in Cambridgeshire came either side of the English Civil War, in 1630–37 and again in 1650–52, which reflected both the disruption wrought by armed conflict and the limited success of Vermuyden's original plan. It had involved the digging of a deep, dead-straight channel, seventy feet across, from Earith in Cambridgeshire to a sluice at Salter's Lode just south of Downham Market. It was intended to shorten the course of the River Ouse by twenty miles, and involved a titanic earth-moving effort. When filled with water it became the Old Bedford River and ran for twenty-one miles. Together with a wider system of sluices, gates, embankments and the excavations of further artificial water-courses totalling an additional twenty-eight miles, Vermuyden had sought to raise the gradient of the River Great Ouse and so hasten its outflow into the Wash at King's Lynn.

When the whole task was completed in 1637 it was the largest drainage scheme ever attempted, but it ran up against the central challenge of all such projects. It was essentially the pursuit of a single human goal and its imposition upon an immensely complex non-linear ecosystem. The Fens would not conform to ruled lines and a simple man-made vision and, while the massive excavations of the Old Bedford River filled with excess water, they did not speed the flow of the Great Ouse. On the contrary, a report in 1634 said that 400,000 acres that were supposed to become dry land were still inundated in the winter months.[17]

The second and later phase of work began when Vermuyden was fifty-five and, by the standards of the age, already an old man. Nevertheless he set about a supplementary scheme that was no less impressive or ambitious than the first. His workforce dug a trench equal in length to his Old Bedford River – known today as the Hundred-Foot Drain or, with comparable lack of imagination, as the New Bedford River. Much of it was done by outside workers, either Scottish prisoners of war or Vermuyden's imported navvies from the Low Countries.

The Dutchman's second attempt to reduce the Great Level to terra firma eventually replaced reed and mire with corn and dry pasture and provided fresh impetus to reclamation projects throughout the Fens. Yet not all the outcomes of these immense endeavours were quite as the adventurers had hoped. Nor did Vermuyden himself reap the profits he had anticipated. He died in poverty and almost complete obscurity in London in 1677, at the grand old age of eighty-seven.*

Another consequence of drainage that few of the adventurers had predicted was the massive siltation of the lower reaches of the Great Ouse, which was so serious it made the upstream parts of the river unnavigable for larger merchant ships. The problem was that sluices had been inserted to prevent tidal surges running back upstream. While these immense stop valves halted the inundations, they also massively impeded the scouring effect of the current as it forced its way downstream. The changes to the river profile had deeply negative consequences for the commercial life of ports such as King's Lynn, and for the region in general.

However, one impact of the drainage work was more predictable. It aroused deep opposition from local farmers and the poorer elements of many communities, whose livelihoods were threatened by loss of opportunity. In fact, almost every large drainage scheme in the Fens met with unrest. The countermeasures included the physical dismantling of the flood-defence works, destruction of crops, occasional violent assault upon the 'adventurers' themselves, and even murder. More typically the protests took the form of rowdy gatherings, 'tumults' in the language of the day, as men, women and children brandished the tools of their various fenland trades – scythes, rakes, pitchforks – to make their grievances known.

The complaints were far more than simply the discontents of an ignorant populace in the face of progress. In 1650 a Lincolnshire knight of the realm, Sir John Maynard, put the case for the existing conditions of his county's wetlands:

---

* Some authorities give Vermuyden's date of birth as 1595, which would have made him eighty-two at his death.

Our Fens as they are, produce great store of Wooll and Lambe, and large fat Mutton, besides infinite quantities of Butter and Cheese, and do breed great store of Cattell, and are stockt with Horses, Mares, and Colts, and we send fat Beefe to the Markets, which affords Hides and Tallow, and for Corne, the Fodder we mow off the Fens in summer, feeds our Cattell in the winter: By which meanes wee gather such quantities of Dung, that it enriches our upland and Corne-ground … Besides, our Fennes relieves our neighbours, the Uplanders, in a dry summer, and many adjacent Counties: So thousands of our Cattell besides our owne are preserved, which otherwise would perish.[18]

While he may have articulated the benefits of farming within the grain and the natural flow of the ecosystem, Maynard omitted to mention the extraordinary natural abundances of wild vegetation and protein – reeds, sedge, herbage, flags, fish, ruff, plovers, godwits, cranes, herons, duck, geese, swans – that were also reduced or even lost entirely as a result of drainage. These too were crops as well as constituents of the region's biodiversity. These too were integral to the region's economy as well as its ecology.

One of the most enduring laments for this destruction was an anonymous poem from about 1620 called 'The Powte's Complaint'. Its impact derives not only from its rehearsal of the case against intensification, but also because the complaint is made by a non-human fenlander, a once-abundant fish known as the 'powte'.

Come, Brethren of the water, and let us all assemble,
to treat upon this matter, which makes us quake and tremble;
for we shall rue it, if 't be true, that Fens be undertaken,
And where we feed in Fen and Reed, they'll feed both Beef and Bacon.

They'll sow both beans and oats, where never man yet thought it,
Where men did row in boats, ere undertakers bought it:
But, Ceres, thou, behold us now, let wild oats be their venture,
Oh let the frogs and miry bogs destroy where they do enter.

Behold the great design, which they do now determine,
Will make our bodies pine, a prey to crows and vermine:
for they do mean all Fens to drain, and waters overmaster,
All will be dry, and we must die, 'cause Essex calves want pasture.

Away with boats and rudder, farewell both boots and skatches,
No need of one nor th'other, men now make better matches;
Stilt-makers all and tanners, shall complain of this disaster,
For they will make each muddy lake for Essex calves a pasture.

The feather'd fowls have wings, to fly to other nations;
But we have no such things, to help our transportations;
we must give place (oh grievous case) to horned beasts and cattle,
Except that we can all agree to drive them out by battle.

'The Powte's Complaint' has had an enduring place in British culture, surviving as a protest folk song until the twentieth century. It was sometimes renamed 'The Fowlers' Complaint' (one assumes because the word 'powte', like the fish to which it referred, had passed from common knowledge). In the 1950s, the original ten stanzas were used in a cantata called *Fen and Flood*, composed by Patrick Hadley, and arranged for orchestra and choir by Hadley's former teacher, Ralph Vaughan Williams. Today the poem makes an ongoing appeal precisely because it grants insight into the ecological loss to one of the very creatures most affected. It is a piece of environmental art *avant la lettre*. What makes it doubly resonant is the exact identity of the animal.

Powte or 'pout' was an old term used for at least four types of fish. One, sometimes cited as the creature mentioned in the song (for example by H. C. Darby and Ian Rotherham), is the sea-lamprey (*Petromyzon marinus*).[19] The word 'pout' refers to the circular configuration of the mouth parts that are deployed in the lamprey's flesh-sucking parasitism upon other prized fare, including trout or salmon. As the name indicates, however, the sea-lamprey spends much of its life in saltwater and, while it spawns in rivers, it had only modest presence on the English dining table. The seventeenth-century Norfolk scholar Sir Thomas

Browne noted that some specimens 'are very large and well cooked are counted a dayntie bitt collard up butt especially in pyes'. Yet he refers to them specifically as 'lampries', while in the next line he writes of another 'eel poult' and clearly intends a very different species.[*]

The creature named – surely the most likely candidate – is the weirdly reptilian, oddly bearded burbot: the same fish that gave its name to Whaplode, and was an abundant fenland resident of high commercial value in the region's markets. It was found in ten of the fenland rivers, and there are records of a harvest dating to the twelfth century.[20] The creature can grow to 8 lb in weight and enjoyed an extremely high culinary reputation – akin to caviar in some cultures – for both its flaky toothsome meat and massive vitamin-rich liver, which Browne wrote, 'well answers the commendations of the Ancients'.[21]

If the burbot is the powte, then the author of the eponymous lament could not have been more prescient. Burbot has been considered extinct in Britain for decades, partly because of habitat loss. It is equally telling that the last proven record was an individual caught in 1969, in the Great Ouse catchment area at Aldreth, within three miles of Vermuyden's Old Bedford River. One of the first modern sightings, which gives hope that pout may one day return to complain in English waters, was an individual fish seen downstream on the same river and close to the Eel and Pike pub at Needingworth.[22]

'The Powte's Complaint' may not have been intended as an argument against ecological change in its modern sense. However, it remains a fascinating statement about the human forces that turned a region from a place fit for burbot to one suited for flower bulbs. In some ways, the

---

[*] The fact that Sir Thomas Browne already knew of, and used, the name 'lamprey' is surely good evidence that 'powte' was not used for this species as some claim. There is little evidence to support the idea, and I can find no connection between the two. The name 'lamprey', or versions of it, have existed for at least 700 years and were well established and recognisable as referring to a single distinctive fish group, all of them possessed of blood-sucking parts. There are two other fish species with definite 'pout' associations. Both can be instantly dismissed as possible sources of inspiration for the song because the eelpout (an aggregate of 300 species in the family Zoarcidae) and the pout whiting (*Trisopterus luscus*) are marine species without any cultural place in the Fens.

poem is akin to the song, 'The Manchester Rambler', Ewan MacColl's contribution to the campaign for the right to roam. 'The Powte's Complaint' and 'The Manchester Rambler' come at very different moments in the history of land privatisation, but they are both spirited expressions of defiance by the dispossessed. At a time when the poor are becoming ever poorer while the rich get richer, the resonances of both are undiminished.

'The Powte's Complaint' carries another message about the consequences of wholesale conversion of landscape and the need to be mindful of, if not obedient to, the underlying ecological conditions. The most important, if unforeseen, effect of drainage in the Fens was loss not of water but of terra firma. The region is roughly separable, on a line south of Wisbech and running west to a point north of Peterborough, into silt and peat fen. The silt zone north of the line, underlying the most fertile and productive farmland in Britain, forms South Holland.

Most of the area drained by Vermuyden lies south of the line in the peat zone. Once it oxidises, peat deteriorates, and the rate of dispersal is something that fenlanders have come to recognise. The best-known measure of its loss is an iron column at Holme Fen, south-east of Peterborough. In 1851, when it was hammered into the freshly drained peat, the column's top was level with the ground. Today it stands 13 feet (3.96 m) above it. Peat is being lost at the rate of over half an inch (1.5 cm) a year, and in some areas is predicted to disappear completely. Vermuyden's profits were based on soils that seem every bit as exhaustible as fossil fuel. Their usage also has the same impact: it releases carbon into the atmosphere.

Farmers now try to mitigate the effects of soil loss. Equally there are further layers of silt soil, which pre-date the last ice age, underlying the peat. While few would yet argue that farming is doomed in the Fens, nevertheless the loss of peat is deeply troubling. A society that neglects its most precious and fundamental resource is surely on a self-destructive course that lacks basic agricultural common sense. It is well, perhaps, to heed the lessons of a humble fish.

15

WHAT COUNTRYSIDE?

I have long loved the lapwing's cry:
it is wildness walking on the wind.
It sidles into clouds, pennywhistles
its way to heaven, routs the lower
eddies, tells wind-high tales of nests
and speckled eggs, fills hearts
when bleakness comes full-on
in withering blasts. It is bright metal
cast in moulds of air: its uprush
and its plummet leave the sky
astir with plaintiveness, plunging
death-songs, descants and lies.

Giles Watson, 'Lapwing'

Life on Earth is an open system of unimaginable complexity. Its engine room is a star 93 million miles away that we know as the Sun. Its emitted light in the red and blue spectra travels over the course of eight minutes to our planet. There it is harnessed and converted to nutrients by green plants and marine phytoplankton through the process of photosynthesis.

The protoplasmic resources yielded by this near-magical, life-nourishing mechanism, which has so far been found to exist in no other part of any galaxy, and which has been in operation here for more than 3 billion years, disperse into a multiplicity of outcomes. One name that we have given those outcomes is biodiversity. It is the sum of genetic variation across all planetary life as represented in forms of amoeba, plant, fungi, arthropod, amphibian, reptile, bird and mammal. To date, humanity has named between 1.5 and 1.8 million species and there may yet be another 99 million of them.[1] Those organisms have developed into communities, which we call ecosystems.

Agriculture, by contrast, is a closed system of life initiated and developed by our human ancestors since the Neolithic period, with a single planned goal. It concentrates the energies from natural processes into a targeted suite of edible or economically important animal and plant crops: cattle, chickens, sheep, wheat, barley, sugar beet, daffodils etc. For much of the approximately 12,000 years of its operation, agriculture was inefficient, and there was a strong element of entropy as energy generated by farmers escaped human control and was recaptured by wild plants and animals.

Farming, therefore, delivered its intended foodstuffs to humans, but also gave rise to wildlife communities that were sometimes every bit as rich as natural systems. It is worth reiterating a point made by the ecologist Colin Tubbs, that his native Hampshire probably achieved maximum biodiversity, not prior to the impact of agriculture, but in the late eighteenth century after it had been subjected to farm practice for thousands of years.

We were, we are, what the environmental campaigner and writer George Monbiot would call a keystone species. Like the sea otter, the wolf and beaver, humans create abundant opportunities for other life forms. Farmland is just one of the biotic communities originating from our actions. Yet in Britain it is fundamental. An estimated 42.8 million acres are under crops or permanent pasture, roughly three-quarters of all the land in these islands.[2] It is farmers who have shaped and nurtured the complex array of semi-natural habitats. The skylark, whose heaven-sent voice is so emblematic of Britons and the British countryside, is just one of those species that depends on farming. It is common in this country precisely because it profits from our actions. Larks love farms. At least they did.

Almost entirely within my lifetime a transformation occurred in farming methods and, like so much technical innovation, some of it was a result of armed conflict. In the post-First World War period scientists investigated peacetime uses for the ingredients of artillery shells and other armaments. It turned out that the nitrogen-rich compounds used in explosives had a similarly supercharged impact upon plants. Hitherto, the crop-boosting effects had been supplied by time-honoured fertilisers – animal dung or decayed plant matter – but the Victorians also experimented with other organic sources. Among the most effective was bird guano, which was collected from seabird islands off the coasts of Chile, or South Africa and Australia.

These early forms of nitrate- and phosphate-rich materials were highly limited, and soon fell far short of agricultural demand.* However, the new inorganic chemicals delivered by industrial factories, such as the ICI plant on the River Tees, knew no such restrictions. Instead of being extracted from the ground, the nitrogen in the new compounds was captured from the air, where it makes up almost 80 per cent of our atmosphere. The stuff now seemed limitless, and in very short order farmers were applying greater and greater quantities to their land.[†]

The historian Professor Chris Smout points out that there was a twentyfold increase in nitrogen use by British farmers in the half-century to 1980.[3] Today they apply 1.5–2 million tons every year.[4]

---

* The fertilising power of seabird dung, which the Inca people who first exploited it called *huana* (whence 'guano'), was commercially extracted from the 1840s. Unlike the South Americans, the Western mining companies, which shipped it to Britain and elsewhere, used methods that were entirely unsustainable. Vast concentrations of guano, in some places more than 160 feet deep and the product of thousands of years of seabird occupation, were scraped down to bare rock in a quarter of a century. (See *Birds and People*, pp. 147–8.) An even earlier source of phosphorus for British crops were the bones of the fallen from European battlefields, including Waterloo, Leipzig and Austerlitz. Of this macabre trade, one German chemist complained, mainly it seems on nationalist grounds, that 'England is robbing all other countries of their fertility.' Presumably he would have been happy to fertilise Teutonic crops with German bones. (See Henry Williamson's *The Story of a Norfolk Farm*, p. 140.)

[†] The nitrogen may come from the atmosphere, but the hydrogen used in production of the base fertiliser ingredient, ammonia, comes from natural gas. The energy consumption in fertiliser production is huge, and Marion Shoard suggested that it requires the energy equivalent to 2 million tons of oil annually. (See Shoard, 1980, p. 20.)

Possibly more than any other single innovation, fertilisers have allowed global production to keep pace with the phenomenal growth in human population: from 1.5 billion at the start of last century, to 6 billion people by its close and 7.3 billion today. Yet the new-found dependence upon the chemical additives is in many ways as shocking as their achievements have been impressive.

A report entitled the Millennium Ecosystem Assessment, commissioned by the UN and published in 2005, calculated that half of all nitrogen fertiliser ever applied has been spread on fields since 1985. In the last 50 years, overall fertiliser use has increased by about 500 per cent.[5] Humans have doubled the biologically active nitrogen in the world today. While nitrate-rich fertilisers indisputably boost crop yields, they do not remain compliantly locked into the places desired by farmers. They have a life cycle of their own, leaching from the land back into dykes or streams.

As nitrogen impacts upon soil fertility, so it also affects our river systems, only there it leads to choking, toxic blooms of algae which starve the waters of oxygen and kill off many of the aquatic life forms. Nitrates then accumulate in dissolved form in underground aquifers and, before these sources can be used for human drinking water, the nitrates have to be stripped out at high cost. They then make a further journey out of our control, converting to nitrous oxide, a greenhouse gas 200 times more potent than carbon dioxide. A European report on the total costs of this 'escaped' nitrogen concluded that it was between €70 and €320 billion, double the value of its boost to crops.[6]

Another key agricultural development that came out of a wartime laboratory was pesticides. Among the first major steps was the exploration of an unforeseen potential in a compound synthesised as early as 1874 and entitled dichlorodiphenyltrichloroethane, or DDT for short. It was a Swiss scientist, Paul Hermann Müller, who unlocked DDT's hitherto overlooked insecticidal properties and who was eventually awarded the Nobel Prize for his work. During the Second World War the chemical was used as a means of controlling lice and mosquitoes, carriers of typhus and malaria respectively.

From there it was a short journey to using it wholesale on crops. Such was its cure-all efficacy that post-war American farmers fell in love with DDT, deploying aeroplane crop dusters and tractor-sprayers against their old invertebrate enemies like weapons of war. There were advertisements for the compound showing a cartoon farm 'family' – dog, apple, farm wife, cow, potato, cockerel – all with beaming smiles beneath the musical jingle, 'DDT is good for me-e-e!' The subsequent revelations of its negative effects would eventually lead to its specific withdrawal from most agricultural nations (see footnote on p. 141).

Yet the idea there were smart new chemical solutions to old pest problems was here to stay. In 1944 there were 63 pesticide products approved for use on British farms. In 1976 it was 819. The base chemical ingredients numbered just 37 in 1956; in less than thirty years that figure had risen to 199.[7] Measured by weight, the total pesticide usage in the UK doubled in the 1970s alone, while those used on cereals have doubled again since that decade.[8]

In half a century farmers had made a psychological journey from viewing an entire chemical arsenal – herbicides, fungicides and pesticides – as an expensive and technical line of last resort, to a prophylactic stand-by. Chemical sprays are often deployed regardless of need, while the tractor-mounted sprayers used to deliver them have also flourished in direct proportion. In 1940 there were 1,100; by 1981 it was 74,000.[9] Today they are everywhere. I saw one just down the road from the daffodil fields at Gedney Fen. And what happens at Gedney recurs everywhere that arable crops are grown with chemical assistance, both in Britain and worldwide.

We should not think that farmers are unique in adopting chemical solutions to ancient problems of crop pests or loss of harvest. It is a symptom of Western society's now axiomatic presumption that all of life's problems should have near-instantaneous redress that the same reliance on antibiotic chemistry is found in both the household interior and exterior. The pesticide addiction manifest in American gardens is nothing short of shocking. The Audubon Society publishes a leaflet on guidance to US gardeners. It reports that American lawns receive three times the pesticide applied to its own agriculture: a grand total of 28,000 tons of herbicide and insecticide.

One of the historical developments allowing for a shift towards intensive and clean agriculture was the astonishing improvement, in terms of complexity, speed and sheer muscle power, in farming's key implement. The machine is still known by the same twentieth-century name (first used in 1901) – 'tractor' – but it has gone from being a basic hand-cranked vehicle, like those arranged in evolutionary order across the lawn near the Famous Farm Café, to a technology of space-age sophistication. The biggest have double arrangements of caterpillar tracks like military tanks or bulldozers, with fifty gears and display panels of computerised instruments that would not look out of place in an aircraft or even a spaceship.

In the 1920s there were 10,000 tractors in Britain. Within sixty years there were half a million.[10] In the 1930s the most widely available models had a lifting capacity not too much greater than those white-fetlocked beasts plodding across the walls in The Famous Farm Café. Today the biggest tractors boast 1,200 horse-power, although machines of 150–250 horse-power are more typical on British cereal farms. Even these more modest examples have a price tag of £70,000, while a new tractor costing £100,000 is nothing exceptional.*

The new tractors, along with ever more sophisticated and flexible accessories, enabled farmers to deep-drain, plough, flatten, uproot, excavate and infill fields until they were uniform, even, rectilinear spaces, often without hedge borders and sown and cropped to within a couple of feet of their boundaries. A late friend of mine used to cite the famous lines from Oberon's soliloquy in *A Midsummer Night's Dream*, 'I know a bank where the wild thyme blows', adding that it was now not only difficult to see wild thyme, it was also hard, on most modern farms, to find a bank (see below, p. 114).

Equipped with a mid-range model, two men – a farm manager and his full-time hand – can run an entire 500-acre arable holding. Small wonder that by the 1950s real horses had ceased to exist as working stock, but since the late nineteenth century human labour had also been

---

* The super machines used for specialised work, such as a beet harvester or a cereal combine harvester, can have a price tag for a new machine of £250,000. With a grain-holder capacity of eight tons, the latter vehicles can have a combined operational weight of 18 tons.

in a prolonged decline. In 1881 the agricultural workforce stood at 1.7 million men, one-tenth of the entire national total. Just after the Second World War this figure had dropped to 563,000. It continues to fall. According to the Department for Environment Food and Rural Affairs, in 2007 the number was 526,000 and less than 2 per cent of the British labour force. More than half of this total comprises part-time workers.[11]

Nor has the contraction impacted only upon the humble farmhand. The British farmer has become a scarcer species too under the collective impacts of intensification. The need for economies of scale, the higher capital requirements, the demands imposed by ever-larger equipment and the more intensive and expensive use of chemical inputs, and the relentless downward pressure on farm-gate prices by the supermarkets and primary buyers of raw produce, have shifted conditions in favour of large landowning operations. Graham Harvey, agricultural consultant to the long-running radio soap *The Archers* and author of an excoriating condemnation of industrial farming, *The Killing of the Countryside*, pointed out that in 1938 there were 226,000 British farmers with holdings of fewer than 50 acres. Thirty years later 64,000 of them had gone out of business.[12] Richard Body, the former Conservative MP for Boston and South Holland area, offered an alternative audit of the process. In 1964 there were 250,000 farmers with fewer than 100 acres; by 1982 the total was 120,000.[13]

The reduction in the overall numbers does not truly reflect the scale of concentration that has occurred since the Second World War. In 1983 there were almost 86,000 farms of 50 acres or less, yet all of these combined represented just 4 per cent of farmland in Britain.[14] Today 10 per cent of farms account for half of all Britain's agricultural production, and in the sphere of cereal production it is even more specialised. Just 9,000 big producers generate 60 per cent of the grain.[15]*

---

* It is intriguing to compare the British phenomenon of agricultural concentration into the hands of fewer and fewer producers with the situation in other countries. In her book *This Land is Our Land* Marion Shoard pointed out that average farm holdings in this country are far higher than in Europe. The year of her comparison is 1983. Then the mean British farm size was 170 acres, compared with 63 acres in France, 38 acres in West Germany and 17 acres in Italy. (See Shoard, 1997, p. 112.)

For the farmers, but especially for the advocates of 'big farms', there was an unassailable logic to underpin these developments. British agriculture might be profitable and efficient, yet the numbers of mouths to feed was rising constantly. Following the First World War the UK had a population of 43 million people; at the close of the century the figure had risen to 57 million. British farming had to keep pace with the increase in one of the most populous countries on the planet, and the national challenge was agricultural every bit as much as it was economic or cultural.* What had allowed British farmers to meet the needs of the age was the rise in yields delivered by all of the post-war innovations described above.

The figures on increased production are nothing short of extraordinary. In 1937 when the author of *Tarka the Otter*, Henry Williamson, reaped the barley off one of the best fields on his Norfolk farm at Stiffkey, he was proud to record a first harvest of a ton for every acre.[16†] Across Britain as a whole that was roughly the pre-war average. The subsequent innovations, however, more than trebled this figure. Today the average for East Anglian cereal farmers, whose yields are invariably

---

* Since 1963 the British population has risen from 53.65 million to just over 65.5 million by 2017, with much of the increase occurring in the new millennium and partly as a consequence of immigration. This, however, is less than the increase in France, which incurred a rise of 17.33 million people over the same period. Proportionate to area, Britain is still one of the most densely populated countries in Europe with 700 per square mile, a figure that is only exceeded by the Netherlands (1,056 per square mile). In France, for example, the equivalent figure is 265. If one measures only England, however, then it is revealed as among the most densely occupied regions on Earth (1,053 persons per square mile), with a density greater than that in India (1,005 per square mile) and far higher than China's (373 per square mile).

† Few things better indicate the pace of change in farm methods and in farming mindset during the last seventy years than the system used to calculate harvests. For Williamson did not tally his yield in tons, but coombes, a unit of dry volume equivalent to four bushels (i.e. 32 imperial gallons). Both coombes and bushels are part of a measuring system dating to a time when occupants of this land spoke Middle English. My own personal encounter with an agricultural vocabulary from the age of Chaucer comes via my 93-year-old neighbour, who gave me a scythe that he had used to harvest his rain-soaked cereal crop in the summer of 1948. He vividly recalls computing his Norfolk wheat crop in coombes.

calculated in metric figures, is 7–9 tonnes a hectare for spring barley (2.8–3.6 tons/acre) and 8–10 tonnes (3.2–4 tons/acre) for winter-sown barley. Winter wheat yields, meanwhile, are now 10–12 tonnes a hectare (4–4.85 tons/acre).[17]

Such is the sophistication of today's combine-harvester technology that the man in the cockpit can follow mathematically precise lines mapped by GPS technology, and then read the cereal volumes on any single part of any field. In the richest sections the figure can be 14 tonnes. The overall national rise in cereal production in the fifty years from 1936 was nine-fold for wheat and thirteen-fold for barley. Those increases have been reflected across other sectors. In the fifty years from Williamson's first barley harvest, beef yields rose by 60 per cent and eggs volumes by 90 per cent.[18]

Throughout all of these changes the farmers' case seemed both unanswerable and straightforward. They are, they had to be, more efficient. We needed it. We willed it. And they did it. Yet we must also acknowledge that there was a price to pay.

The agricultural changes outlined above have brought about a wholesale reordering of the British farmed environment in three generations. And the key to that process has been specialisation.

The average pre-war farmer had pursued a time-honoured agricultural programme that was buffered against poor performance of any single crop. If the corn or the beef was not as they had expected, then at least there were chances to make up any shortfall with other more profitable yields. Between them the multiple harvests compensated for any one loss. It was an agricultural hedging of bets against seasonal fluctuations in yield, and it resulted in the classic organic mixed farm: a self-sufficient blend of cereals and livestock, pasture and plough, fruit and vegetables, pigs and poultry.

It was not just a robust economic model: the mixed farm created the environmental integrity of the British countryside, which was rooted in that very same principle of diversity. Intensification and specialisation, however, cut across that time-honoured ecology. Instead of variety, the prevailing ideology was uniformity. Not only did agrochemicals reduce a field to a single clean crop but, field by field, the whole farm was converted to produce just two or three commodities. Sometimes only one or two. In aggregate the impact of all these individual specialisations has been massive. Essentially the British countryside has been radically simplified. What was once a complex ecosystem has been turned into a monoculture in a production line. While that industrialising process may have reduced it to profitable order and efficiency, it stripped away the environmental intricacy.

In wildlife terms the wholesale simplification of Britain has inflicted what is probably the most sustained loss of biodiversity since large swathes of the country were unlocked from a smothering carapace of ice at the beginning of the Holocene. Measuring such declines without a comparable mathematical audit of wildlife populations is difficult, if not impossible. The *State of Nature* report in 2013 is the closest we have come to a fully synthesised assessment. However, therein lies a problem.

For statistics and columns of figures do not begin to express the effects of the changes at a personal and interior level. For some people, agricultural intensification has triggered an emotionally charged, even visceral response, at the root of which is a baffling confrontation with local extinction and loss of meaning. The effect is powerful enough to alter an individual's personality and their entire view of life. It amounts to a persistent low-level heartache, a background melancholia, for which there is little remedy short of emigration.

I know this because my best friend Tony Hare, the person who more than anyone else awakened my own awareness of biological loss, killed himself in 2010 shortly after attending the Copenhagen climate conference. Co-founder of the British botanical charity PlantLife, Tony adored flowers. They were the subject of his doctoral thesis, and the more-than-human parts of the world that appealed to the deepest parts of him. I once saw him fall to his knees, as in an act of worship, before what seemed to me the commonest, most ordinary, most insignificant plot of inch-high plants: a square foot of turf dotted with minuscule scarlet fungi and prostrate lichens. 'Worlds', he called them, and went on to argue that what was happening here was the same as in any rainforest.*

It was bold stuff; but I never took these responses lightly. On the contrary, for he was an extraordinary person, a relentless, centrifugal dynamo of energy – a film maker, television presenter, author, scientist, businessman, DJ, a musicologist of narrow enthusiasms and eclectic tastes, an intellectual, but also a witty, often hilarious creator of madcap humour, whose laugh, which I can hear clearly as I type these words, was a machine-gun burst of uncontrollable mirth that came directly from the solar plexus. It made you smile simply to hear him.

His speciality was pet names for everything. My name had been converted, through much rough handling, from 'Cocker' to 'Blobber'. Don't ask me why. But then the plant ragged robin was always known as 'Radioactive Reg'. Again, who knows what associative process triggered it. Frogs were always 'fgogs'. To go in search of flowers was to go 'worting' (from the Anglo-Saxon *wort*, still present in the names of many plants such as a common Blackwater resident, marsh woundwort).

As well as funny names, he had funny voices in which he greeted not just people but the creatures and plants he met. The classic on seeing a species he hadn't anticipated was 'Ooooo, 'ello!' One almost expected it to honour him in the same intimate vernacular, and the overall effect was that the living non-human world seemed animated with personality as in children's stories and folk tales. The other stock mode of address, proffered to moths or beetles he'd lured onto his palm, was a Leslie-Phillips-like 'Hell-*eau* … '

Tony Hare was no fool, though. He was a man whose lighthouse brain beamed fierce light into the obfuscatory guff spouted sometimes on all sides of the environmental debate. He could be hard on farmers and their works – for me, often, too hard – but he was equally hard in his dismissal of what he saw as the timidity or intellectual shoddiness of his own side. An 'anti-environmentalist' was his own sometime

---

* I have described the occasion in an earlier book, *A Tiger in the Sand*, which was dedicated to 'Tony Hare and his "world"'. The piece about that specific moment can be found on p. 125 of the book.

self-classification. It was he who composed the satirical document entitled 'Towards Focusing' (that I mention in Chapter 5, see p. 71) to mock the winding circumlocutions of eco-speak.

No one who knew him well doubted his clarity, his prescience, his grasp of what was happening to our landscape. Some of the most memorable words I ever heard him say were in the early nineties. 'Whenever people talk to me of the British countryside, Mark, I ask, "What countryside?"' Sweeping and rhetorical it might have been, but this radical, quintessentially Hare-like interrogation was rooted in his own lifelong forage across the landscape. Tone, as I always called him, knew what he was talking about. No director of the National Trust or the RSPB ever spoke with deeper knowledge or more passion than Tony Hare on his theme.

Yet I cannot speak for Tony on what pained him most. I can only recount my own deepest sense of natural loss, which stems from my encounters with the birds of my childhood. What has impressed itself upon me in the last forty years is that what I feel, and what Tony felt, reflects the experiences of thousands, probably tens of thousands of people.

The birds that have been most affected by agricultural changes are, as I noted in this book's opening chapter, a suite of largely ground-nesting species that are specialists of farmland: grey partridge, lapwing, turtle dove, skylark, yellow wagtail, corn bunting and yellowhammer. It is these that are the subject of the Farmland Bird Index. As I have already pointed out, Britain's FBI figures are the worst in Europe.

One of those species, the lapwing, was the alpha and omega of my spring days in Derbyshire, where I grew up. Behind our house in Buxton, when the winter snows burnt the hills down to a lion's flank of dead tawny grasses, the lapwings would return and nest. On every field the high-glossed aerial display of the males produced the sounds I heard as I got ready for school. They were there when I set out, and they were there the moment I returned. At night before I went to sleep, with the windows open and the river humming carelessly as it unfolded down the valley, I could hear the heart-piercing cry of nervous lapwings on their eggs or crouched with their young, and in the morning I awoke again to their high-flung song and dance.

In the 1970s, during my teens, I kept detailed notes. While lapwings seemed far too common for me ever to think that these records would be significant, the notebooks have eventually revealed the tragic losses. When I was young, any farmland area in that part of north Derbyshire, east Cheshire and northern Staffordshire held lapwings. They were part of our collective birthright. In fact, they were part of everyone's. Look at the map for the species in *The Atlas of Breeding Birds in Britain and Ireland* (1976), the first major census of our avifauna, and the UK is a solid, uniform pattern of large red dots, with spaces for their absence only in north-westernmost Scotland and the Cornish extremities, and then a round twenty-mile hole for London. The rest, 85 per cent of Britain, was lapwing country.

My own first personal sense of something seriously wrong came in 1985, when I not only counted the birds, but also found most of, if not all, the nests in the fields visible from our back window. On 13 April 1985 and again the following day I located five nests, but logged in my notebook respective lapwing totals for the two days of 39+ and 30 birds. Since I lived in Norfolk from 1979, my visits to Buxton were intermittent, but the note-taking pattern was so ingrained I would always record my findings on any home trip. On 3 June 1989 I noted not just 5–6 pairs of lapwings but also the fact that the fields held 84 sheep and more than 40 cows, and I added: 'Noticeable decline in lapwings, probably because of higher level of stock.'

By the mid-1990s those same fields held occasional lapwing pairs. For almost all of the last twenty years thereafter a perennial topic of conversation between my family and myself is the absence of lapwings. There are now few in the immediate vicinity of Buxton, although they persist on the ring of hills above the town, especially on the high moors to the north and west. My own hunch is that they are surviving in some of the highest fields where the ground is wettest, stock densities and grazing pressure are lowest, where no silage crop is taken and where the ground is least likely to be drained. Today I know one field on the other side of the hills from our house where this spring I counted thirteen pairs.

My experience replicates not just a national pattern, but the picture for an entire continent. Lapwings have lost 34–49 per cent of their population across Europe in less than two human generations (and what are judged to be three generations of a relatively long-lived species). In effect, half of Europe's lapwings have gone in forty years. It is now technically classified as 'near-threatened' with global extinction.[19]

The British figure for lapwing losses is substantially above the European average, with a decline of 65 per cent since the 1970s.[20] The problem with offering you such figures is that they can give the impression that the decline has ceased. It hasn't. The process is live and ongoing, and the downward direction of travel will almost certainly continue.

What we know incontrovertibly now is that cold stains of absence have spread across the once solidly red map of lapwing distribution. Big holes have appeared across roughly two-fifths of central Norfolk. The worst losses, however, are in the western highlands of Scotland, much of Wales and in the English south-west, where almost the entire peninsula from Land's End almost to Bristol has been vacated.[21] Wales, with its high sheep-grazed hill country, rough moors and small mixed-farm landscape, was once lapwing heaven. Not now. The editors of the recent bird atlas (2014) for the Principality propose a breeding total of just 600 pairs.[22]

These losses to date have been largely driven by agricultural intensification. The species-rich hay crops that covered England in the early decades of the twentieth century and until the Second World War were not just wonderful for flowers: they grew lapwings too. These hayfields have been almost systematically drained and homogenised, enriched with fertilisers and re-seeded with monocultures of rye grass for silage. Stocking densities of cattle and sheep, meanwhile, have hugely increased and led to shorter grass swards, lack of cover for chicks, higher risks of trampling and general loss of habitat. In arable areas the use of pesticides has decimated the lapwing's invertebrate prey, while a switch to autumn sown cereals (winter wheat) means that the crops are often too tall come spring for lapwings to nest.

These are primary factors, but some prefer to point to other issues, such as the increase in crow and fox populations with the decline of gamekeeping and innovative methods of rearing gamebirds that don't require relentless persecution of the broad-spectrum predators. In some areas predation by animals such as foxes is a problem. Yet anyone arguing the importance of increased predation must substantiate their case to explain the losses across Europe.* And they must take account of another factor that is significant and pervasive.

In 1963 two American ecologists, Robert MacArthur and Edward O. Wilson, developed a model of island biogeography. Essentially what it showed was that populations of plants and animals on islands were in a state of rough equilibrium. Over the course of time, vagaries in the success of isolated island communities meant that some species went extinct, while other new species moved in. Smaller islands, however, experience a more rapid turnover of new and old inhabitants because they are more susceptible to perturbation.

Bigger islands, by contrast, support higher diversity and larger populations of any particular organism. The authors' rule of thumb is that ten times the area gives double the diversity of species. Or, to put it in its negative form, if you reduce the area tenfold, you halve the species range. So large islands are more diverse, more stable, less susceptible to species loss. This groundbreaking work was of fundamental importance, and it has shed light on the underlying processes involved in species declines.[23]

This includes my patch at Lightwood in Buxton, because it too, in effect, is an island. Now that 'my' lapwings are concentrated on a single higher-elevation field, rather than the dozen where I saw them breeding in the 1970s, it means that one successful raid by a single fox could wipe out all success for an entire season. So predation becomes overall more significant.

We have lapwings still, spread in pockets across the former blanket distribution mapped in that original 1976 atlas, but each is an island and more vulnerable to change. In south Lincolnshire the main lapwing

---

* In my experience, farmers' insistence on predation as the primary factor for lapwing declines is typical. Mike Shrubb, author of The Lapwing and himself a farmer, points out that the subtlety of the effects of habitat change 'makes it difficult for many farmers to accept that farming change is responsible for the decline of farmland birds such as Lapwings'. Nonetheless, he points out that change in agricultural methods and technology ... have been the main determinants of decline in farmland bird populations.' See p. 180.

breeding populations for the whole county are at just two sites, Frampton and Freiston, both of them on the shore of The Wash, 15 and 21 miles from the Famous Farm Café.[24] Both are RSPB reserves. It is particularly tragic to see lapwing losses in Lincolnshire, because the bird is the emblem of the Lincolnshire Wildlife Trust. There could well come a time when they are forced to choose another symbol, because lapwings will be completely extinct in the county.

The same pattern – concentration in a few areas and mainly in pre-existing sanctuaries – holds true for Norfolk. The editors of the recent county bird atlas note that all the high three-figure counts are on wetland reserves: Holkham, Welney, Berney and Buckenham, the last immediately across the river from where I live.[25] This picture obtains equally in Wales, where the birds are focused in a twelve-mile wide belt on the country's eastern boundary.[26]

Based on such developments, my guess is that by mid-century vast areas of Britain, but especially in England west of Norwich, east of Bristol and south of a line from the Tees to the Ribble, will be free of almost all ground-nesting farmland birds (except skylarks).* That scenario will be mitigated by our lymphatic system of dedicated nature reserves, and improved if there is a substantial remedial programme.

We know that nature is in a state of perpetual flux. Any person's life coincides with patterns of abundance that can be entirely natural or declines that are completely outside of the effects of agriculture. To make a claim for any set of childhood wildlife encounters could be said to be privileging one scenario before others. Nevertheless it strikes me that a country has reached a critical benchmark when its lands support no native ground-nesting birds above two ounces in weight. And the reason is simple. There is so little real ground left.

There will, of course, be red-legged partridges and pheasants, but both are non-native introduced gamebirds reared for sport in artificial batteries and with a status not too dissimilar to free-range chickens. I would suggest that farm-bred fowl develop a more integrated

---

* And let's not get overly optimistic about skylarks. They too have declined by almost 50 per cent across Europe. In Britain it is 60 per cent.

relationship to British conditions than many populations of pheasants. Today about 35–45 million pheasants are reared for shooting, which represents a doubling of hand-reared stock since the 1980s.[27]

The figure for red-legged partridges, meanwhile, has risen a hundredfold in the last half-century. Today it is 6 million. The unleashing every summer of so many is the equivalent by weight of releasing 1.7 million Thomson's gazelles into our country. Together these two gamebirds account for more than half of all the avian biomass in Britain. There are shooting estates of perhaps 500 acres that are rearing 100,000 pheasant poults.[28] In its mass-production methods and lack of real connection to place, the minimum total of 41 million non-native species is perfectly emblematic of the places in which they flourish. They are alien birds in an alienated landscape.

To suggest that they flourish, however, is to overstate their fortunes. Approximately 20 million birds are lost each year. Road fatalities must represent a significant proportion of these. Around us in east Norfolk the birds' default habitat is on the country lanes, where they run in complete confusion before oncoming cars. Many are so devoid of survival skills that they cannot even recognise the dangers from such mechanical predators, and at who knows what cost to motorists.* I often wonder, however, if the pheasants' suicidal preference for roads lies in the fact that the tarmac at least has characteristics of the rectilinear structure in which they were reared, and on to which they are imprinted.

In the last few years I have played a macabre game whenever I have to go to other parts of the UK. On these journeys I look out for any native ground-nesting birds that one can assume to be breeding. One such road trip involves me driving from Norfolk to Criccieth on the edge of the Lleyn Peninsula in central Wales. It is almost a complete east-to-west transect through our island, cutting across a dozen counties. Major roads are, of course, not areas where native ground-nesting birds are concentrated. Even so – and taking this into account – I suggest that it is significant

---

* Another overlooked cost to the country of pheasant shooting is the amount of grain used by farmers to rear them. The nation's inflated sports flock of 41 million free-range fowl is consuming in the region of 236,000 tons of cereals annually.

that on these trans-national journeys I see no breeding native ground-nesting birds other than skylarks. In recent years I have made a similar south – north trek of 560 miles to the Moray Firth, and it is invariably not until Perthshire that I break the ground-nesting bird embargo, with something like a lapwing, curlew, snipe, or grey partridge sighting.

In case you think I have opted for the lapwing to make a special case over-emphasising the processes of loss, I must point out that this species is by no means the only or worst-affected of my childhood fixtures. I could have chosen from a suite of birds that were once present at Lightwood and have now gone. The spotted flycatcher was another I saw from my bedroom window. Since 1970 it has fallen by 87 per cent. Common sandpiper and tree pipit and cuckoo and whinchat and wood warbler were Lightwood favourites too. None now breeds. The national declines are respectively –50, –68, –59, –54 and –58 per cent. The first three are since 1970, but the last two have declined only in the last 22 years, since 1995.[29]

The yellow wagtail, which I used to find among those beautiful limestone-wall-bounded fields between Chelmorton and Sheldon, that I mentioned in Chapter 9 on p. 116, is down 67 per cent since 1970. Grey partridge, corn bunting and turtle dove, three more on the Farmland Bird Index, have incurred losses of over 90 per cent. The latter is thought to be at risk of complete extirpation from Britain as a breeding species.

Extinction seems the ultimate terminus for any bird, flower or insect, yet there is perhaps this perverse merit to extinction. It can occasion the power of a headline; it enables a campaigning organisation or individual to summon the interest and attention of the public.* To use

---

* Wild British Lazaruses resurrected from their graves include the white-tailed eagle (reintroduced 1980s), red kite (extinct in England; reintroduced in the 1980s), large blue butterfly (1980s), large copper (1913 Ireland, 1927 England, died out again in the 1950s and 1960s respectively), European beaver (2009) and short-haired bumblebee (2012). However, one that perhaps best illustrates the tremendous galvanic powers of the E word is the great bustard. The bird was lost as long ago as the 1840s, and while it is one of the most magnificent ever to grace these islands, and while I would love to see it restored, the chances of reintegrating the largest-flighted bird in the world to so reduced a national environment are slim indeed. To date, the complex, expensive and ambitious campaign to restore it, which was begun in 1999, has had small success.

the terminology of literary criticism, it is a drama with an 'objective correlative' – an appropriate set of background conditions which enable anyone, even without technical knowledge, to understand the feelings of sadness and the urgent motives for action.* In short, extinction serves as a rallying cry for radical countermeasures.

Most of the declines in our country, however, are of a more complex *Hamlet*-like nature, where the resulting emotional effects are more difficult and more exquisitely painful. It is more problematic because semi-extinction or mere decline of a species brings no possibility of closure for the resulting melancholy. For my generation, Tony Hare's generation, that is precisely our fate.

We are suspended in a landscape of losses. Living in this island entails awareness of a systemic haemorrhaging of life, complexity and texture from the very sweep of Britain. It implies a triple drainage of beauty, colour and meaning from our sense of place. In a way we are denied some of the simple pleasures entailed in our love for wildlife. For as Helen Macdonald has put it:

> The rarer they get, the fewer meanings animals can have. Eventually rarity is all they are made of. The condor is an icon of extinction. There's little else to it now but being the last of its kind. And in this lies the diminution of the world. How can you love something, how can you fight to protect it, if all it means is loss?[30]

To blame our landscape of loss for the death of my friend is almost certainly to overstate its role. I know there were many complex reasons why Tony Hare took his own life, but I also know for a fact that the disappearance of wildlife that he had cherished as a child weighed heavily upon his soul. His sense of pain and bitterness were omnipresent and palpable, a permanent part of who he had become. In this, Tony's

---

* The phrase was popularised by T. S. Eliot in his critical essay on Shakespeare's *Hamlet*. He suggested that a problem with the play was that the prince's intense emotions were not rendered comprehensible to the audience by the life circumstances of its central character. The drama had a missing element because Hamlet's sense of grief lacks what Eliot called an 'objective correlative'.

life and death bear witness to the experience of every single person concerned for nature in Britain.

Some might argue that this is little more than a form of middle-class urban angst that has no true relationship to the things that matter. Worrying about the birds and flowers in our meadows is a luxury most of us cannot afford. Nor is the sense of loss peculiar to our own age. The Victorian naturalist the Reverend F. O. Morris experienced much the same as he watched Victorian reclamation works salvage one of the last parcels of untamed fenland at Whittlesea Mere. It lies just twenty miles south of Gedney in the classic peat fen area, in what is now Cambridgeshire.

In fact, the exposed iron spike measuring fenland soil loss that I mentioned in Chapter 14 was driven into the ground at Holme Fen with the complete drainage of Whittlesea Mere in 1851. It was one of the last great dramas in the area's transformation, allowing Whittlesea's conversion to productive farmland. It simultaneously sealed the fate of one of the great treasures of Victorian entomology, a fiery beauty called the large copper butterfly, whose last stronghold had been destroyed with these measures and whose extinction was declared barely a decade later.

Morris's reaction to the loss of his beloved butterfly was one of Christian forbearance. 'Science', he wrote,

> with one of her many triumphs, has here truly achieved a mighty and valuable victory, and the land that was once productive of fever and of ague, now scarce yields to any in broad England in the weight of its golden harvest ...
>
> The entomologist is the only person who has cause to lament the change, and he, loyal and patriotic subject as he is, must not repine at even the disappearance of the large copper butterfly, in the face of such vast and magnificent advantages.[31]

Is this a reconciliation we all must now make with the transformation of the British countryside? Has agricultural intensification been a triumph of science? Were the gains truly vast and magnificent advantages? Is it disloyal and unpatriotic to lament the loss of lapwings or large copper butterflies? Or can we ask legitimate questions about whether it was necessary?

16

Subsidies I: The Sorcerer's Apprentice

B ritish farmers have not always been so empowered and efficient. On the contrary, the rural community in this country went through a depression that lasted from the 1870s until the late 1930s. For landowners it has been represented as an economic disaster when prices plummeted – wheat, for example, halved in value in the thirty years to 1890 – while agricultural rents fell to unprecedented lows. In 1936 they were the same as they had been when George III was on the throne.[1]

One of the key drivers was a massive increase in the international trade of agricultural products in the second half of the nineteenth century. Huge areas of the world had been opened up for arable crops, especially in the USA, Canada, Argentina, Australia and New Zealand. The availability of cheap continental cereals bore heavily upon British farmers, but they had at least managed to delay the full consequences of this globalisation through what were known as the Corn Laws.

They were introduced in 1804, renewed in 1815 and not repealed until 1846. Their original purpose was to stave off an earlier slump in grain prices at the end of the Napoleonic War. French embargoes at the turn of the nineteenth century had kept the value of English cereals artificially high but, at the close of hostilities, farmers and landowners were faced with the effects of cheap imports. The Corn Laws blocked them until the domestic price for grain had reached 80 shillings a quarter (a unit of capacity equivalent to 8 bushels or 64 gallons).

The measures were naturally welcomed by landowners, but vehemently opposed by an urban industrial middle class, whose Anti-Corn Law League, founded in 1839, portrayed the legislation as the work of an *ancien régime* holding back trade out of narrow self-interest. The legislation was blamed for forcing up the price of bread and other staples and, in the eyes of Britain's entrepreneurs, obliging wages for labour to remain unnecessarily high.

The Corn Laws were a reactionary response to international developments, but they were also an attempt to avert deeper, systemic change in British society. The historian David Cannadine has observed of the nineteenth-century House of Commons that it 'was essentially a landowners' club – Irish peers, sons of UK peers, baronets, or country gentlemen.'

As late as the 1860s, it was claimed that three-quarters of all MPs were patricians. The upper house was even more of a monopoly of landowners, and during the nineteenth century these hereditary, aristocratic legislators remained at the apex of the power elite.[2]

Given that the wealth of Britain's political masters was integrally linked to an older agrarian economy, it was not difficult to see how and why they had voted for protective tariffs.

Yet the tectonic plates were shifting, and taking power and wealth away from the countryside towards the towns and cities. The transfer is mapped precisely by changes to Britain's national productivity. At the time the Corn Laws had been introduced a third of the country's workers were involved in agriculture, and farming yielded 40 per cent of the country's wealth. When they were repealed in mid-century by the Conservative Prime Minister Robert Peel, who was denounced as a traitor by many of his party and jettisoned from office because of Tory splits over the issue, agriculture had shrunk to 20 per cent of national production. By then only a third of workers were in its employ.[3]

At the century's close the rural labour force had fallen to less than one-tenth of the total and British farming had entered its infamous nadir. By the 1890s, agriculture contributed only 6 per cent to the gross national product. In the period when the Corn Laws had been a key instrument of control, Britain had been largely self-sufficient in food; by the turn of the next century the country was producing just 60 per cent of its domestic needs and four-fifths of the wheat needed was imported.[4] Late-Victorian farmers had managed to stave off some of the effects of depression by moving away from grain and into stock-rearing, which was more profitable because of the increased meat consumption by workers in British towns and cities. However, the ultimate effects of decline could not be disguised.

Even at the end of the Victorian era the rural community still had an essentially feudal tripartite structure, with a dominant top tier of landowners, then a broader middle made up of the people who actually produced the nation's food. These were largely tenant farmers who did not own land but rented it from the rural gentry. Broadest and deepest of all was the base of this social pyramid, which supported them all, supplying all the muscle and sweat that tilled the ground, weeded the fields, milked the cattle and harvested the crops. They were the rural workers – peasants, more or less – and precisely the noble men and women depicted in the paintings on the walls of the Famous Farm Café.

Theirs was not an easy lot. In his classic book on Suffolk rural life, *Akenfield*, Ronald Blythe gives us the story of Leonard Thompson, a farm worker born in the same year as my grandad – 1896. Thompson's own father, also a farm labourer, earned 10 shillings a week before the First World War. With this modest sum he fed and clothed a family of nine (the eldest boy had been killed in the Boer War). His tied cottage had a scrubbed brick floor, one rug made of scraps from old clothes, a larder and a living room. Leonard shared one of the two bedrooms with five siblings. Their food was apples, potatoes, swede and bread. Their drink was tea without milk or sugar. Water had to be fetched up the hill from a mile away. Two of his brothers also laboured. The youngest was eight years old and earned three shillings a week (15 pence today).[5]

For these rural folk it was Armageddon that brought blessed relief. As Leonard Thompson noted, he and his pals were more than happy to enlist at the outbreak of the First World War, because 'We were all damned glad to have got off the farms.' [6] Another of the positive outcomes for farmers – the German naval blockade of British waters – served to force up commodity prices and demand for home-grown produce. Yet the most significant development was the trial of guaranteed prices by government for essential crops, as well as powers of compulsion over aspects of farm management.

For farmers, these were some of the most favourable government measures since the Corn Laws. During the twenties and thirties central planning was given an additional fillip with the creation of the Milk Marketing Board. Similar bodies were set up for pigs and potatoes, but it was the impact of the first upon dairy farmers, boosting milk output by almost 25 per cent in the four years to 1938, that showed the way for state intervention. In the inter-war years the first 'deficiency payments' were also established. They amounted only to a modest total of £104 million, and were dispersed to producers to make up shortfalls between the actual wheat price and a guaranteed minimum (ten shillings per hundredweight). In themselves they were small developments, but very soon the principles on which they rested would become mainstream.

Once again, it was war and its aftermath that changed everything. At the outbreak in 1939 Britain imported all but a third of its food requirements. The renewal of a German blockade and the devastating impact of Nazi U-boats triggered a wholesale shift in planning, methods and morale of British agriculture. In only the first year, 2 million additional acres were ploughed and sown with crops for human consumption. Between 1938 and 1942 gross output went up two-thirds, and by the war's end commodity prices had doubled in six years.[7]

Such was the gratitude of a victorious nation for the heroic efforts of its farmers that the same post-war Labour government which would found the Nature Conservancy and institute the National Parks Act of 1949, would also pass the Agriculture Act in 1947. As the historian Michael Winter has noted, the legislation 'enshrined the dramatically altered role of agriculture in the economy and polity resulting from the experiences of the Second World War'.[8] There were now comprehensive subsidies across all major farm products, especially milk, cereals and sugar beet.

There was a secondary, but nonetheless key, development from the earlier era that should not be underestimated. It concerns the seemingly unbreakable bond of shared values and common cause – Graham Harvey calls it a 'cabal' – that had evolved between the government's Ministry of Agriculture* and the representative body for many British producers, the National Farmers' Union.[9]

The latter had been founded in 1908 following the creation of a local farmers' collective in Lincolnshire in 1904. In the interwar years the NFU had come to speak for all producers. Technically it was an independent body devoted to the needs of one special-interest group, but according to Winter the 'NFU–MAFF axis became so strong that relations between ministry civil servants and NFU officers could be closer than between civil servants and government ministers'.[10] Farmers were in effect partly driving in their own interests the very state policies that impacted upon them. As the historian John Sheail has pointed out, the links between landowners or farmers and post-war governments were 'so strong that conservation and recreational interests had the greatest difficulty in penetrating, let alone influencing, the policy-making process'.[11]

These social and political developments were as fundamental to the post-war agricultural revolution as any technological or chemical innovation described in Chapter 15. However, they should not be seen as separate from those processes. For all parts functioned as an integrated whole, and created the self-reinforcing cycle that locked into place an irreversible drive towards intensification.

On the ground the order of the day was draining or infilling, uprooting, clearing, deep-ploughing, re-seeding, spraying and fertilising much of the ground that now attracted subsidised payments. For farmers had nothing to lose and everything to gain from pursuing the path of increased productivity. All that they harvested carried a price guarantee, and many of the measures that increased their yields were

---

* Technically it was MAFF, the Ministry of Agriculture, Fisheries and Food, now replaced by DEFRA, the Department for Environment, Food and Rural Affairs.

further underwritten by government grants, or could be offset as expenses against tax.*

Before tackling its consequences, it is worth addressing one myth about the period. It centres on the notion that it was with the nation's entry into the European Common Market and consequent adoption of the Common Agricultural Policy that farmers had protectionist and interventionist policies forced upon them. In truth, they were already in place. In his book *Nature Conservation* Peter Marren shows that Britain's EC membership did not so much change overall policy as reinforce it. He goes on to suggest that more wildlife sites probably went under the plough between 1940 and 1973 than afterwards, 'but there was no monitoring process to put the losses on record'.[12]

At a simple habitat level, what we know to have gone is half the ancient woodland, nearly three-quarters of heathland, three-quarters of the country's ponds and almost all flower-rich meadows. Yet the diminishing part of the countryside that eventually caught the public's imagination, the one that has come to symbolise this entire phase of rural history, was the loss of hedgerows. For some reason, everyone notices them. Or more to the point, people notice when they are absent. It is this lack, undoubtedly, that is one of the most striking and disconcerting features of south Lincolnshire. It somehow compounds the impression that here is England's most 'un-English' landscape.[†]

Much ink has been spilt on exactly how much hedgerow was lost in those post-war decades. The issue was extensively covered in two of

---

* Through a mechanism known as the Annual Investment Allowance farmers can deduct the total value of any capital expenditure in a single tax year, sometimes wiping out their entire fiscal liability.

† Not that we would have thought that in the Middle Ages, or even until the eighteenth century. In a broad swathe of country – a north-east-to-south-west wedge running from Bridlington to Bournemouth and across west Norfolk from Sheringham to Southampton – hedgelessness was once the norm. The predominant agriculture was an open-field system almost entirely lacking in them. Enclosure during the eighteenth and nineteenth centuries was the development that brought so much quickset thorn boundary to the landscape, as the private lands were divided among their new proprietors. It was exactly this violation of his old home territory that John Clare railed against in poems such as 'Remembrances' when enclosure came to his beloved Helpston.

the most important and impassioned environmental audits of the period. In *The Theft of the Countryside* Marion Shoard opted to dwell on the finer-grained detail to make her case, pointing out that between 1947 and 1972 in an 8-square-mile patch of Huntingdonshire, 2,300 hedge trees were grubbed out, while Norfolk as a county was losing 8,000 hedgerow trees every year during the same quarter-century.[13]

In the opening pages of *The Killing of the Countryside*, Graham Harvey hits us with the bigger picture. He also explicitly links losses to subsidies, pointing out that since they were introduced England's farmers had cut down 150,000 miles of hedge and continued to grub them out at 10,000 miles a year.[14]* For Harvey these changes entailed not only a dissolution of the very idea of countryside – he redefined it as 'an industrial site set in a rural location' – but also a systemic breakdown in the relationship between the British and the very food they consume.[15]

Central governmental interference through the subsidy system had disrupted the farmer's direct links to his or her own regional markets. Instead of producing food for local people, farmers became the manufacturers of raw materials in a new international industry. In Harvey's words, the UK had been inducted into a 'technology-driven race to intensify farming, to re-fashion nature into what has been called "a global assembly line"'.[16]

In the new food order, it is the middlemen, the giant multinational corporations – Kelloggs, Cargill, Unilever etc. – that are the real beneficiaries of what farmers produce. Almost 80 per cent of all food items are now processed in some way. In 2015 British agricultural products were estimated to be worth £26.9 billion when they left the farm gate, yet in the same year British consumers spent an estimated £198 billion in store

---

* For what it is worth, Peter Marren quotes a figure of 99,000 miles between 1950 and 1995, and suggests that it represents half the hedgerows of Britain (see *Nature Conservation*, p. 137). Elsewhere, Marion Shoard puts the total losses at 120,000 miles between 1946 and 1974. John Sheail, for the period 1947–72, cites 10,000 miles a year and suggests that it involved half of all hedges in parts of the eastern counties. What we can conclude is that it was a significant percentage of the total hedge boundary in Britain. Moreover, for the last decade and a half we have been paying farmers subsidies, not to grub them out, but to replant them.

on groceries. It is this adding of so-called 'value' that yields the big profits. The other chief winners in the new supply chain between field and plate are the supermarkets. Today seven big stores – Aldi, Asda, Lidl, Morrisons, Sainsbury's, Tesco, Waitrose – sell us all but 12.5 per cent of our groceries.

Capitalism has not only captured the profits of farming; it also decides in large measure what we place in our mouths. One need only walk down the aisles of manufactured cakes, biscuits and assorted sweets – often by far and away the largest single section of any supermarket – to witness this process at work, and also the baleful health consequences and ludicrous illogic of the new food-delivery system. Massive increases in public sugar consumption are at the root of national epidemics in obesity (two-thirds of men and almost six in ten women are overweight or obese) and type-2 diabetes (4 million people by 2025). The latter alone is said to cost the country £14 billion in NHS treatments. Yet in 2010 five major European sugar producers netted £500 million in CAP subsidies.[17]

Although things had not reached such a pass by 1 January 1973, many of the developments described above were already well in train on the day that the Conservative Prime Minister Edward Heath signed the documents at the Egmont Palace in Brussels. With the fateful stroke of Heath's pen, Britain became a full member of an elite trading arrangement, technically known as the European Economic Community (in everyday parlance it was more usually known as the Common Market) and, from 1993 onwards, as the European Union.

It had been brought into existence by the Treaty of Rome in 1957, and since its inception a substantial part of the monies received and dispersed by the Community's bureaucracy was given to the farmers of the six original country members through a mechanism known as the Common Agricultural Policy. Britain and its rapidly changing postwar landscapes were soon to be subjected to its forceful prescriptions. The original Treaty of Rome spelt these out under its Article 39:

1. to increase agricultural productivity by promoting technical progress and by ensuring the rational development of agricultural

production and the optimum utilisation of the factors of production, in particular labour

2. to ensure a fair standard of living for the agricultural community
3. to stabilise markets
4. to ensure that supplies reach consumers at reasonable prices.[18]

Contained within this vague, even anodyne, bureaucratese was a set of goals whose impacts would be unleashed on the European landscape in a *Sorcerer's Apprentice* blend of perfectly fine intentions and unforeseen but devastating consequences. Eventually the process would acquire all the manic tempo and cymbal-clashing insanity of Paul Dukas's famous symphonic poem.

It has long been said that the original CAP had been fashioned primarily with the large and diverse agricultural communities of France in mind. French farmers have always received a disproportionately large slice of the EU's subsidy cake. Even today, in the context of the enlarged European Union of twenty-seven national members, France gets approximately €11 billion and 17 per cent of the total budget. However, in that country too, the fallacy that one can manage a continent's agricultural policy from a highly centralised supranational bureaucracy is well exposed. Since 2000, French farmers have declined in number by a quarter, while the number of its agricultural workers has fallen by about 334,000 in the same period.[19]

What did increase, as a consequence of the CAP's inviolate assumptions that central management equals 'reason' and more reason equals 'progress', was the output in farm products. Wonderful though these boosted yields seem in a technical sense, by 1972 the six countries were producing more food than their populations required. In the year of British accession to the European Community, it was already spending a billion *écus* (the precursor of the euro) just on the storage of these excesses. And by 1986 that figure had climbed to 7 billion *écus*. One example was the 1.5 million tonnes of unused and unwanted butter that was held that year in refrigerated cold rooms across the continent.

The scandal of farm subsidies dawned on the British public through increasingly surreal press stories from the late seventies until the mid-eighties that told of European wine lakes and cereal mountains. Yet in the mad *Sorcerer's Apprentice* world of agro-support, the net effect of overspending on storage was not an end to subsidies. It was to trigger far more expenditure to cope with the mounting surpluses. By the mid-1980s the CAP was absorbing more than 70 per cent of the entire EU budget, and by 1992 the price of underpinning Europe's farmers had risen from 12 to 31 billion *écus*.[20] Today it is €47 billion.

One of the most depressing aspects of subsidies was their impact upon the relationship between farmers and the land, unpicking the very idea that agriculture is centrally an enterprise about good soil management. At its worst, Britain's terra firma became little more than a symbolic medium, an investment vehicle and a source of leverage, through which farmers could realise substantial profits. Sometimes they were not husbanding fields or stock primarily to generate food: these were secondary to the form-filling enterprise of state-administered payments.

The clearest example of the process is in the uplands, where sheep became eligible for what were known as headage payments. In effect, the more sheep you kept, the more subsidy you received, because it was paid per animal. Between the 1970s and 1990s some hill farmers pushed the system to its limits, so that stocking levels were sometimes way above the carrying capacity of the ground they farmed. As we saw, that was what happened around Kinder Scout, where sheep numbers rose from 17,000 (1914) to 60,000 (mid-1970s). Nationally the figures challenged the very idea of the hardy fell farmer as rightful custodian of his (or her) bleak and beautiful upland landscape. In effect, hill farmers violated the very soil on their farms for money. Between 1980 and 1995 sheep numbers almost doubled.[21]

By 1996 headage payments on sheep and cattle were worth £655 million to British hill farmers and far outweighed the value of carcases or wool.[22] Although they were eventually cancelled at the turn of the millennium and farmers were paid thereafter on the basis of the land acreage they managed (technically known as the Single Payment Scheme and later the Basic Payment Scheme, and often known informally as 'area payments'), the principle of subsidised agriculture was inviolate. Nonetheless many even in the industry now willingly accept that hill farms are widely unsustainable, or receive most of their profit in some form of government grant.

For the environmentalist George Monbiot the relationship between subsidies and sheep in his former home country of Wales represents a distillate of the general toxin spread by the EU's farm policies in the last half-century. As he points out, the whole of the Welsh countryside is managed in the farmers' minority interests, yet they represent just 5 per cent of the rural population. The contribution of sheep farms to the Welsh economy of £400 million is substantially less than that from recreational walking (£500 million), and is only a fraction of that generated by all wildlife-based activity (£1,900 million). Neither of the latter two income streams is directly subsidised, but the average Welsh sheep farm receives £53,000 a year. Given that the average income per farmer is £33,000, the business of keeping sheep and cattle on the Welsh hills loses £20,000 per annum per unit.[23]

Nor does this encompass the true cost of those over-grazed slopes to the British taxpayer. Most underlying soils in the Welsh uplands have been denuded of their carbon content by over-grazing, while the impact of rain run-off on fells stripped of their vegetation has been directly linked to the increased incidence of flooding. In England and Wales the annual cost of these disasters and their prevention is in the region of £1.8 billion. Such was the downstream cost to one insurance company that they seriously investigated the idea of buying and re-foresting the largest Cambrian mountains, because it was cheaper than their pay-outs on 'carpets in Gloucestershire'.[24]

The central psychological effect of subsidies has been to build up a generational dependency on hand-outs, which are now an unchallengeable fixture of the group mindset. We cannot blame farmers for this. Nor can we blame subsidies alone for all the changes to the British environment, yet it is indisputable that they primed the engine and are integral to the entire system. Their impact also entails a peculiarly bitter irony for anyone who has been obliged to watch the processes unfold. For not only have they had to endure the inexorable reductions in landscape: they were also made to pay for them. The precise monetary figure given through taxes by the average British family towards the CAP has long been an issue of dispute. That it came out of their wallets, however, is not, and because the poor spend a disproportionately higher amount on food than the wealthy, they have been the hardest hit. As Graham Harvey observed, 'the CAP takes cash from the most disadvantaged members of the community and puts it into the pockets of the wealthiest.'[25]

If one had to summarise the overarching effects on wildlife of state-funded intensification in British agriculture, then two environmental data serve as a handy measure. One involves the loss of 44 million breeding birds from the British countryside after 1966. It is worth repeating the number to dwell on its magnitude. *Forty-four million breeding birds.* The British Trust for Ornithology, whose volunteers assembled most of the census information on which the assertion is based, can even pinpoint the period when most of the decline occurred. It was between 1975 and 1987.[26] The other key indicator is the loss of all but 1–3 per cent of 4 million acres of flower-rich meadows in the twentieth century.

Setting aside the environmental consequences, we can see that there are strong grounds to argue that state support for agriculture has been a failure even on its own terms.* Farmers, and especially small farmers, have been among its chief victims. If a core goal of subsidies was to keep a diverse farming community on the land, then they patently have *not* worked. In almost every European country where they have been rolled out, subsidies have cut swathes through the numbers directly involved in extracting goodness from soil.

Another thing they have failed to do is to ensure that Britain is self-sustaining in agricultural output. True, we obtain from our own fields about 60 per cent of our food, but this is completely dependent upon the chemicals – oil, fertilisers, herbicides and the other assorted '-cides' – most of which are imported. It is the manufacturers of this essential chemistry-set and of the equipment used to dispense it that are the real winners in the entire process.

---

* One of the more tragic and least-regarded outcomes that should exercise even the NFU is the fact that the subsidy-fuelled inflation in land prices has more or less debarred any young aspiring farmer who is not already possessed of the necessary acreage from entering his or her desired profession. It is pretty much a closed shop except for the very wealthy.

The overriding question that all this raises is: why have we not ended subsidies? In his extraordinary book *Who Owns the World*, Kevin Cahill notes that at the heart of the CAP payment system are 77,000 recipients who represent 0.7 per cent of the whole farming community. In turn, they amount to a trifling 0.022 per cent of the population. Yet this fortunate few own a quarter of the region's land and receive collectively €12 billion a year for no other reason than that they are the most land-rich people on an entire continent. This is compelling enough but, as Cahill points out, the statistics disguise the fact that at its pinnacle the system doles out money to an inner corps of aristocratic and royal families, our own included, who are not millionaires but billionaires. Their individual annual hand-outs are calculated in millions. Cahill calls the process 'the heist of heists', a judgement with which it is difficult to disagree. Setting aside all the other impacts, why is the CAP not challenged merely on the grounds that it is fiscal injustice of the most medieval kind?[27]

The critics of subsidised farming have repeatedly raised the question of the public's response to these issues. In *The Theft of the Countryside* Marion Shoard argued that 'If the people of England knew what was happening to their countryside, they would not stand for it.'[28] It is almost forty years since she wrote these words, and perhaps the more troubling truth is that people still do not know what has happened, or is happening now. Even more shocking is the fact that most of them probably do not really care. There may be nearly 7 million members of the key environmental NGOs*, but it means that there are at least 58.4 million people in Britain who are not. For the vast majority, nature barely registers. And it does not do so for perfectly acceptable reasons. They are simply too busy, too assailed by the preoccupations entailed in modern life. They are consumed by the need to sustain their marital or family relations, especially those of parenthood, and enjoy their precious leisure moments and their surplus wealth, with a barbecue or an hour at the match on a Saturday afternoon. In short, their lives are already full. There is no room

---

* Let's remind ourselves that the figure is not a simple sum, since many individuals will be members of multiple organisations. The truer number is probably around 5–5.5 million.

for the fate of the fly orchid or the pine hoverfly and the prospects of the large blue butterfly. However much it may have been diminished in recent decades, the countryside is no more than the incidental background to their lives. It is a temporary green blur that counts for little and to which they pay scant attention. If there are fewer sparrows in the garden, at least they seem to continue to chirp merrily and their songs still form part of that subliminal hymn arriving through the window during Sunday's extra hour in bed, that says things are pretty much as they were.

As a consequence of this indifference to the fate of non-human life in these islands, it is pitiful to observe how little real discussion or concern for environmental matters surfaces in British political discourse. In the election of 2015 I watched and listened to as many debates and news items as possible to make a personal audit of references to nature. Apart from the issue of climate change, I recorded its discussion on just one occasion. It was during a live public debate on ITV between the seven leaders of the main political parties. After one hour and 48 minutes of a two-hour debate, the Green Party leader Natalie Bennett tried to raise the issue of global species extinction and the loss of 50 per cent of all wildlife in the last thirty years. The programme's chair Julie Etchingham crushed Bennett's emerging point like a troublesome cockroach. And the subject never re-surfaced.

There is one more very good reason for public indifference to the fate of British nature. In *The Killing of the Countryside* Graham Harvey argued that 'Decades of watching their local environment despoiled has bred a sort of confused resignation among country people. They see no logic to the degradation going on around them, but they know the landowning lobby holds most of the cards.'[29] Harvey further noted how the Common Agricultural Policy effectively bound the country into a federal farming state, against which there was no redress, apart from internal reforms instigated by the EU itself.[30] If it was not entirely unalterable, the larger system at least rebuffed public criticism with ease and, though it has made attempts at rectification, as we shall see, they have been immensely convoluted and glacially slow.

There is a further key factor that acts as a drag on any possible change. It is that the central engine of modern life and of the British economy is urban and industrial in character. Today 53.6 million Britons live in towns and cities. This bias has been the case for nearly 200 years. In that time, we have somehow come *not* to see the extent to which land was once the very foundation of power in Britain. Much of that centrality has diminished, but by no means all. Land and its ownership still confer power and influence in this country. Just to offer the briefest glance at these issues, it was not until the twenty-first century that 750 hereditary peers, many of them landed, lost their time-honoured rights to sit in judgement over all legislation in this country. Even now ninety-two hereditary peers continue to do just that, inserting themselves and their self-interests into what is assumed to be a completely democratic process. Why?

Whatever your own private answer to the question, it is indisputable that landowners' continuous self-assertion in British life occurs not just in Westminster, but at all levels of society, down to the village hall. Marion Shoard has done a masterly job of analysing the disproportionate presence of farmers/landowners in almost all fora and regional and local power structures, from county councils and internal drainage boards, down even to the various committees of the National Trust.*

The people of this country, subjects rather than citizens, have an inbuilt deferential reflex to the landed, and have allowed the same powerful minority to continue to enjoy massive unequal fiscal benefits and political privileges for seventy years. We may all have the vote, but those who own land have more votes than others.

---

* In both of her books, which are indispensable studies of British farming and land practice in the late twentieth and early twenty-first centuries, Shoard highlights the privileged status of landowners in all layers of public life. One small part of her analysis looked at six counties – North Yorkshire, Suffolk, Oxfordshire, Lincolnshire, Buckinghamshire and Cornwall – and the percentage presence of farmers or their wives on the relevant county councils. She then compared that number with the percentage that farmers represented of the overall county population. Farmers made up 18 per cent – nearly one-fifth of all county councillors – in the six counties, but just 1.4 per cent of the adult population. She also looked at farmer representation on the boards of three Welsh national parks, where they made up a third of all members. Yet the tourist industry, which was and is the greater source of income in these areas, had members on only two of the three boards. See Shoard, 1997, pp. 185–95.

17

SUBSIDIES II: THE SEQUEL

Like the rest of Britain, I was dumbfounded by the events that occurred overnight on 23–4 June 2016. Against almost all the expectations of the political pundits, the nation learned during those quiet hours of summer darkness that, after forty-three years of membership of the European Union, it had chosen to leave. Unlike the rest of Britain waking to the aftershock on the Friday morning, I was overtaken in the middle of writing this chapter. I was also, by chance, twenty miles south of Gedney and the Famous Farm Café, riding back and forth along those dead-straight fen roads in a Range Rover, talking farm policy and farm practice with farmers.

It now seems completely fortuitous that on the day the Common Agricultural Policy was effectively terminated as a guiding mechanism of land management in Britain, I was assessing an environmental prize for an agricultural society at the invitation of my friend and co-judge Jake Fiennes. Such events are now a widespread staple of the nation's farming community, but they are also, in a way, a product of subsidies.

For the CAP scandal that had come to the fore towards the end of the century, with its tales of butter mountains and olive-oil lakes, triggered a gradual movement away from straight production support for Europe's farmers. The first stage in the journey began in 1988 and was called 'set-aside', whose absurdity could only be rendered rational when filtered through the institutional mindset in Brussels, because it involved paying producers *not* to farm. Eventually 10 per cent of land was compulsorily set aside, as the name makes plain, and left fallow until late May or June, when the uncropped fields, then full of weeds and often with breeding skylarks in mid-nest cycle, were sprayed with herbicides or ploughed up.

It could hardly rank as the best use of public money, yet set-aside continued to function into the new century and was not officially terminated until 2008. From an environmental perspective, its chief merit was to break the previously unassailable linkage between production and state payments. It also provided, however hazily, an initial administrative framework and intellectual stimulus, out of which new kinds of economic incentive could be devised to support farmers to produce food less intensively and to let wildlife happen on their land.

In the ensuing decades a whole series of new subsidy prescriptions – the various British avatars have been called Environmentally Sensitive Areas, Countryside Stewardship, Entry-Level and Higher-Level Stewardship and now back to Countryside Stewardship mark II – were developed and rolled out. The funding for them was initially very modest in relation to the full CAP. By 1993/4 in Britain it had reached just £107 million, 4 per cent of the entire national CAP figure.[1] But as they increased they were accorded at least nomenclatural equality with the standard giveaway to farmers. The main CAP area payments, the farmers' natural entitlements, so to speak, sit under Pillar One. The new monies for nature, awarded under competitive tender and collectively called 'agri-environment schemes', make up Pillar Two.

Today Pillar Two represents 9.3 per cent of the total national CAP figure, and in 2015 it amounted to £368 million a year for wildlife-friendly farming. The new brand of subsidy continues the old idea that agriculture needs state support, but the Pillar Two payments at least enshrine the ideal of public money for public good. Agri-environment schemes pay farmers to deliver wheat, lamb or sugar, while simultaneously supplying more green-winged orchids, more lapwings and more nectar-rich habitats for butterflies, bees and moths; in short, food and real countryside.

Theoretically anywhere can be entered into an agri-environment scheme, from the RSPB's Minsmere reserve to an arable prairie in fenland, as long as it meets the criteria and satisfies those who judge the applications that it delivers demonstrable wildlife benefits. There is hardly a nature reserve in Britain, and certainly not in lowland England, that is not covered by some agreement. Some of the major beneficiaries of agri-environment culture are the main wildlife NGOs. The landscapes around Kinder Scout and the fields that throng with waders and flowers about Widdybank and Cronkley Fells in Upper Teesdale are typical of places that now benefit from such schemes.

The question that hangs over them, however, is not just: can they work, or even, could they be made to work better, but, most tantalising of all, could they possibly provide us with a partial long-term remedy for what has happened to the British countryside in the twentieth century? On the day that the nation voted to terminate its EU membership, I learnt one possible answer from my co-judge, Jake Fiennes.

Jake is brother to the actors Ralph and Joseph Fiennes (the latter is his non-identical twin), to the film-maker Sophie Fiennes and to the Los-Angeles-based composer Magnus Fiennes. Although he has something of his brothers' film-star looks, Jake chose a radically different path to the rest of his cinematic siblings. Yet his career still has roots in the Fiennes' deeply unconventional childhood experience, part of which included rural life on their parents' Suffolk farm. All the children grew up imbued with an instinctual connection between the food that was placed on their table and the animals that lived – and died – in the fields. Jake recalls an occasion when he and the rest of the family were all sitting round the kitchen table skinning the Fiennes' home-reared rabbits, when a friend happened to arrive to witness the happy scene of shared activities, and promptly fainted at the carnage.

After a post-school year on a ranch in the Australian outback, Jake did a stint as a gamekeeper with his friend Charlie Burrell, who is now celebrated for a rewilding project at his family estate, Knepp Castle in Sussex. Jake then took his new trade to Raveningham, the 5,500-acre family seat of the Bacon family, just downstream from my Blackwater 5 acres in east Norfolk. He has been there ever since and is now estate manager for the owner Sir Nicholas Bacon. Long before I ever met him I had heard of Raveningham's head keeper, who was developing a reputation for the environmental work, to which he and his boss have had longstanding commitments (the latter has served, for example, as president of the Norfolk Wildlife Trust). A distinctive feature of the regime at Raveningham, or 'Rav' as the locals all call it, is that since the Second World War the gamebirds are wild-bred. It means that their pheasants and partridges are completely unlike the headless 'chickens' that throng the Norfolk roads every autumn, which are incubated under battery heaters and reared in pens.*

From small beginnings in the late 1980s, Rav's keeper took advantage of an early agri-environment scheme to develop the needs of his wild-bird shoot. Later, as estate manager, Fiennes expanded the scale of the operations so that nature assumed a central place, not only on land directly managed by him for the Bacon family, but also on adjacent properties run by four of the estate's five tenant farmers. It means now that the whole landscape is administered in an integrated way for conventional farm crops and for wildlife. Jake has not dispensed with all intensive methods of farming, but he has reduced chemical inputs to an absolute minimum and, for example, uses no fertiliser on the pasture for Rav's grass-fed beef herd.† The entire approach accords with Fiennes's belief that while 'organic farming cannot feed the world, intensive farming as currently practised is completely unsustainable.'

---

* A day's shoot in December 2014 at Raveningham, at the invitation of its owner and estate manager, is the only time I have ever gone to war personally with Norfolk's gamebirds. It must be said that I was armed with nothing more lethal than a camera. I was impressed by the extent to which slaughter was a minor part of the full day's enjoyment. At the end of the drives, more than a dozen guns had killed barely two dozen cock pheasants. Even the journalist got to take home a brace, not to mention a haunch of Chinese water deer. Contrast this with a shoot that Jake had worked in Shropshire, where his employers required him to pick up 60,000 pheasant eggs in preparation for the autumn's heroic campaign.

† It was instructive listening to Jake Fiennes interrogating numerous farmers over the two days of our judging stint to understand the kneejerk, prophylactic approach adopted by many to pesticide use. Every single one of them was asked whether they had sprayed for orange blossom midge, a species that Jake explained was almost entirely absent that spring as a potential threat to crops. Yet every one of those he had asked had already sprayed for orange blossom midge just in case!

I remember my first visit to witness this place, which is only a few miles from Claxton. As we drove down to the Yare marshes my initial astonishment was at the sheer number of hares. They were everywhere: in the cereal fields on either side, or squeezing through holes in the hedge as they bolted from the engine's growl. The act of momentary compression when the animals lowered themselves to make headroom seemed to store extra tension, and out they would pop at the other side, the limbs and ears re-expanding, the awkward roll accelerating and those ridiculously long legs thrumming in uneven free flow over the field horizon.

When we reached the floodplain proper, the hares were joined by Chinese water deer.* I see the latter at Blackwater in ones or twos, but nothing like the numbers at Raveningham. There were a dozen all around us. We stopped to look at them by a wet scrape and, suddenly, there, spread across a plate of blue water was a flock of gadwall, mallard, shoveler, lapwings, redshanks and avocets purified in the evening sunlight. Right at the centre of them was a brief sphere of the most beautiful deep orange-red, layered below with linen white and chequered above in black. All at once a hunting marsh harrier crossed overhead and this compressed inner pool of brightness atomised as thirty migrant black-tailed godwits took flight in a white-banded thresh of wings. I was on a farm, but it looked and felt like a nature reserve.

Perhaps the most remarkable thing about the achievements at Raveningham is that it is neither. Nor is it the case that an economically driven enterprise has withdrawn wildlife-unfriendly methods from parts of the land and thus allowed nature to return of its own accord. What is striking is that the whole place is run in a highly

---

* Chinese water deer is not, as some assume, the same as a muntjac, although both species originate in the Far East. The former is a labrador-sized primitive deer that has fang-like tusks rather than antlers and was first released in Norfolk in the 1950s. Since then it has spread and built up a well-established feral population in the Broads. Unlike many non-native species, it appears not to have had an adverse effect on the British fauna and flora, except perhaps for its frequent roadside quarrels with moving cars. The introduced population is now thought to be a significant percentage of the world total because of serious declines in China.

intensive fashion. Because the estate manager is nothing if not driven. Jake jokes openly about his obsessive- compulsive disorder.* He works a sixty-hour week and on summer mornings he is often out by five.

It is when you hear him talking about the thrill he gets from seeing dandelions coming up on his cattle pastures – *his* dandelions, where dandelions had never occurred before – that you know you are dealing with an agricultural original. The most memorable sentence I can recall him uttering was when this land manager proclaimed, 'Once you have the insects right, you have everything else.' Reflect a moment on the prolonged, baleful history of insecticide use in Britain and all its consequences – loss of swallows from large areas of the English lowlands, the decline of grey partridge from several million to a few thousand in fifty years, the withdrawal of bumblebees from the countryside and their retreat into urban and suburban environments – to understand the radical nature of what he said.

A perfect index of Fiennes's approach is his 6-metre margins around some of the fields. The idea is to mitigate the effects of the prevalent farm practice whereby crops are sown often to the very field boundary. Sometimes the uncultivated gap by the hedge, if there is a hedge at all, can be a matter of inches. While 6-metre margins theoretically create corridors for wildlife, many of them I have walked in Norfolk are little more than a uniformly mown sward of rye grass with wildlife flowers pocked at infrequent intervals, and usually involving just one or two species such as dandelions and germander speedwell. In wildlife terms, they represent the absolute minimum value – but, no matter, they are better than nothing at all.

---

* Jake suggests it is a family trait, and that it probably helps to explain the trajectory of success enjoyed by all the siblings. He tells a great tale about having dinner a couple of years ago with Ralph and moving the salt and pepper pots on the table three inches to the left while his brother wasn't looking. Lord Voldemort would then subliminally register how the fundamental structure of his universe had been minutely altered and move them back the exact three inches to their allotted spots. It was only after about six rounds of this mind game that Ralph realised he was being tested.

At Rav the 6-metre margins are astonishing. Some are sown with fourteen species of formerly common meadow flowers, such as knapweed, trefoil, yellow rattle, campion, mallow. With the various grasses and other naturally occurring annuals the diversity rises in some areas to twenty to thirty species. In June they are interlacing ribbons of colour and diversity, filled with the sights and sounds of pollinating insects – bumblebees, hoverflies, beetles and butterflies. Their richness accumulates with the passage of time, and they represent years of hard work and experimentation with the cutting regime, the methods of seed drilling and the precise mixture of the plants.

As margins they are the very best they could be. They gladden the heart of any naturalist. But let us be clear. They are not meadows in the sense of the adventitious 4-million-acre patchwork that once covered the English countryside as an indirect consequence of an older agricultural dispensation. Those margins are, in a way, intensive crops – deliberately engineered and rigorously, even obsessively, maintained and, via the mechanism of an agri-environment agreement, they yield an annual 'profit'. Yet given our age and our circumstances, they are surely as good as meadows.

What is most radical about Fiennes's approach is the professionalism and profound sense of obligation he brings in equal measure to both the conventional parts of the farm and its wildlife component. Equally telling is his refusal to accept a standard binary definition of himself as either 'farmer' or 'environmentalist'. Being dyslexic, he dislikes labels, but especially their power to limit our understanding of any situation. He insists he is neither. Both roles are part of a unified process, which he reduces to a single fundamental goal. As he says, 'I am just passionate about life.'

Another marked characteristic of the practice at Rav is that all crops on the estate yield a harvest, not just the beef, lamb, barley and beet – and he operates a seven-crop rotation both to help manage soil fertility and to control weeds and pest issues with minimal chemical interventions – but also the pheasants, deer (c. 400 a year), hares (300–700 a year), rabbits, partridges, wigeon, mallard, teal, pink-footed geese and woodcock. There are parts of such a regime that no nature-reserve manager would contemplate. At certain times of year what gamekeepers like to call vermin – weasels, stoats, foxes and carrion crows – are strictly controlled. Jake Fiennes has also faced repeated public and media assault – critical articles appearing in the *Daily Mail* and *Daily Mirror* – over the killing of hares at Raveningham.

The question I would ask of anyone troubled by what happens is: what do we want from our farmed landscapes? You cannot crop a surplus of anything, be it cows or deer, hares or lambs, barley or yellow rattle, without there being a sustainable abundance. Even the weasels, stoats, foxes and crows that are summarily despatched in the interests of the pheasant shoot are there precisely because the agricultural ecosystem is as intact as it could be.* For some it may not be perfect. To most of us it is surely good enough. The achievements at Raveningham should be judged not by any one element, but on their totality. Recall the words of Aldo Leopold, who was himself a passionate sportsman, cited in the frontispiece. 'A thing is right when it tends to preserve the integrity, stability and beauty of the biotic community. It is wrong when it tends otherwise.' I would argue that in the context of modern agriculture, Raveningham is definitely 'right'.

Crucially, the estate also makes a profit. Yet an important aspect of this is that one part of the farm does not compensate for the other – the intensive conventional crops for the wildlife. As Fiennes points out, what he calls the 'environmental farm' – the section under agri-environmental measures – accounts for one-fifth of all the land and generates the largest gross margins.[2] In effect, subsidies pay. More to the point, we pay Fiennes to deliver knapweed and bumblebees, just as we still pay him partly to produce sugar beet. What is most

---

* Some of the biodiversity on the estate is professionally monitored and would do justice to any SSSI or nature reserve. There are at least eight species of breeding predator, including hobby, sparrowhawk, marsh harrier, common buzzard, kestrel, barn, tawny and little owls. In a single year an entomologist recorded 400 species of moth, more than one-sixth of the entire British moth fauna, including nine species of high conservation concern. There is no full audit of all wild species present, but based on this last census one can surmise that it would run to several thousands. Raveningham, in short, is the classic old mixed farm, and a fully functioning agricultural ecosystem.

noteworthy is that the estate manager takes a consistent approach to all parts of its economy.

Wildlife farming is not a government giveaway that is viewed as an unscrutinised bonus. Jake delivers on his agri-environment payments with the same sense of obligation he would bring to a contract with Tate & Lyle. It is this that is so different from many places – that offers us a vision for all subsidised agriculture. Not to suggest that Raveningham is the *only* farm where best practice occurs: there are hundreds, if not thousands, up and down Britain, applying the same high standards. The challenge is to make their yardstick the measure for everyone.

Jake is passionate about his wildlife, but he is just as meticulous about the conventional side of his trade. On the day the country voted for Brexit it was fascinating to watch him as we went to judge the various nominated farms. Like an insatiable mustelid he ferreted into every detail of their practice. They thought they were being assessed for what they did for nature; Jake was prying into everything. One of his key anxieties, which I was at a loss to understand until he explained, centred on the condition of their grain stores. It was that same totality of approach which he pursues at Rav that he was searching for in his candidates. Most came up short.

Even Bob, to whom we eventually awarded the prize, did not quite satisfy his quest for perfection. Bob and his wife had a classic old mixed fenland farm, its soil that extraordinarily black peat earth of the Cambridgeshire fens. Judging by the steady flow of cars down the dead-straight fen drove to the farm, their shop selling their own meat and eggs was a community asset as much as a thriving part of the business.

We both had Bob down as what Jake Fiennes called a 'dirty farmer'. The place was indisputably untidy, something I both identified with and cherished in him. Its unkempt qualities nourished the biodiversity: the slew of weeds that had escaped notice in various bee-loud corners; the outbuildings with their half-open doors and windows the swallows sailed in and out of; the spilt cattle feed on which the tree sparrows thrived. We were meant to judge the man on how far he had farmed in accordance with a set of written rules. He may well have fulfilled that brief. In truth, all the farms Jake took me to had among their crops some wonderful, well-tended habitats. But what impressed us most about our winner were not even the turtle doves and corn buntings breeding on his patch, or the unsprayed riverbanks where his cattle grazed.

What we saw was something intangible and largely emotional. One surmised that he had probably come on board the agri-environment scheme for the usual money-for-nothing subsidy ride. Slowly, as he had engaged – possibly for the first time ever with the more than human parts of his farm – the man had become fired with a pride in what he was doing. Above all there was a willingness to learn from anyone, and to do better in a cause that he had slowly come to own personally. His farm and what he was doing to improve its environmental quality did not amount to perfection. But he was a worthy winner.

Beholding that dead-level fenland farm with its pitch-black, bog-begotten soils on the day that Britain resolved to divorce from the EU and uncouple from the CAP, I reflected that we had come a long way from when subsidies first began. They were products of a different age, when command economies in the Communist bloc and state intervention in matters of western capitalist markets were commonplace. At their origin, guaranteed prices and government support for farmers were seen as legitimate instruments for underpinning private farm production.

Not now. Ours is a world dominated by the ideas of a free-market economy, where commodity prices are set not by governments but by the normal fluctuations in a global chain of supply and demand. In this form of economic natural selection, subsidies have come to be viewed as out-dated, inefficient and unfair. In the new world order, state agricultural payments are particularly unjust, because they place at greatest disadvantage the poorest developing countries, for whom raw agricultural products are their main trade commodities.

Ironically, what may come to rescue British farm-support payments from the oblivion that should have been inflicted by the rules of global trade – what may indeed enshrine them as fixtures of our rural landscape – are not the arguments of farmers, but of those who once opposed subsidies. In the period that Oliver Rackham defined as the 'locust years', environmentalists made a case against the state-sponsored drive for production at any price: that the countryside could not and should not be treated in the same way as the other parts of a capitalist economy; that earth was not an industrial aggregate out of which crops could be pulled like products from a factory press; that land had values that were not calculable in columns of profit and loss; and that from its underlying soils came intangible goodness that included beauty, culture, wildlife and happiness.

If, in a post-Brexit world, British farmers wish to go on receiving special treatment, then perhaps it is time for all to recognise truly that land itself is a unique and special asset. Some will learn to farm it – intentionally, profitably, efficiently even – for nature and its multiple inspirations for us all to enjoy.

18

BOG

I have never seen such a desolate landscape. It far eclipsed
Galloway and other Highland areas I had visited. The sheer size
of these great flat bogs … was so daunting … a continuous sweep
of low, gently undulating moor … It was bisected by the Thurso
and Wick railway, but this did little to detract from its appearance
of wilderness. Away out in the middle of these flows, miles from
the nearest road, there was a great feeling of solitude. The distant
views of higher peaks rising abruptly above these low moorlands
helped greatly to keep direction, but also emphasised the scale
and sense of spacious emptiness.

Derek Ratcliffe, *In Search of Nature*

Of all the geographical nomenclature used to describe the parts of the
British landscape, I love best of all the technical terms for bog. Despite
the potent simplicity of the monosyllable, which is so beloved of children, bog has around it a complex, precise vocabulary that includes
diplotelm, catotelm, acrotelm, ombrogenous, ombrotrophic, soligenous
and topogenous.

Even the simpler parts – 'bog burst', or 'blanket bog', or 'sphagnum
moss' – are laden with sound sense as well as meaning. Another favourite
is the Danish term *mooratmung*.* It refers to the ways in which the

---

* The surfaces of some American bogs have been recorded to rise or fall by as much
as 36 cm (14.1 in) in a single day. The latest research suggests that the main cause
of these fluctuations is exchange of methane, or – and here's another suggestive
bit of bog vocabulary – gas ebullition.

entire substrate expands and contracts in response to climatic and seasonal conditions. Literally it means 'bog breathing', and it conjures a vision of a landscape as a single, almost sentient organism, and suggests how a person's encounter with bog might be a mutual exercise.

Before everything else the vocabulary helps me to appreciate how so much of the creative process that generates this land form is seldom visible. And without the formal precision of the lexicon, not to mention its poetry and suggestiveness, one could easily struggle to 'read' boggy places. Because of all landscapes in Britain bog is the least legible. When Daniel Defoe spoke of Kinder Scout as a 'waste and houling wilderness' it was largely a hostile dismissal of its qualities. Visually the land can appear bleak and uninviting: open, flat or gently folded country that is usually devoid of humans and their works, and which is invariably treeless and perhaps wind-blasted and wet underfoot, and often lacking in the kinds of plants or animals that trigger instant engagement. For bog-dwellers are often at low densities, and encounters with them are few.

Bogs are also notable for being almost devoid of primary colour. At a macro-level the most varied parts are shades of brown but always mingled with other tones – tinged purple wherever heather grows, or rust and sand if rushes and sedges are present. At a micro-level – say in a clump of russet-headed moss (especially red bogmoss *Sphagnum capillifolium*), or among the slender blossoms of bog asphodel or the scarlet-crowned reindeer lichens (in the genus *Cladonia*), or the carnivorous sundews with their crimson-jawed fly-traps – there are minute stipplings of brighter colour. Yet what characterises it overall is the continuously modulated and harmonised sameness. I sometimes wonder if tweed, the world-famous handwoven cloth of the Scottish Highlands, with its wool-ply of infinite hue, is itself a cultural analogue and creative response to the chromatic blendedness of bog.

More certain is that bog is made truly captivating if you understand a little of the processes that are locked away beneath its surface modulations. The bogs of Caithness and Sutherland, which are among the most extensive, environmentally rich and ecologically important not just in Britain, but in the world, are comprised of a community of temperate, water- and acid-tolerant plants, pre-eminent among which are a group known as the sphagnum mosses or bogmosses. Even the word *sphagnum*, loose-centred and closed by that globular last syllable – like a gas bubble at the swamp surface, perhaps – seems to evoke their aqueous condition. With twice the absorbency of cotton wool, the rootless phytoplasm of sphagnum mosses rests at the surface like a loose waterlogged carpet. If you wanted to you could just pick up great hanks of sphagnum and squeeze it out in cold and juicy handfuls.

There are about ten sphagnum species in British bogs, and many are anonymous in appearance, difficult to tell apart and without widely recognised common names.* They are so low in nutrients, such as nitrogen or phosphorus, that normal soil micro-organisms cannot easily break them down. At the end of a growing season the bottom layers of dead sphagnum collapse into their watery grave, where the unicellular fauna and flora that normally decompose such materials operate with equal inefficiency. However, even in the completely anoxic conditions, bacteria metabolise at least some of the sphagnum remnants. Those that are undigested – and I love the fact that the experts speak of the 'palatability' of the dead vegetation as if micro-organisms savour their boggy diet – accrete in an expanding layer of peat.[1]

The whole vertical community of a bog is defined as an interactive two-tier system (known as the 'diplotelm'). The upper aerobic and rain-fed layer is called the 'acrotelm' ('acro' a version of the Greek ἄκρος, 'topmost') and refers to the exposed surface skin of photosynthesising vegetation – the mosses and the other plants – that binds the whole thing together. The acrotelm, which can be remarkably shallow, and no more than 18 to as little as 3 inches, is essentially the engine room of bog production.

Below this is the bog's storage facility, entitled the 'catotelm' (from the Greek for 'downward', κάτω), a midden of accumulating peat which, unlike its upper sphagnum skin, can be very thick indeed. Occasionally blanket bogs are as much as 10 metres (32.8 ft) deep. People sometimes assume that bog is an inert deposit laid over impervious bedrock. While

---

* One exception is the rather wonderful, if informal, name for *Sphagnum cuspidatum*: drowned cat sphagnum (more usually called feathery bogmoss), because its submerged leaves resemble the fur on a really wet moggy.

there is often little water exchange with the underlying mineral layer, and while it has no aerobic micro-organisms, it is far from dead. The entire diplotelmic bog structure – its depth, shape and development – is the outcome of biological processes akin to organic growth. In short, bogs are alive, dynamic and ever-changing, but very slowly.[2]

By a happy accident of arithmetical convenience, bogs lay down fresh peat, like growth rings on a tree, at a rate of about a millimetre a year. (It is why, in the context of this landscape, I alternate between the imperial and metric systems.) Bogs are thus timekeepers, and in a manner readily assimilable by us. A 10-metre thick blanket bog has been growing for the last ten millennia, and almost since the end of the last ice age.

It means that as you walk through mire landscapes and come to a sheer peat bank a metre deep (3.3 ft) at the sides of the track, it is a straightforward calculation that you are looking at the last 1,000 years. In the vertical column of that humble earth you may read the decades and centuries like words on a page. Once you understand a little of this extraordinary process, you are always aware of time as one of its creative dimensions. You can intuit both the bog's venerable condition and, in turn, plot your own modest span in relation to it. Bogs swallow you down in more ways than one.

It is worth noting here that the word 'bog' itself is cognate *not* with a barren waste or stinking cesspool or, even less, with some treacherous morass like the Grimpen Mire in Conan Doyle's *The Hound of the Baskervilles*. Bog comes from a Gaelic word for 'soft', and its essential precondition is water. Bog softness is made both of and by liquid. In fact, it is the stock cliché of bog talk that the whole thing contains fewer solids than a mug of milky cocoa. The layers of accumulated peat in the catotelm are made up of 94 per cent water and just 6 per cent solids. It is for this reason that peat shrinks rapidly when it dries and, in turn, why the land surface at Holme Fen in Cambridgeshire fell by 13 feet (3.96 m) after it was drained in 1851.

Most commentators emphasise the unfixed, quaking qualities of bogs as you tramp across them, but what strikes me is not the instability, but their remarkable firmness. Bogs let us all walk on water.

Very occasionally they can swell up in conditions of intense rainfall until their watery bowels can hold no more. Then the whole thing ruptures and spews out hundreds of thousands of tons of liquefied peat, in an event known as a 'bog burst'. One such incident occurred on the Isle of Lewis six days before I was born, in November 1959. The deluge caused the drainage of an entire loch, and it was so powerful it was assumed to be the impact of a meteorite.

The source of the water that leads to bog formation accounts for some of the more complex taxonomy associated with it. As a land form it is inevitably partial to places where surface water collects naturally. Localities that give rise to a high water-table, such as depressions or extensive flat areas, including coastal plains, are known as topogenous bogs. The peat formations in the Lincolnshire and Cambridgeshire Fens are of this kind.* If water is channelled by sloping ground into a particular localised track or area, then the resulting formation is called a soligenous bog. Often the two forms intersect and coalesce.

My favourite among the categories, however, is ombrogenous bog. It describes areas of mire that are rain-born and rain-fed. They flourish in districts that have an average of 160 wet days a year, a minimum precipitation of 1,000 mm (39 in) and a mean temperature of less than 15°C in the warmest months.[3] It is the category that occurs most frequently in Britain's north-west, but especially in Caithness and Sutherland, in the area that Derek Ratcliffe described at the start of this chapter and which he christened the Flow Country.

At 4,000 square kilometres (1,500 square miles) this is among the largest continuous areas of blanket bog in the world. The default comparison is with the great regions of polar tundra further north but, while these parts of northern Scotland are almost as close to the Arctic Circle as they are to London, there are fundamental distinctions in the environmental factors creating the two landscapes. The northern tundras actually experience remarkably little rainfall: their wetness is a product of shallow meltwaters held at the surface by subterranean layers of arctic permafrost. The Flow Country, meanwhile, results from waterlogged surfaces gener-

---

* These lowland bogs or fens are distinct from the bogs of the Scottish north-west, however, because the ground water is often base-rich (neutral or alkaline) and the vegetation is usually dominated by sedges, tall herbs and reed, rather than by sphagnum mosses.

ated by cool wet oceanic conditions that have persisted in the region since about 500 BC, in a period that is known as the Sub-Atlantic.[4]

The dark, heavy qualities of the very word *ombrogenous* seem able to conjure the default weather of the Flow Country whatever the season: the soft grey *smoor* layered over a misted brown plain. A handy technological index of the place is that as you drive through its oozing sameness, having the windscreen wipers neither on, nor switched off, fully masters the prevailing conditions. The Flows are often some mid-meteorological ground between wet and dry. *Dreich* is the word my Orcadian wife Mary would use for its temper.

My first encounter with the Flow Country was because of Mary. In the December of 1983 I hitchhiked to Orkney from Derbyshire to spend New Year with her on the island where she was born, North Ronaldsay. A single lucky lift took me from Knutsford to Perth but, marooned at year's end on the latter's outskirts, I was eventually obliged to catch a train to Wick for the flight to Orkney. Once north of Inverness the single-track line followed a picturesque route by the North Sea until, at Helmsdale, it took a curious inland detour, wending westwards away almost from my destination, before it eventually turned back towards Wick and the topmost corner of Britain. The whole of that last leg was across pure bog.

At the time I had no idea I was passing through a place called the Flow Country, nor, for many years, did I even know that it had such a title. It seemed too featureless, too anonymous, to have a separate name or identity. Over the years, as we headed back as a family to Orkney, we stopped on various occasions, and once stayed overnight in a lodge that billed itself as the most remote in Britain. Its isolation turned out to be almost its only quality. It was a grim, comfortless place at the end of a track beneath a hill slope enfolded in low cloud, amid an immense and palpable solitude. Later, as we lay abed in our spartan room, the blurry half-light of the Celtic summer veiled from us by the thinnest of net curtains, we could still feel the great muffled presence of the bog beyond. Incessant rain clattered at the windows in the night so that at times it felt as if we might no longer be attached to terra firma. Come dawn we would rise to find ourselves adrift at sea.

Come the morning, however, and, like all naturalists who know themselves to be in an area famous for wildlife, I went out in anticipation of what I might find. Eventually I arrived on the shores of a mist-veiled water called Badanloch where, despite the claggy August cold and a coat and hat and jumper sleeves pulled down as far as my fingertips, the midges assailed me in smothering hordes. I recall them particularly ravaging my forehead, inside the cockles of my ears, the corners of my eyes and down my upper arms. I am long accustomed to midges, but nothing from my northern-upland childhood had prepared me for such pestilential numbers. I lifted binoculars to scan the loch for the divers or scoters that might breed in the area, but I could bear their plague for seconds only, before reclaiming the sanctity of the car's interior. Later in the morning as we sailed to Stromness from Thurso, I found my hands and wrists were a rash of continuous bites.

The one reward of the outing was to see a place more dissolved in liquid than I had ever known. The most compelling details were the after-effects of the deluge. The vegetation was weighted and fringed with multiple drops of moisture, and in aggregate the grassy banks looked as if some weird rain-plant had suddenly fountained out of the ground overnight and set blooms of a billion coruscating beads of water. To walk through it was to be soaked instantaneously. Each boot-fall across open ground left its semi-circular puddle in the surface water-table. I wrote about it later in the *Guardian*. 'To risk environmental heresy,' I suggested, 'it's the only British landscape that I have enjoyed driving through as much as walking in. It gave to the bog's eternal stasis a human being's necessary if feeble sense of forward momentum, like a tiny vessel in an ocean of land.'[5]

*

In a new year in a different season I went back to tackle the great RSPB landholdings in the Flow Country from a northerly direction. Down from my coastal digs through Achvarasdal and then Shebster, cutting right to Broubster and Shurrery, I then drove as far as Shurrery Lodge and parked. The approach track to the Forsinard reserve cuts over the northern edge of Blàr Dearg and then skirts the southern slopes of Beinn nam Bad Mór. Finally it rose to let me look across, under high cloud and bright skies, the largest, most un-British landscape I have ever seen in my life. There was nothing but more and more of the same brown ground on which I stood, yet away it flowed from me, for five, ten, maybe fifteen miles in all its oceanic sameness. How could this be, I wondered, on the same island as Claxton, or, more bizarre, the Strand and Pall Mall?

Teasing out the continental quality of the Flow Country, I concluded that there are two interlocking factors. The northern half of our islands is full of places with high relief and prospects of mountain scenery. Precious few, however, are as level or quietly rolling, as uniformly coloured and as vast in scale as the panorama south of Beinn nam Bad Mór. The view reminded me not of the montane north but of the desert south. I've seen such bleached and featureless expanses in Jordan or Morocco. Nor am I alone in this sensation of its immense foreignness. Two ecologists who know it better than almost anyone, Richard Lindsay and Des Thompson, have described it as 'a huge plain resembling the limitless grasslands of Inner Mongolia. Its surface is as restless as the sea, because beneath the steady wind, the short sward of grasses and sedges constantly sways in a relentlessly renewed pattern.'[6]

The other element that smacks of Mongolia perhaps is its silence. Key into any British place and somewhere in the sum of its parts – the troposphere overhead, or even from the audible margins beyond the physical horizon – one has the infrasound, the white noise, of human traffic, either from cars or aeroplanes or some other internal combustion engine. On the slopes of Beinn nam Bad Mór the quietness was a plastic and tangible presence. We were all steeped in its immense clarity: the breeze, the songs of the birds, the slow-breathing bog, my own heartbeat.

There was a sense not of self-conscious isolation in it, but of being enwrapped like everything in its strangely comforting totality. There were skylarks sizzling and, overhead, ravens rolled out their calls as they rowed high across the heavens, and somewhere out on that burnt-brown plain were golden plovers singing sadly – the sweet music rising and falling – to their own melancholic home. Like a semi-permeable membrane the silence filled in behind this glorious music. Its vastness did not belittle the constituent parts of the soundscape: rather the songs of the birds swelled up to fill it and each of us was enlarged by the same creative process.

The extraordinary thing about walking in such stillness is that you are somehow liberated from the inner ear's relentless motorway of random thoughts to dwell on the qualities of the bog itself, which all seem to trend towards paradox. Reason is somehow unmade in bog. For is this not a landscape composed of water, and water translated into land? As I wandered further into its midst, I composed my own haiku to try to reconcile the contradictions.

> Peat is made of moss,
> And moss is grown from sunlight.
> Is earth, therefore, sky?

Bog looks the simplest and even the dullest of places but it is, in truth, among the most complex of land forms. It might appear bleak or desolate, but the whole thing is a living and breathing organism. Often one thinks of it as empty, but it is rich in life. The Flows hold some of the most important and largest breeding populations of upland birds in Britain. They look so anonymous, amorphous, so without feature or tangible part on which our minds can gain purchase, yet they are actually a precision mechanism, a slow-dripping chronometer archiving its own history in minute increments of peat. Every day is logged in that substrate, should you care to look, at a rate of 2.7 micrometres of new earth.

I can understand why bogs might appeal to poets. I'm thinking especially of Seamus Heaney, for whom bog held a central imaginative place from the very start of his career. It is there, for instance, in the single most-loved Heaney poem, 'Digging', from his first collection *Death of a Naturalist*. We shouldn't be surprised. He was bog-born and bog-raised in Northern Ireland, growing up near Castledawson and within walking distance of the great peat landscapes surrounding both Lough Neagh and Lough Beg. His life on a local farm became one of the great themes for all his poetry. In 'Digging' he writes about peat as the family's key source of fuel, and links the physical prowess of his father and grandfather in their handling of the turf-cutting spade, to his own practice as a poet excavating those same childhood landscapes with his pen.

The most important of the verses on this subject are known simply as 'the bog poems', and appear in his collections *Wintering Out* ('The Tollund Man') and *North* (e.g. 'Bog Queen', 'The Grauballe Man', 'Punishment', 'Strange Fruit' and 'Kinship'). All of these, as well as other parts of Heaney's poetry, are lovingly attentive to the physico-chemical properties of bog and especially to its astonishing preservative powers.

For the catotelm conserves not just the remains of sphagnum moss in its anaerobic tomb: it also resists the decomposition of any organic materials that somehow find their way into the watery depths. Bog oaks have been retrieved from the rotting peat of the Cambridgeshire Fens that are many thousands of years old. Yet the timber is still perfectly fresh and sound and can even be worked by a sculptor. I know this because I have on my desk, watching me as I write these words, a wonderful thousand-year-old bog-oak rook, carved by the artist Claire Guest. In Heaney's poem 'Bogland' he recalls how hundred-year-old butter has been retrieved still 'salty and white' despite the mire's enveloping black liquor.

The key bog poems were written about the time of or shortly after the publication of an international bestseller called *The Bog People: Iron Age Man Preserved* (1965, and translated into English in 1969), by the rather appropriately named P. V. Glob. Heaney was presumably captivated by this Danish academic's account of almost intact Neolithic human remains that were retrieved from mires in central Denmark. They included one eventually known as Tollund Man, who is perhaps the best-preserved of all ancient human corpses, and who had been lifted from peat diggings near the town of Silkeborg in 1950. Other finds in the same region included the so-called Grauballe Man and a female corpse that was initially believed to be Queen Gunhild, both of which inspired separate Heaney poems.

What was striking about many of these pre-Christian corpses was that they bore evidence of ritualised slaughter. Some had had their faces or heads crushed with blunt weapons, or they carried visible wounds where their throats had been slashed prior to burial. Tollund Man, for example, was disinterred with the rope still intact about his neck, which was assumed to have been used to hang or strangle him. Heaney traded on the historical examples of quasi-judicial or, at least, socially condoned killings to explore the murderous tribal exchanges which convulsed Northern Ireland at the time the poems were written.

For all its contemporary political resonances, what captivates me most about the poetry is the way the language re-enacts the processes of transformation as body and bog coalesce. In 'Bogland', which pre-dates publication of the poems on the Danish bodies, Heaney suggested how the ground itself is 'kind, black butter/Melting and opening underfoot'. The word that really arrests you is 'kind'. Who would think of a desolate and inhuman habitat as somehow yielding and generous? Yet at the heart of all the verse is an indigenous Irishman's recognition of bog's original sense in Gaelic. Bog is 'soft' ground. He goes on in the poems to develop the interplay of catotelm and human corpse as a mutual blending, one into the other, until it is depicted as a full-blown loving and erotic relationship.* In 'Tollund Man', a 2,400-year-old Neolithic person, with his unforgettable look of quiet repose upon his astonishingly intact and still-lifelike face, is reconfigured as a bridegroom to a goddess whose 'dark juices' swallow him down until he is turned into the parchment-skinned body of an ancient saint.

What Heaney's bog poetry does best for me is to recover not just the elemental closeness of the human body to the bog at our feet, but the quiet, sensual, slow ways of the stuff. For bog cannot be rushed in any sense. Even coming to appreciate it personally has been a 30-year-long process. Its revelations, like its appeals, are hard won. Bog works upon the imagination in increments. My discoveries have all taken time, as the weight of evidence gathers patiently like sediment and the known facts acquire the power of lived truth.

*

---

* One wonders if Heaney's imagery was partly inspired by his readings of the Danish poet Steen Steensen Blicher and his 1841 poem 'Queen Gunhild', in which Blicher wrote:

> Now you lie naked, shrivelled and foul
> With a bald skull for a head
> Blacker far than the oaken stake
> That wed you to the bog.[7]

Two truths came to me in one memorable day in late May the year after my walk south from Shurrery Lodge. On that occasion I wanted to see Forsinard from the south and from above. The tallest relief in the southern sector of the reserve is a conical hill, whose beautiful Gaelic name is Ben Griam Beg. At 1,900 ft (580 m) it commands a similar panorama to that obtained on Beinn nam Bad Mór to the north, but just from the opposite direction. From Loch Shurrery, in fact, Ben Griam Beg is the dominant peak looming over the bog plain 15 miles away.

To reach the summit it was a pleasant walk along a track to the single isolated croft at the foot of the hill. Despite the sunshine and quiet air my perpetual distrust of Caithness weather meant I had ventured forth with thick jumper, waterproofs, gloves, scarf and woolly hat. During the final ascent to a saddle just below the top of Ben Griam Beg I was obliged to strip down, layer by layer, until I finished the climb in shirtsleeves. At the brow, just below this lower summit, I was breathless and overheated. Then all changed as I breasted the crown.

Over that whole hill a north wind hammered us all down and sent Atlantic clouds high overhead, one white galleon after another, racing hard to the east. It flattened the vegetation to the curve of the slope. I slumped under the lea of a lichen-smothered monolith and pulled all my clothes back on, layer by layer, and pressed in tight to the ground and tried to get out my map to match the names to the places that I could see beyond. But it was a comical wrestle with the power of that wind. As I folded the thing to the correct section, which involved unfurling the whole flapping sheet, it was like wash day in the backyard on a gusty spring morn. In the end I could manage only two small faces of the OS 10 clamped taut between the opposed pull of two gloved hands.

What compelled me more than anything in those moments of intimacy, moulded hard to the hillside, was the cushion of vegetation against which my whole body was weighted. I gradually realised that I was lying on a garden of montane flowers and shrubs. Here in one square turf – my friend Tony Hare would have called it a 'world' – were crowberry, bearberry and mountain bearberry, common heather, cloudberry and sphagnum mosses and lichens. As is the way with montane shrubs, it was a wonderfully air-filled, soft-sprung mattress, and had the sun been hot and the place 15 degrees warmer it would have made a perfect bed to sleep on.

As my head lay in intimate connection with this pillow I began to follow the strands of bearberry in their creeping habits over the ground and unpick their entwinings with all the other plants in the ground-hugging tangle. Given that it was blasted even on this mild late-May afternoon – and I tried to conjure my world of shrubs and lower plants in winter when the gales were murderous and ice-edged and the days two-thirds shorter – I realised that one had to see its life through all seasons.

It dawned on me then that this was not a paltry, inch-high lawn, a temporary bed for a passing stranger: it was a full-canopied Lilliputian forest, luxuriant and complete, but shaped and tended by the savage Atlantic gales and the rain and the northern sun and the niggardly acidic soil and the deer's grinding molars. It was all this hillside would ever be or ever wanted to be in such conditions. It had all of life's indivisible blend of charity and meanness. It was clothed in its own full-blown regalia.

In this country we are accustomed to places with little woodland. After all, we have one of the lowest percentages of tree cover of any nation in Europe. There are over 40 million acres of agricultural fields, many of which are now devoid of trees, but an entire panorama without hedge or coppice of any kind is virtually unknown in these islands. Rarer still is the place where trees *naturally* do not occur. Because most of Britain still aspires to be a forest, and if it were ever left to get along without us, that is what our country would do: re-cloak almost its entire body in woods.

But not here. Not these blanket bogs, and not Ben Griam Beg. They possess what is known as a 'post-glacial climax vegetation'.[8] 'On the extensive flows of east Sutherland and Caithness', reads a major report on the area from 1988:

> the record in the peat itself demonstrates irrefutably that a treeless blanket bog landscape barely distinguishable from that of today has existed for at least the past 4,000 years ... There are few places in Britain now where it is possible to look across a landscape and share much the same view as Neolithic man. Up to 1979, this was still possible over much of Caithness and east Sutherland.[9]

On that day I finally realised the meaning of all this. I was seeing the bog through Stone Age eyes.

From this prospect, which must have stretched over 100 miles from north to south, I also understood fully what we have done, and what we had intended to do to this treeless place. Below where I was sitting on Ben Griam Beg was a complex mosaic of tree cover. The regimented lines of lodgepole pine in the foreground formed thick green blocs, but any colour diminished with distance, just as all complexity was lost through foreshortening, until it melded on a far horizon into a solid black shroud lying on the land. It was made entirely of non-native conifer.

Most of the plantations I could see had been sown in the early 1980s. In order to grow them in such unsuitable ground, the operators had first to drain and plough the bog. They used the latest, massive, ground-cutting machines with new super-wide apical track shoes that could virtually skate over water. In the process the equipment scoured out deep trenches where no straight line had been known, except perhaps in an old peat-digger's plot. The new incisions, however, were so deep and so precisely aligned that when he saw them from the air for the first time, the television presenter and RSPB president Magnus Magnusson likened them to the scars left by some god who had scraped their claws across the surface of the Earth.[10]

At that time vast areas of the Flows were being sketched out for further development in this manner. Looking ahead half a century, a spokesperson for private forestry in Scotland suggested that 'In the year 2026, I do not foresee blocks of forestry on a moorland landscape, but the stark moorlands of SSSIs and common grazings isolated in a forest scene.'[11]

Had they had their way, in the fullness of time, these tree-growing professionals and their business financiers would have covered most of the Flows in a vast county-sized rectilinear plantation. In keeping with its constitution, the bog was brewing a crisis, but slowly. A furore of human controversy would eventually be poured onto all this watery silence, and in the catotelm the bog would lay down an archive of its unfolding.

19

A LOATHSOMENESS OF CONIFERS

In the last 100 years the woodlands of Britain have probably undergone more change than in any century since the time of the Romans. And those developments have brought profoundly mixed fortunes. As Oliver Rackham noted in his classic study *Ancient Woodland*, 'For a thousand years England, at least, had less woodland than most European countries and has taken correspondingly more care of its woods.'[1] In the twentieth century that state of affairs was substantially reversed.

The once cared-for places, especially the ecologically important and largely deciduous ancient woods, were felled at an unprecedented rate.*

---

* Ancient woodland is a precise term used by ecologists to denote tree cover that was in existence before 1600 (or 1750 in Scotland). The benchmark date by no means indicates the actual age of any of our ancient woods. Some of them were probably working environments by Roman times. Most, if not all, were managed according to a well-established system known as 'coppice with standards'. Contrary to popular belief, deciduous trees don't generally die once felled. Instead they throw out a fountain spray of new growth from the ground stump, or stool. These pole-like lengths of re-growth are harvested on a rotation of 4–20 years and once supplied a multitude of purposes including firewood and charcoal. Managed in this way, some coppice stools can continue their productive lives well beyond the usual span of the free-growing tree. Some ash stools in Oliver Rackham's beloved Bradfield Woods, for example, are 1,000 years old and among the oldest living things in Britain. Yet they still produce a good crop. 'Standards', on the other hand, were trees left to acquire their customary height and size and then felled irregularly to supply larger timber cuts, such as the major roof joists in house construction. The system of coppice with standards is still used, and has probably been operated in British woods for 6,000 years.

One commentator thought that more native woodland had been destroyed in England in the thirty years after the Second World War than in the previous four centuries.[2] By the end of the clearance programme the country had lost about half of all the habitat. However, the destruction would be matched by a period of intensive re-stocking that would expand the nation's standing timber by millions of acres. Few of the new plantations, unfortunately, had anything like the wild-life value of the old grubbed-out woods.

The turn-around in these woodland affairs, like so many of the changes to the British landscape, had its origins in military conflict. Our chronic deficiency in woodland meant that the British had been importing their timber requirements since the thirteenth century. Indeed, during the First World War German submarines had sunk so much of the country's merchant fleet that the authorities feared it could threaten the entire war effort. Without lumber to create the necessary pit props in the coal mines, Britain risked running out of the fuel that drove the nation's industrial-military complex. It was said that in the four years of fighting the country had felled a sixth – 450,000 acres – of its entire woodland cover to meet its expanded needs.[3]

In the aftermath of war the Lloyd George coalition government responded by creating the Forestry Commission (FC) and backed it with fresh legislation, a specific Forestry Act in 1919. The goal behind both measures was to prevent such timber shortages ever recurring. Its long-term impact was a tree-planting programme that would eventually leave almost no part of the nation unaffected. In fact, some places were entirely – radically – transformed in short order. Among them was Breckland, an area of largely treeless heath infamous for its infertility, its shifting sandy soils and its prodigious populations of rabbits, on the borderlands between Suffolk and Norfolk. Within two generations a region that had once been likened to the deserts of Arabia became a densely packed 47,000-acre plantation of largely Corsican pines. It is still so today.

Unfortunately, before Britain could reap the benefits of the inter-war afforestation it was overtaken by yet another major conflict. On this occasion the drive to keep the nation in pit props and other essential wood products – including the Sitka-spruce panels used to build the super-fast, super-light de Havilland Mosquito bombers – was said to have caused the loss of a further 500,000 acres of standing timber.[4]* The time was ripe for radical new measures. Forthwith, the desire for trees unleashed in 1919 evolved after the Second World War into a veritable obsession. It paralleled precisely the singlemindedness that was then overtaking agriculture, for, as Oliver Rackham pointed out, modern forestry largely means 'the extension of arable farming to the growing of trees'.[5] Everything now was subservient to productivity and output.

Deciduous species, and especially the oak tree, may have been the stuff out of which the people of these islands had carved their sense of national identity, but from here on the nation's private landowners-cum-foresters, backed by the Forestry Commission, would hear of nothing but conifers. Conifers were the future. The logic justifying them was simple and seductive. By volume, hardwoods such as our native oaks, beech or ash yield over the same period of growth about a half or even a third of the timber supplied by the faster-growing conifers. For the new forest managers it was not just any conifers either, but non-native species largely from the American north-west, such as Sitka spruce, Douglas fir and lodgepole pine.

The tenacious evergreens would adapt to the wettest climate and even, in the case of the last species, to the most waterlogged ground. In the eyes of the early Forestry Commissioners such hardihood made the American imports perfect for their needs. Because modern forestry was not intended for the country's mild southern lowlands – the traditional locale of both its ancient woods and its cornfields – rather the

---

* It is worth noting that Oliver Rackham rejected the claims of major woodland loss in the 40 years from 1914, and suggested that these bouts of wartime clearance in Britain did little more than make up for a lack of felling in the half century prior to 1914. As he repeatedly argued – without, it has to be said, truly denting the prevailing public myth that felling equals clearance – cutting trees down does not kill them, it simply allows them to re-grow. See his *Woodlands*, p. 459. What truly destroyed the woods was the Forestry Commission's programme of grubbing them out.

point now was to avoid competition with agriculture, and thus take the conifers to Britain's windswept and largely treeless hill country to the north and west.

In the post-war period there is something brutally impressive about the pace and efficiency of the Forestry Commission's operation. At the end of the 1950s it had planted more than a million acres.[6] By 1985, almost 5 million acres of the country – a tenth of its land area – were under such plantations. All but 2 per cent of them comprised exotic conifers. The Forestry Commission alone accounted for 2.9 million acres of the total, making it the single largest landholding institution in the country, with a territory greater even than its monarch.[7]* From the very beginning, there had been opposition to the insensitivities associated with this industrialised tree production, especially in scenically renowned regions such as the Lake District.

Dark cubist blocs of spruce or pine – for which the Welsh author and environmentalist William Condry coined the collective noun 'a loathsomeness of conifers' – intruded their alien geometry upon the nation's scenery from Cornwall to Carmarthen to Caithness.[8] In the 1960s the FC tried to soften some of the opposition by more sensitive measures that reflected the recommendations of the landscape architect Dame Sylvia Crowe. She proposed that trees should be planted in alignment with natural contours and kept off watercourses, while edges and more sensitive parts should be fringed with attractive deciduous species or larch trees. There was also a programme of measures to accommodate walkers and visitors, including picnic tables, guided walks, trails and campsites.[9] None of this largely cosmetic change, however, did much to assuage environmental criticism.

The numbers were unassailable. The two native deciduous species of oak in Britain have been recorded to support an invertebrate fauna

---

* In the post-Thatcher years of privatisation, the Forestry Commission was the object of regular government sell-offs, until its massive fiefdom was much reduced. Even so, in 2011 it was still the largest single land manager in Britain, with 637,000 acres. The Crown, in comparison, has a combined estate of 283,000 acres including the Duchy of Cornwall (133,000 acres), the Duchy of Lancaster (50,000 acres), Balmoral (50,000 acres) and Sandringham (20,000 acres).

of no fewer than 423 species. Spruce, meanwhile, is home to 37. In many ways, the results were worse than those figures suggest, because of the stocking methods. The conifer saplings were placed on ploughed ridges six to eight feet apart, and when they linked arms overhead the space between became unpassable, while the overarching plantation thicket was soon so dense and dark as to obliterate any ground flora beneath a sterile carpet of needles.

It was soon discovered that conifers also scavenge atmospheric pollution and concentrate such elements in their needles. Roderick Leslie, a former chief executive of Forest Enterprise (the business arm of the FC), fairly points out that, while the conifers were often blamed, it was industry that created the pollution, not the trees themselves.[10] Yet no moral niceties alter the fact that the trees pass on their pollution load to the surrounding drainage systems, so that some rivers rising in conifer country could contain concentrations of acid that are fourteen times higher than previously.[11]* And if the foresters could not be blamed for atmospheric toxins such as sulphur dioxide, they were indisputably responsible for the fertilisers and pesticides that also leached into the hydrological systems where none had ever been used before.

The loss of deciduous woods normally took place in a separate part of the country to that undergoing expansion of conifers. There was however, one form of operation where the two processes came into devastating alignment. The Forestry Commission may have been oriented towards the uplands, but it did not completely abandon tree-planting in the south. There it was regular practice to operate within existing woodland boundaries, with the foresters ringbarking and poisoning deciduous trees or clearing them wholesale with mechanical

---

* Another key effect on rivers from forestry ploughs was the rise downstream in sediment loads, sometimes to as much as 50 times greater than before the establishment of a plantation. It could take years for a river system to settle down, and this was often at a level four times higher than the original. It should be noted, however, that the issue has abated in some river systems because of small improvements in water quality and larger changes in air quality, as a result of the historical removal of industrial pollutants at source. In turn, this has had beneficial effects on wild salmon or trout stocks, which plummeted in many areas that were heavily influenced by conifer plantations.[12]

diggers. Then they would re-stock the resulting *tabula rasa* with the anointed evergreens. Even the National Trust had been persuaded at times to take part in this particular form of vandalism. For that is exactly what it is. While it may have made sense on some Forestry Commission balance sheet – and, as we will see, only when major subsidies from the public purse had been included – in environmental terms it was an act of desecration comparable with dismantling an ancient library to supply oneself with kindling.[13]

As with agricultural intensification, the appetites of those committed to afforestation seemed only to increase with their consumption. In *Forestry in Crisis*, Steve Tompkins maps out the arithmetic of this expansionist programme. The original 1919 goal for the Forestry Commission had been 1.8 million acres of plantation, but in 1943 it was increased to 3 million, and then 4.4 million in 1977.[14] By the last date, and in an era of intercontinental nuclear missiles, the whole chain of argument that posited timber for coal for war was obsolete. Yet the foresters sidestepped any resulting inconvenience and adopted a new mantra. The aim was not war supplies but national self-sufficiency, irrespective of the fact that the country's existing 5 million coniferised acres were then meeting just 12 per cent of the country's needs.[15]

Successive governments had been susceptible to the arguments made in a Forestry Commission report, and then in a second study by a group of forestry academics at the Centre for Agricultural Strategy (CAS). Based on an analysis of historical timber prices and the size of UK timber imports, the latter had predicted in 1980 that global timber stocks would fall while international demand would continue to rise. They suggested that by 2025 international timber prices would have increased by 30–135 per cent relative to other commodity prices.*

This analysis, with its predictions of 'soaring import bills', became part of a default case for ever-more afforestation in Britain. Unfortunately, a second wider study that paid detailed attention to both the effects

---

* A team of economic consultants subsequently judged the higher estimate of timber-price increases in the study to be 'a highly unusual outcome, which is almost without parallel in the price of any major basic commodity'. [Tompkins, 1989, p. 163.]

of inflation and the value of sterling relative to other currencies, showed that between 1960 and 1978 UK timber imports had actually fallen in value by 45 per cent. Furthermore, successive predictions made by the Forestry Commission about UK demands for wood products were shown to be consistently well above the actual figures, while a UN investigation into global timber demand concluded that there would be no such shortage, and foresaw only moderate international growth in consumption.[16] One of the original authors of the 1980 CAS report eventually disavowed the document's conclusions, but the foresters' rhetoric of world shortage and rising import bills was what carried the day on British timber policy.

The new Thatcher government soon removed all consideration of a hypothetical total afforested area and replaced it with an annual quota for new plantations of 50,000–60,000 acres. Through the 1980s the figures were revised upwards, until the afforestation target was 81,500 acres annually, an area of trees that would have covered nine-tenths of the county of Rutland. However, as Marion Shoard points out, had it been implemented as originally conceived, then by the middle of this century such a policy would have blanketed an area the size of Kent, Lancashire, Nottinghamshire, Northamptonshire and Warwickshire combined.[17]

In the golden years of post-Thatcherite privatisation it was not the state-owned Forestry Commission that was encouraged to lead the charge for trees: it was independent business. And, as in agriculture, what ultimately helped to unleash their appetites for evergreens was not any intrinsic profitability in timber, but the money to be made from tax concessions and subsidies paid out by government. It had long been the case that in financial terms the commercial growing of trees had been more art than science, and more guesswork than hard calculation. To ease the unforeseen market changes that were at play with a product that took thirty to forty years to mature, the authorities had offered inducements to private foresters.

By the time of the crisis in the Flow Country, a number of wealthy investors had developed securing these tax breaks into a fine art. It was based on a loophole first spotted in 1952 that had allowed newly afforested land to be assessed under a part of the tax code known as Schedule D. This enabled a person with substantial tax liabilities arising from another enterprise to redirect monies otherwise destined for the Inland Revenue to underwrite the start-up costs in a new plantation. Above and beyond the tax concessions, the private investor was also entitled to substantial grants issued by the Forestry Commission. Between them, the offset contributions made up as much as 70 per cent of the entire expenditure required to establish new trees, while the ongoing costs of management could be similarly discounted against other taxable incomes.

Eventually, independent forestry companies undertook on behalf of individual investors the land purchase, the technical paperwork and the supply of labour on the ground. Later the owner could further enhance their returns by a final legal manoeuvre. The one drawback of registering lands under Schedule D was that owners were eventually liable for tax on profits from any mature timber. However, existing British woodlands were normally registered under a separate taxable regime known as Schedule B, and this system did allow an owner to fell and sell timber free of tax on any profits.[18]

Thus the new breed of investors usually sold their land outright before the plantation matured, or they re-registered it in the name of a spouse or offspring, or an independent trust, at which point the woods could revert to the more generous Schedule B. This late transfer meant that an investor could enjoy tax-deductible expenses in the early days, then tax-free profits once time had come to harvest the trees. In their relationship with the Inland Revenue it was a case of tails I win and, later, heads you lose.

For almost two generations forestry became an enterprise not truly about growing trees, but of strategic tax avoidance and substantial profits underwritten by government grant. As in so many recent trans-actions that involve land – and the parallels with subsidised agriculture are precise and obvious – money was transferred from the public purse into the hands of those who were already well off, and, in some cases, extremely rich absentee landowners (in 1986, for example, it was found that of Sutherland's new brand of foresters, almost three-quarters had addresses in London or the Home Counties).[19] It amounted to a form of modern feudalism, whereby the privileged few received tribute from the ignorant or, at least, the ill-informed many, with the government serving as middleman.[20]

In comparison to the rest of Europe, in Scotland, according to the author and Green MSP Andy Wightman, this has led to 'by far the most concentrated pattern of private forest ownership [being] dominated by large holdings and by far the lowest proportion of the population involved in owning forests'.[21] In Europe, trees have traditionally been the business of a much wider cross-section of the community, including in many instances local and municipal cooperatives. The largest Finnish producer, for example, with a turnover of €8.4 billion, belongs to 130,000 forest owners. In Scotland, in contrast, forestry is the preserve of the state, landed estates and wealthy investors. A detailed analysis of eight countries – Austria, Belgium, France, Hungary, Latvia, Lithuania, Norway, Poland and Slovakia – shows that forest holdings above 124 acres are 55 per cent of the Scottish total, while the equivalent European figure is 1.6 per cent. Meanwhile parcels of less than 2.5 acres make up 60 per cent of the European woods, but just 6.3 per cent in Scotland.

Not only are trees concentrated in the hands of the few, but that minority also does everything it can to obscure the pattern. In Sweden there are detailed inventories of forest owners, including their gender, age and place of residence. In Britain, the Forestry Commission collects minimal information and publishes nothing.[22] Part of the way in which foresters have perpetuated the arrangement is an effective, highly aggressive challenge to any kind of probe or query of their fiscal self-interest. In 1978 a shadow Conservative minister caught the full tenor of the attitude when he spoke at a timber growers' AGM about the risk of forestry appearing to be a 'tax haven', lest it should, in his words, 'invite the attentions of the "*envious* and *malevolent*" [my italics]'.[23] No scope in this moral equation for any genuine inquiry into the full public costs of low-quality afforestation: opposition to it was motivated solely by outworn class resentments or, worse, by evil plain and simple.

Another strong suit of this vested interest had been its ability to lobby at the highest levels. Many of the personnel involved in private forestry are, or at least were, politically powerful, sometimes with an office in the House of Lords. Steve Tompkins, a lifelong forester himself, pointed to the special role previously played in the matter by the Forestry Commission. At the time of the Flow Country dispute it comprised two separate parts: Forest Enterprise, with responsibility for its own profitable timber production, and the Forest Authority, with a duty to oversee and regulate national tree-growing policy and practice. (In the early 1990s this latter component was transferred from the FC to the Department of Forestry.)

The double remit meant that the institution looked in two occasionally contradictory directions. It was a business and the business regulator. Added to this binary structure was the fact that its ranks, its various regional committees and its inner board of Forestry Commissioners were deeply entwined with those who worked for, or even owned, the various companies engaged in private forestry. Occasionally they were one and the same thing, and certainly they shared the same core values and attitudes. As Marion Shoard had pointed out, the government had almost always assumed that the national forestry agency was something best overseen by big landowners. After its creation in 1919, five of its seven leaders had been from the same background.[24]

The Forestry Commission could always use its intimate links to government personnel to further the strong financial self-interests of its wider community. Testament to its resilience in the face of public criticism was the organisation's survival despite two independent reports in 1972 and 1986 conducted respectively by the government's Treasury department and the National Audit Office (NAO). The first concluded that state-administered forestry was poor value for money, and its only justification was the generation of employment opportunities. These, however, could have been better delivered by other means.[25]

The soundness of the judgement was proved just fourteen years later, when the NAO's findings on the FC's economic performance were, if anything, worse. The average return on investment of 2.25

per cent was 7.75 per cent short of the norm expected of any public-sector trading operation. In some parts of its planting operations the FC yield was just 1.25 per cent.[26] On the tax allowances and public monies given to private investors, the NAO concluded that they were a subsidy 'which could only be justified in national economic terms if there were social benefits from the expansion of forestry'. What they meant by social benefits was the provision of jobs. Unfortunately for this argument, the report pointed out that private forestry was worse at generating employment than the Forestry Commission.[27]

It is a mark of how deeply entrenched the forestry lobby was in Britain's political-power structures that none of this halted upland afforestation. The tax dividends continued regardless, and prompted the private forestry outfits to look further and further north for fresh opportunity. By 1989, 90 per cent of all afforestation took place in Scotland, to which country the FC had moved its headquarters as early as 1975. It was not just the tax loopholes driving the speculation: there were also improvements in tractor technologies to enable timber planting or extraction even on the most unlikely slopes and bogs. There were further developments in planting regimes, using a cover crop of lodgepole pine to dry out the sodden mire and leave it relatively suitable for the marginally choosier, but more valuable, Sitka spruce.

The innovations enabled one company called Fountain Forestry to scout out areas previously dismissed in the trade as MAMBA – 'miles and miles of bugger all'. Notwithstanding any inaccessibility and apparent emptiness, some of these Scottish places were rich in wildlife and already designated as Sites of Special Scientific Interest. However, the Forestry Commission had previously refused to accept these conservation designations as a barrier to planting licences. Thus a series of test skirmishes on the issue was inevitable once the Nature Conservancy Council sought to check the unbridled development.

Among the most high-profile was a quarrel over a dramatic mountain place called Creag Meagaidh in Inverness-shire. It lay at the heart of an area beloved by botanists for its montane flora, and cherished by walkers for its impressive Munro, complete with a spectacular corrie, called Coire Ardair. And all of it was within easy reach of the A86 road between Kingussie and Fort William. Yet what gave final resonance to the case for protecting Creag Meagaidh was the fact that for twenty miles around it had been encircled by a dense conifer shroud.

Fountain Forestry had bought it in the early 1980s and promptly received approval and the offer of planting grants from FC that would have virtually obliterated Creag Meagaidh's slopes in Sitka spruce. The NCC challenged the decision and, after various compromise options were proposed and rejected, it bought the mountain and designated it a National Nature Reserve, having reimbursed Fountain Forestry with £430,000. This was £130,000 above the price the company had paid just two years earlier, and the increase was directly attributable to the inflationary power of the planting licences granted by the Forestry Commission.[28]

In many ways, it was the speed of the private operations that caught the conservationists off-guard. There was also another factor at play. Although the Nature Conservancy Council was waking up to the increased threat posed to Britain's upland landscapes by grim dark blanket afforestation, when the locus of discord moved 100 miles further north from Creag Meagaidh, into the last mainland counties of the British Isles, the environmentalists were not entirely sure what was at stake. But they had a strong hunch and they were catching up quickly.

If the word 'explorer' had any kind of meaning in Britain in the late twentieth century, then it might have been attached with an element of justification to the field ecologists who undertook the detailed investigation of those wide-open bogs. In the early 1980s the Nature Conservancy Council, under the direction of its chief scientist Derek Ratcliffe, had begun a five-year study of the Flows. One of his devoted footsoldiers, the ecologist Richard Lindsay, called them 'fire-brigade surveys', because they knew their work was sometimes only weeks or months ahead of the foresters' plough.[29]

Very often the only way to access the areas was on foot, and they were so remote from roads that they had to camp on the bog and stay for days to survey a peatland system, and then trek back out, only to repeat the process elsewhere. Who knows if any person had ever preceded their excursions, but Lindsay recalls how

Sometimes the experience was simply awful, with day after day of relentless, soaking, driving rain or thick, soaking cloud, but sometimes things were good, even extraordinary, and all the more richly memorable for that. One particular midsummer's eve amidst the Forsinard flows will stay with me forever – common snipe ... drumming, distant dunlin ... trilling and hoarse-whistling, a Merlin ... hunting below us, and a spectacular len-ticular cloud capping Ben Griam Beag. That very scene was to vanish the following year, replaced by ghastly deep furrows and seedling trees, and now all we have are the memories and data sheets recording what was lost.[30]

What this field work proved definitively was that the Flow Country was hugely important in a host of ways. For one thing, it turned out to be the largest relatively natural landscape left in a country where human impact has been almost universal. The over-used phrase for the place was 'Britain's last wilderness'. It was not only incorrect: it was potentially insulting to local people. For 'wilderness' conjured a place of wild beasts and 'savages'. In truth, people had been happily living in and working on the landscape for thousands of years. To them it was and is still home.

Most of them would probably acknowledge, however, that the trad-itional crofters' lifestyle treads lightly upon the region, with farms concentrated on the more fertile and productive ground, especially along the straths, as the river valleys are known. The population is also small and, in fact, smaller than it had once been.* For, like most Highland communities, they had themselves been the victim of clearances when

---

* At the time of the evictions the Duke of Sutherland owned the best part of the entire county and was Britain's largest landed magnate by area, owner of an aston-ishing 1,362,343 acres. In 1870 his estate yielded an annual income of £68,398, which had a purchasing power equivalent to £6 million today. Yet His Grace's ancestors had been keen to improve on these by converting the estate to sheep farming. One effect of this was to drive tenants out of the beautiful Strathnaver and re-settle them on the coast at Farr, squeezing thirty families onto an area previously occupied by twelve. The factors overseeing such work were apparently still notorious 150 years later.[31]

the nineteenth-century Dukes of Sutherland decided they wanted sheep rather than human tenants.

The Flow Country was not only our most extensive natural and *naturally treeless* landscape: it also turned out to be among the rarest forms of habitat that these islands possess. Blanket bog of this kind is found in remarkably few places worldwide. There are representative areas in the Pyrenees, in parts of western Norway, western Ireland and Iceland and, further afield, in the Canadian province of Labrador, in Russia's Kamchatka peninsula, in Alaska, the Falkland Islands and at South America's southern tip in Tierra del Fuego, with additional small patches in the Rwenzori Mountains of central Africa and in New Zealand. The entire total is just 38,600 square miles (24.7 million acres), and it has suffered mixed fortunes.

A country like Ireland, for example, had substantial areas totalling almost 3,000 square miles, but most of it had been lost by the 1980s to commercial peat digging or had been earmarked for further exploit-ation. Britain, on the other hand, was estimated to hold between a tenth and a seventh of the world total, more than any other country. More significant was the fact that the Sutherland and Caithness bogs were easily the most extensive and richest area, representing more than 1,500 square miles prior to afforestation.[32]

Another key revelation of the fire-brigade surveys centred on the ornithological significance of the Flow Country. In a way, it is easy to see how, hitherto, even environmentalists had underrated its ornitho-logical interest. For many of the birds are at low densities and many of the best bits of habitat lack even dirt tracks. It was only when a prolonged ecological audit had assembled a complete picture that conservationists grasped the truth. The Flows held one of the country's most important wader populations, as well as a wider avian assemblage that was typical of the Arctic tundra, except that these Scottish popu-lations were 500 miles further south, and its most southerly outpost in the entire northern hemisphere.

Most significant were the internationally important populations of greenshank (630 pairs), golden plover (3,980 pairs) and dunlin (3,830 pairs), with nationally important totals for common scoter, black- and red-throated divers, not to mention 5 per cent each of Britain's short-eared owls, peregrines, golden eagles and merlins. Perhaps the most critical finding of all, however, was that afforestation was already having a profoundly negative effect on them. The surveys conducted over the period 1979–1986 showed that some of the finest wader-breeding areas had already been ploughed, resulting in declines of up to 19 per cent in the three key species.[33]

This alone was grounds for a major campaign, but there was an additional complexion to the environmental argument. It wasn't just that the conifer schemes threatened the nation's last and least-altered landscape: this was a place for which we had international obligations. How could we make representations to Kenya for its government to protect that country's magnificent savanna landscapes with their extraordinary migrating megafauna, or urge India to safeguard its tigers in the subcontinental jungles if, when called upon to protect *our* most special places, we had covered them in an intensive monoculture? That very point was implicit in a statement produced by the International Mire Conservation Group – a worldwide consortium of peatland specialists from eight countries – which had held a field symposium in northern Scotland in 1986. It compared the importance of the Flow Country to that of the world's other outstanding natural places – the Serengeti and the South American rainforest.[34]

For the NCC, from its chairman down, the future course was plain. Yet it would also go a step further. A decade earlier its own blueprint for the British environment, *A Nature Conservation Review* (1977), had identified some of the finest representative parts of the Flow Country and earmarked these for protection. Now its officers adopted a different approach. Such was the very nature of a bog environment – its complex hydrography, its extremely low nutrient levels, with its specialised avifauna thinly distributed through all parts – that the NCC concluded that it should not and could not be treated as a cake to be divided. It was the totality of the place that mattered. A decision was taken to call for recognition and protection of the whole lot. It was all or nothing – a strategy fraught with risk.

20

THE MOST MASSIVE SINGLE LOSS OF IMPORTANT WILDLIFE HABITAT

Given the scale and frequency of disputes over land-use elsewhere in Britain, and given the remoteness of the Flow Country from mainstream national life and the public's almost total ignorance of the place until that moment, it seems ironic that it should have become the focus of such environmental controversy. However, 'the Battle of the Bogs', as it was widely known, resulted in a dispute that arguably did more to change the conservation scene in Britain than any other single event in the twentieth century.

A key trigger for the whole furore was a Nature Conservancy Council publication in 1987 entitled *Birds, Bogs and Forestry: The Peatlands of Caithness and Sutherland*. It was the culmination of all the research the organisation had initiated since the end of the 1970s. Despite the rather innocuous title and sober format, the report was probably the nearest thing to weaponised data that the NCC had ever issued.*

It reiterated all the arguments about the importance of the northern bogs. It stressed the threat from non-native conifer plantations and, as

---

* There was a fuller, more technical, though no less uncompromising, report entitled *The Flow Country: The Peatlands of Caithness and Sutherland* that appeared in 1988. Both made the same substantive case and are still crucial documents to understanding the entire debate and its consequences. An overlooked element in each was the remarkable photographs of the massive landscape changes, especially the rectilinear scars left by the ploughs as afforestation was inflicted on the area.

early as page 9, declared that government policy on upland afforestation had already caused 'the most massive single loss of important wildlife habitat in Britain since the Second World War'.[1] Just in case anyone missed the point, it was reasserted in the penultimate sentence to the entire document.

Yet there was an additional delayed charge buried on page 106. There, the report's authors wrote:

> The remaining extent of the Caithness and Sutherland peatlands as a whole should therefore be regarded as the desirable nature conservation area for its national and international importance. A significant and important fraction of the total has already been lost to afforestation in an extremely arbitrary and haphazard way … and there is no rational and scientific or conservation basis for making a further arbitrary selection from the remainder, to surrender additional areas to afforestation.[2]

This was uncompromising stuff – in fact, it was outright opposition to the official line – and not calculated to go down well with the NCC's political masters. Essentially it was saying that there was no scope for the usual British compromise: the one where you concede the construction of a reservoir and lose a tenth of a supremely rare habitat, then industry gives a £100,000 donation for ecologists to study the importance of the landscape thus diminished. Here the official environmental adviser to the government was arguing not just a case for protecting a substantial part: what it wished to establish was a moratorium on planting on any peatland habitat across 1,500 square miles of two counties.

In effect, the Battle of the Bogs was the first full articulation of landscape-scale conservation, a concept that now stands at the heart of so much modern action, and which is integral to the present 're-wilding' ideology. At that moment in its history the NCC had finally recognised the limitations of the SSSI system. The consequences of cherry-picking and protecting representative samples had led over the decades to an Indonesia-like archipelago in this country of nature-rich islands amid an increasingly uniform ocean of chemically treated mono-cultures. In such a marginally populated part of the country, and with one of the UK's most important landscapes at stake, the NCC had finally stood up to save at least one place relatively inviolate.

To underline the point, the study stressed how the International Union for the Conservation of Nature and Natural Resources (IUCN) had recommended that the NCC nominate the Flows as a UNESCO World Heritage Site. The area already qualified on all three key criteria. At that time there were but a handful of such places in Britain, and most that had been honoured were buildings (Durham Cathedral) or human artefacts (Stonehenge). Of natural landscapes, only St Kilda would be accorded the same prestigious status in that same year.

Yet for the Flow Country it was not to be, and even now its lack of recognition, and our apparent lack of national pride to see the place designated under that UN convention, is hard to understand. We should pause to reflect how the status of our finest blanket bogs as a site of global significance still seems to subvert our reflex assumptions about exactly which parts of these islands should be considered important. Roman walls, feudal fortifications, royal palaces, ruined abbeys and perhaps bluebell woods – fine; but remote bogs? Our ongoing national inability to see the designation implemented seems a continuation of the attitudes of Andrew Steele, who in 1826 described bog as a 'blot upon the beauty and a derision to the agriculture of the British Isles'.[3]

The international status of the Flow Country was stressed by the NCC chair William Wilkinson, when he launched *Birds, Bogs and Forestry* at a London venue on 23 July 1987. 'We all see the need to look after Westminster Abbey,' he announced, 'St Peter's, Venice, the Taj Mahal … We are right to give such consideration to these man-created masterpieces of civilisation. Do the masterpieces of God and nature deserve anything less?' There were times when a good old British compromise was sensible, he continued, but there were also moments 'when "absolutes" must prevail'. His final message was straight from the text of the report. The historical destruction of our richest environ-mental landscapes such as the Cambridgeshire/Lincolnshire fens was in the past when we thought little of it, but today, he said, 'the situation is different; the picture and issues are clear; any further losses will be deliberate'.[4]

To some people the launch of this nature-championing document was a red rag to a bull. In fact, it was probably this moment more than any other that doomed the NCC as a pan-national institution. The eventual response from Malcolm Rifkind, Secretary of State for Scotland, was an outright veto on any halt to afforestation. Even less willing to compromise was the MP for Caithness and Sutherland and the former leader of the Social Democratic Party, Robert Maclennan, who dismissed the NCC's claims as 'preposterous', and saw the launch of a report on the Flow Country in London as a direct snub by distant bureaucratic mandarins to both local opinion and to the very Scottishness of the whole issue.

Unfortunately, an internal dispute within NCC about the venue for the event had led to its London location, against the wishes of its own hierarchy, but the local MP was more concerned about conservation's perceived threat to the economy of his own constituency. The forests were 'a godsend', according to Maclennan, 'and the NCC seemed bent on "sterilising" the land, just like the Highland Clearances of evil memory'.[5*] That reference to things being 'sterilised' was a loaded term used frequently by landowners, or their political representatives, to describe the effects of environmentalists north of the border. Essentially it meant the perceived economic block that conservation designations placed upon Scottish estates. What the locals wanted was freedom to do as they sought fit in their own backyards. Afforestation, in their eyes, had the opposite effect to 'sterilising': it created business and employment in a region that was short of both.

---

* It is worth pausing to examine Maclennan's strange conflation of NCC opposition to afforestation and the Clearances of 'evil memory'. The Clearances expressed a desire by Scottish landowners to erase traditional clan loyalties and supplant the multiple land-use regime of their clan tenants with a monoculture of sheep. If the Clearances were truly an expression of sterilisation then surely so was afforestation: the displacement of all old land-use with a dubiously profitable single-species plantation.

Yet the case for afforestation based on its job-creating benefits, while it may have been routinely made, was not one that bore too much scrutiny. The total Forestry Commission payroll, just as an example, was no greater in the 1980s than it had been in 1935. This was despite its creation since that date of 3,000 square miles of additional plantation, an area substantially greater than the county of Devon. Similarly, in the Scottish borders the local council had pointed out that while the forestry area had trebled, employee numbers had fallen from 614 in 1970 to 440 by 1985.[6] Notwithstanding these existing employment figures, the Highlands and Islands Development Board reacted instantly to the NCC-proposed freeze in the Flow Country with a claim that the measure threatened 2,000 jobs.

If anything was 'preposterous', as Maclennan had argued, it was this silly exaggeration.* The figure of 2,000 represented more than half the entire labour force for the Forestry Commission nationwide.[7] The 2,000 figure turned out to come from Fountain Forestry, but it referred to projections for when the trees were at a harvestable stage several decades hence. The immediate boost to local jobs by this company was just 60, and according to the National Audit Office each of those was costing the taxpayer £60,000.[8] Had that level of public subsidy gone to other sectors of the economy, such as tourism, it is hard to see how the 'boost' to local employment could not at least have been matched.

There was another stock argument that had been made almost since the founding of the Forestry Commission and which had resurfaced in the Flow Country. It was the idea that the addition of trees – any trees – to a place was by its very nature a good thing, and even an environmentally positive development. It appealed not just to a specialist

---

* It is worth pointing out that the local community in Caithness seemed to have succumbed to the forestry's employment line. When the renowned angler Bruce Sandison, who had condemned the afforestation as 'one of the great acts of vandalism of the late twentieth century', debated in person with the chair of Caithness Tourist Board, Lord Thurso, and stated that the latter should be removed from his office for his involvement in forestry, Sandison lost by 102 votes to three. His stance on the issue led to the Sandison family suffering insults and harassment, including a sack being thrown into their garden containing a large, angry adder. See Sandison, *Secret Lochs and Special Places*, 2011.

community, but also to the public at large. In fact, the notion that tree-planting is an unalloyed virtue is as firmly entrenched in general consciousness as the belief that felling trees is somehow wrong. It is this instinctual attachment, which for its adherents can have almost religious overtones, that often sets the public at odds with conservation practice, or even simply with good woodmanship. For there is often nothing better for a wood than a healthy dose of felling.*

To counter this generic sentiment, the Nature Conservancy Council was obliged to devote part of each of its reports to exposing the fallacy that pine trees on blanket bog were an act of environmental enhancement. Not so, it argued. While there was an increase in woodland species such as robins, thrushes, finches and pigeons, these were precisely the birds already abundant and widespread across all of Britain. They in no way compensated for the loss of bog specialists, such as greenshank and black-throated divers.

Conversely there was a significant problem introduced by some of these new woodland-dwellers, because they included egg and nestling predators like crows and foxes. Both acquired nesting or denning opportunities in the plantations and then foraged across the surrounding mire, adding to the pressures faced by the ground-nesting waders. Frequently the ecologists surveying the bogs found that there was a significant 'edge effect', with none of the bog specialists nesting within a quarter and sometimes half a mile of an afforested area.[9]

This was a problem, but so too was a general lack of understanding of avian ecology by the proponents of afforestation. There was a prevailing sense that if the birds could somehow see their way to understand the foresters' case and move over a little on those vast bogs, then there would be room for everyone to get along. Such folksy notions of avian ecology were starkly at odds with the realities of a low-nutrient environment, where the waders were obliged to forage over very large areas to breed successfully. Sometimes, however, the foresters' attitudes were just plain

---

* The muddle over the issue, like so much of the general confusion about woodland, hinges on the fallacy that cutting a tree down kills it off. It does not. Or, at least, it does not kill a deciduous tree. It does, however, end the life of most conifers, with yew being a notable exception.

callousness. Talking of the greenshank population, the then director of Fountain Forestry allegedly pronounced that 'If a bird cannot survive on 650 acres, then it doesn't bloody well deserve to survive.'[10]

As far as the public was concerned, probably the strongest part of the environmental case was precisely the cardinal weakness in the foresters' own: the economics. There was so little financial justification for it. In fact, several of the other private forestry companies refused to get involved in afforesting the Flows precisely because it was such a poor investment. They openly advised their clients not to do so. As we have seen, the usual, expected return on public expenditure was 10 per cent, while the mean profit on FC plantings was less than a quarter of that figure. And this was by no means the worst.

Many of the upland plantations are susceptible to what is known in the business as 'windthrow', when the prevailing weather systems set up a domino effect through the shallow-rooted trees and cause them to fall like skittles. Vast areas can be prematurely felled in this manner. There is a perfect current example in the plantation just south of Ben Griam Beg and the RSPB's Forsinard reserve. As you drive north out of the tiny settlement of Kinbrace on the A897 from Helmsdale, the hill slope just to the west of the road is a porcupine's back of jagged grey quills in a matrix of evergreen foliage. It is like a plantation but upside-down, with the foliage on or near the ground and dead stumps rooted in mid-air. It looks impenetrable and largely worthless as timber, even to a layman's eye.

So it proves. The forester Steve Tompkins suggested that the profitability on windthrown plantation was as little as half of 1 per cent.[11] What he described as 'a tragedy of British forestry policy' was the fact that over the period from about 1957 to 1987 about a fifth of the FC's timber production had had to be felled because of endemic windthrow, in addition to another 6 per cent damaged by 'catastrophic windthrow'. 'Massive subsidies to afforestation', he concluded, 'without adequate scrutiny of the return on the public investment, have given us second-rate forests in the hills.'[12]

This was only half the story, because while there was so little return on outlay for the public purse, there were very handsome profits to be made by a tiny number of investors, not to mention their solicitors and financial advisers. Every year a business such as Fountain Forestry needed about 40–80 wealthy individuals to succumb to the lure of tax and subsidy benefits from the new plantations. Many of the clients, as we have seen, were extremely wealthy, including, in one year (1987) alone, ten of the top twenty earners in the country.[13]

Not only were they rich, but some of the individuals were also public figures. They included the likes of the golfer Nick Faldo, the snooker player Alex 'Hurricane' Higgins, Lady Shirley Porter (scourge of public waste as chair of the council in the borough of Westminster), as well as two pop icons, Phil Collins and Cliff Richard. Perhaps the most widely publicised of all the absentee landlords in Caithness was the BBC's perennially popular source of Irish blarney, the TV host and radio journalist, Terry Wogan.* In fact, a patch of plantation near Broubster, the near-deserted settlement on the road to Beinn nam Bad Mór, was known briefly as Wogan's Wood.

More than anything, it was the involvement of such individuals that drove journalistic interest in what might otherwise have been a rather academic story about tree farming on a remote Scottish bog. Yet the somewhat surreal mix of blanket mire and government tax breaks for the rich and famous, infused through the more substantive issues of fiscal injustice and environmental destruction, produced just the right brew to galvanise public attention. The whole thing smelt of corruption. As one exposé in the *Observer* argued, some of these famous individuals were getting a return of 33.5 per cent a year, which compared rather nicely with what was delivered to the public purse by the worst windthrown sections of public forestry. 'Planting forests is a sure way to grow rich, if you are rich already,' the article's authors noted. 'Through tax relief and grants, the taxpayer will cover up to three-quarters of your costs without expecting any of your profit.'[14]

---

* It is one of the stranger ironies of the Battle of the Bogs that, while not a syllable of Wogan's cheery fifty-year-long monologue on British radio or television is likely to survive the ravages of time and tide, nevertheless a detailed transcript of his impact as an absentee landlord in the Flow Country is archived in perpetuity in the catotelm's subterranean vault.

Among the other media coverage that helped move the public towards outright opposition was a hard-hitting Survival documentary entitled *Paradise Ploughed*. It aired about the same time as the piece in the *Observer* was published – February 1988 – and was presented by self-confessed 'peatnik' David Bellamy. In the programme, a senior figure from the Forestry Commission acknowledged to camera that had he and his colleagues known what they knew then, they would never have agreed to the licences that allowed the area to be afforested.[15]

Perhaps sensing the public mood, the Chancellor of the Exchequer Nigel Lawson notified the House of Commons a month later that the tax loophole that had driven the whole race for evergreens since the 1960s was about to be closed. Rather like the prior announcement by his colleague, the Secretary of State for Scotland Malcolm Rifkind, that there would be a 430,000-acre SSSI in Caithness and Sutherland, Lawson's words made it seem as if the environmentalists' case had prevailed. However, matters were not quite as they seemed.

A leader in the *Daily Telegraph*, hardly a publication sympathetic to the left-leaning greens of the Nature Conservancy Council, astutely diagnosed the government measures as an exercise in business as usual. True, the old tax loophole would be closed by the Chancellor's announcement, but a new form of subsidy would be very quickly substituted that covered 60 per cent, instead of the previous 70 per cent, of start-up costs. And true, a substantial swathe of mire had been set aside for nature, but afforestation was by no means blocked in Sutherland and Caithness. In fact, the Secretary of State for Scotland had given his official imprimatur to plantations totalling 247,000 acres. Of these, an estimated 100,000 were eventually located on the finest blanket bogs in the world.[16]

Under the title 'Half a cheer for Rifkind', the *Telegraph*'s editorial argued that

it still yields too much to those with indefensible vested interests, and allows the further spread of conifer planting which is destroying primaeval peat bog with its wading birds, diminishing one of Britain's scarce and thus precious empty landscapes, and possibly putting salmon and trout fisheries at risk – all to provide tax breaks for absentee millionaires ... An area with immense recreational potential and natural beauty is still at risk of being despoiled at the taxpayer's expense.[17]

Regardless of these reservations, the outcome of the Battle of the Bogs was probably as good as it could have been for the more-than-human parts of nature. In effect, it was a score draw for developers and conservationists alike.

In the decades following the events described above, the various players would experience markedly different fortunes. The RSPB, which had been highly active in the campaign against afforestation, stepped up in a way that should earn it immense credit. So too did its million-strong membership. In the early 1990s large numbers of them responded with great generosity to the Society's appeal to buy swathes of blanket bog. If anything demonstrates the powerful hold of wild places on the public's imagination, then it was the donations made by those who will probably never travel north to see the Flow Country in person. Not only did their efforts result in the purchase of a substantial initial reserve at Forsinard, it kickstarted a process that has continued for a quarter of a century.

The RSPB's cumulative landholding now stands at 52,000 acres, including some of the finest mire habitats in Britain.* The entire intervention must rank as one of the primary achievements in the charity's history, comparable with the National Trust's Operation Neptune. It is by a large margin its most significant single property, and the biggest contribution it has made to the preservation of any habitat. Yet the organisation holds not just pristine bog, but 8,500 acres that had been

---

* The other institution that protects a substantial part of the Flow Country is PlantLife, co-founded by my friend Tony Hare in 1989 in the aftermath of the Battle of the Bogs. As with the RSPB at Forsinard, Plantlife's Munsary reserve in Caithness represents by a large margin their biggest site, in fact two-thirds of all the land that they own. The full reserve is 4,600 acres, including 1,600 that is leased.

planted with conifers. Assisted, it should be noted, by the very people who know the land best – the local forest workers who had been involved in planting the trees decades earlier – the RSPB has achieved miracles on this degraded ground. By clear-felling the conifers, blocking up the drains, raising the water table and pressing the brash residue down into the peat, they have set significant areas of former plantation back on their journey to blanket bog. It is a good measure of how times have changed that some of the afforested sections bought most recently and earmarked for restoration were owned by the Forestry Commission.[18]

The latter is another institution that was profoundly affected by the events of the late 1980s. However, in this instance it was driven by the sting of public opprobrium. Some of its senior staff like Roderick Leslie openly acknowledged that in the aftermath of the Battle of the Bogs it had become a 'public pariah'.[19] In his historical account of the Forestry Commission he has written of the 'twenty years of concerted effort to exit from the stink of the Flow Country, to get close to the people who love the forest and give them what they want'.[20] Part of the new ethos involved a more caring attitude to its own ancient woodlands, and the removal of conifers from these surviving treasure houses of national biodiversity. In all, 86,000 acres of the habitat had been earmarked for restoration.[21]

The FC reforms also entailed a recognition – and one laments that it was not there from the outset in 1919 – that woods have multiple purposes for the whole of society. A good example was the Commission's increased sensitivity to the environmental value of its timber holdings, whether it was measures for sparrowhawks and tawny owls in Kielder Forest, or for woodlarks and nightjars in Thetford Forest, or for dune-loving plant communities on Anglesey's Newborough Warren.

One could argue that it was this post-Flow Country change of heart that ultimately saved the Forestry Commission from extinction. More than two decades of its adjusted policies had slowly won the trust and affections of the British public, so that when the Conservative–Liberal coalition government announced in 2011 an intention to privatise and sell off the whole FC estate, the idea met with massive opposition. In short order a 38 Degrees petition acquired 550,000 signatures. The government then instituted an expert panel to review the plan, including representation from the Wildlife Trusts, the National Trust and the RSPB, as well as forestry professionals. As the group sat to deliberate it received 42,000 individual submissions, all of which helped steer it to an eventual rejection of the government's proposal. To its credit the administration then performed a complete volte face on the issue in July 2012.

One cannot help noticing a cruel twist of fate in this moment. For while the Forestry Commission had lost the arguments in the Flow Country but went on to prosper, the Nature Conservancy Council won the debate and suffered almost instant decapitation. Roderick Leslie has himself acknowledged the irony in this. He claimed that when he heard of the government plans to scrap the NCC, his 'first reaction was "It should have been us".'[22] What makes it doubly painful from an environmentalist's perspective is that the bold stand taken by the Nature Conservancy Council was surely among its own finest moments. Yet its resulting dismemberment has entailed a massive loss for the cause of wildlife in Britain.

The origins of the decision, like its ultimate impact, remain a subject of constant debate among environmentalists. The one indisputable part was the government's conviction that the NCC had to go. Apparently 'without any consultation and without attempting any proper costings or drafting of proposed legislation', the Secretary of State for the Environment, Nicholas Ridley, announced in July 1989 that the existing organisational arrangements were 'inefficient and insensitive'.[23]

Henceforth the NCC would be divided into three, with its duties performed in England by a replacement body called English Nature, and then in Scotland and Wales respectively by two devolved, nationally focused institutions that represented a merger of the Countryside Commission and the old NCC elements in each country. The combined organisations were called Scottish Natural Heritage and the Countryside Council for Wales (the last was re-shaped again in 2013, when it incorporated the Principality's section of the Environment Agency; this revised edition is now entitled Natural Resources Wales, an amendment that by itself speaks eloquently of a dilution of its nature-conservation remit).

One immediate explanation of the NCC's fate was the personality and views of the Secretary of State for the Environment at that time.

Nicholas Ridley came from a long line of landowning political grandees. Following the stock educational path of his class from Eton to Oxford, he had been elected in 1959 to a safe Conservative seat, which he held for almost the remainder of his life. He was stylishly aristocratic, prickly, opinionated, an early free-marketeer and, subsequently, a Thatcherite to his nicotine-stained fingertips (he died of lung cancer in 1993, aged sixty-four). A lover of painting and art, Ridley was once asked by the Prime Minister Edward Heath if he wished to be arts minister, which he rejected on the grounds that 'it involved public expenditure. And I was against all but the most minimal use of the taxpayer's purse.'[24]

Ridley was a conservationist of sorts, having served in various capacities for the National Trust, although even here his loathing of any kind of collective public endeavour that smacked, however remotely, of socialism, put him at odds with the organisation's methods and ethos. 'It was high time,' he once quipped, 'the National Trust was privatised.'[25] His attitude to the Nature Conservancy Council was, according to Derek Ratcliffe, largely hidden from view, but from the occasional remarks that he let slip

> Ridley appeared to believe that conservation problems were exag-
> gerated, state-owned land (as on National Nature Reserves) was
> anathema and should be privatised, conservation was best left to
> that natural custodian 'the countryman', and that management of
> wildlife should be especially for the pursuit of field sports.[26]

I remember vividly how Tony Hare called him 'the Minister *against* the Environment', and if Ridley's attitudes to the NCC were seldom articulated, his actions spoke volumes.* He packed its governing council

---

* One of Ridley's major achievements was the setting up of the National Rivers Authority, forerunner of the Environment Agency. On wildlife, however, he was by consensus among the least sympathetic Secretaries of State for the Environment in living memory. It seems significant that he was outdone for arrogance, if not tenure of office, by his relative by marriage Owen Patterson. The latter infamously referred to environmentalists as the 'green blob'. An appointee to a Natural England committee once told me how he was ushered into Patterson's presence to be interviewed and was left standing as the secretary of state was seated. Patterson refused to look up from his papers at his interlocutor for the whole time that they spoke.

with those of his own ilk. Most of them were exactly the countrymen he thought himself to be: one who 'knew how to catch a trout in the brook and flight a wild duck in the evening'.[27] In 1989 his recruits included an earl with grouse-shooting interests, a forestry lobbyist and a large arable farmer. By the summer of that year, landowners outnumbered scientists and academics nine to six; and of professional conservationists there was not a single one.[28]

Ridley's tenure of office coincided exactly with the Battle of the Bogs. According to Peter Marren, who was himself an eyewitness at close quarters of the whole period, the Secretary of State induced a state of paranoia among the NCC staff. It is in the light of this statement that one must marvel at the principled all-or-nothing and apparently suicidal stance mounted by the Council. Yet perhaps the writing for Ridley's *coup de grâce* had been on the walls for years.

One of the factors that weakened the NCC north of the border was antagonism from a powerful lobby of Scottish lairds, in whose hands are concentrated a higher proportion of land than in almost any other European nation. In 2012, 246 private estates possessed more than 6.5 million acres, roughly a third of Scotland's entire land surface. Half the country is in the hands of 963 owners.[29] We have seen how this same community, with powerful representation at a regional level or within the Scottish Office, had been able to kill off the idea of national parks in 1948. The first such area to be designated north of the border was not until more than half a century later (see also Chapter Eight, p. 116). In 1991 Scottish peers in the House of Lords were able to amend legislation that founded Scottish Natural Heritage so that the new body was obliged to undertake a complete review of all Scottish SSSIs.[30]

The difficulties faced by conservationists in the Scottish countryside had already engendered tensions between bosses at the NCC regional headquarters in Edinburgh and its London office. It was this inter-departmental friction that had accounted for the launch of the report *Birds, Bogs and Forestry* in the latter rather than the former. This presentational mishandling, which was taken as such an insult by the likes of Robert Maclennan, struck wider landed interests in Scotland as a mark of the NCC's remoteness from regional realities.

When the announcement of the split came in 1990 there were howls of protest from all parts of the environmental sector. One NCC board member, Lord Buxton, promptly resigned. Yet there were some benefits. The cumulative resources of the three organisations would eventually far outstrip those of their older parent body. In 1990 the NCC had enjoyed a budget of £42 million and 785 staff; in the new millennium the devolved agencies had 2,245 employees and enjoyed a shared budget of £220 million (2006).[31]

This shift in environmental arrangements would also ultimately be seen in its wider historical and social context, as one of the earliest steps in what is now viewed as a highly organic devolution of responsibilities away from the centre. The new bodies have eventually been judged to be more specifically shaped and adapted to tackle the issues particular to their areas. Tribal loyalties, that were almost certainly latent in the unreconstructed NCC, evolved into clear cultural distinctions. Were they ever to be asked now if they wished to reconstitute as one, it is highly unlikely that the employees of three devolved bodies would ever opt for a single supranational organisation.

The remit of the new institutions also broadened to take on issues that had barely troubled the old predecessor, such as public engagement with the natural world, health, climate change, energy and food security. Peter Marren noted how the changes of direction had been preceded by a shift in tonal emphasis even before the split. At one time the NCC had been accustomed to define itself 'as the government body which promotes nature conservation'. Prior to being disbanded it had started to present itself as the agency 'that advises government on nature conservation'.[32] Sir John Lister-Kaye, who saw the organisational shake-up in Scotland at first-hand, suggests that these nuances in vocabulary acquired substantive meaning in the new era. He argues that while the NCC had existed to argue the primacy of nature, the *raison d'être* of SNH was to engage people with nature.[33]

Although few would now seriously challenge the dispensation that has prevailed for the last quarter-century, probably fewer still of those who witnessed the before and after processes would dispute that something fundamental has died in nature conservation in Britain. Reading

John Sheail's detailed accounts of post-war nature conservation history, one gains a sense that in government circles, almost from its inception, the Nature Conservancy (and later the Nature Conservancy Council) had often been viewed as an indigestible irritant, or as an ungrateful and troublesome foundling that repeatedly challenged or disrupted the settled policies of its paymasters.

Ridley and Rifkind seemed determined to introduce discipline to this unruly child of nature. Henceforth there might be a government sub-department to implement matters pertaining to nature conservation, but its wilfulness was to be curbed. There would be no more independent voice, however small or ineffectual, within government challenging the substance of land-related policy. Inheritor institutions, often of outstanding quality, would continue vital administrative work and operate existing or even enhanced systems of land protection, as in previous decades, but the notion of an official lobby that dared to speak truth unto power on behalf of the more-than-human parts of nature, has been lost.

This has had a curiously pervasive and largely unforeseen effect on the totality of the so-called 'green' movement. From time to time during the post-war decades the voluntary organisations had shown impatience and even annoyance with the NCC, when the latter had seemed to be foot-dragging. An agency whose purse strings were so evidently in the hands of its political masters was ever liable to be castigated as being too timid and compliant. Its unwillingness to deploy the mettle so amply demonstrated over matters in Sutherland and Caithness in other previous, lesser campaigns had somehow stiffened the resolve of voluntary NGOs to take on the more emphatically campaigning role. What was perhaps underestimated in this scenario was the extent to which these more radical, forthright pronouncements required the stolid presence of the NCC as a sounding wall to give the NGO voices their full resonance. After this was taken away, the whole volume of protest faded.

Now an air of quietude seems to have descended and, regardless of the power and content of the *State of Nature* report, the total effort seems inadequate to the needs of the hour. Very often the boldest initiatives and the most far-reaching publicity seem to come from individuals, rather than from institutions. For large memberships are odd things. They are both momentous assets and potential liabilities; or, at least, fear of losing members becomes a liability. Today one occasionally feels that private campaigners – Tony Juniper and George Monbiot are good examples – create as much environmental weather as the RSPB and the National Trust, with their 6 million members combined. Mark Avery, the wildlife blogger and Twitter aficionado, has done more to highlight the issues of chronic illegal raptor persecution and point out the severe environmental costs associated with driven-grouse shooting than any campaign group in Britain.*

Standing on the top of Ben Griam Beg, however, no one could be in any doubt that the fifteen environmental organisations named in Chapter 1 are among our best hopes for a richer countryside. I can also say with certainty that, since the efforts of all those who fought to prevent it being drained and ploughed, the bog below me has only increased in importance.

The contest in the Flow Country took place before the intensifying recognition of the impacts of climate change. Since then ecologists have learnt to appreciate how the catotelm stores raw carbon as well as a record of the past. It is now estimated that peat soils in the UK contain 5.5 billion tonnes of carbon: 31 times the country's entire annual greenhouse gas emissions. Degraded peat environments, by contrast, through deliberate burning on grouse moors or ploughing for afforestation, are still releasing 10 million tons of carbon dioxide.[34]

On this wind-blasted hill, looking over a rain-created plain, I intuit another reason for keeping the Flow Country as it was. But it cannot

---

* Ably assisted, it must be said, by the anonymous individuals who operate the website Raptor Persecution UK. I have on rare occasions spoken to some of the people involved with this first-class and relentless information source and understand their desire for anonymity, when you realise the intimidation and threat posed to them by the agents of illegal raptor killing. Nature conservation is occasionally as red in tooth and claw as nature itself. For a full appreciation of the issues around birds of prey and their persecution as a result of driven-grouse shooting, read Avery's masterly polemic *Inglorious*.

be computed by any of the metrics that capitalist society favours. Nor, indeed, can it be formulated according to any materialist, ratiocinatory argument. On the contrary, it is akin to the logic of Aldo Leopold, when he bade us to think like a mountain.*

What gives value to this place is precisely its inhumanity, its resistance to all that we are – our aesthetic sensibilities, our modern impatience, the linear tabulations of our economic schemes, even the physics of our own bodies. Through its indifference, the bog earths us. It restores our default settings. In this small island of too many people there should have been one last brown god – a land of sphagnum and water and wind and birdsong – that we had not mastered.

---

* Leopold's famous essay 'Thinking Like a Mountain' is to be found in one of the defining texts of environmentalism, *A Sand County Almanac* (1949). Leopold, a previously devoted deer hunter, experienced a moment of apostasy, when he shot a female wolf and watched a 'fierce green fire dying in her eyes'. From that instant, he claimed later, he had understood that there was some new truth revealed to him in those eyes, known only to the wolf and to the mountain, and which humans invariably failed to grasp.

21

OUR GREEN AND
PLEASANT LAND

Suddenly larks are rare. A fertiliser kills
The reasons for their song. Their landscape fills
With whispers that some sharp-eared god enjoys,
Papery music, low botanical noise.

Friends give each other names of fields not drugged, where birds
Still practise their ascensions on transparent words,
Still disappear in light and silence where
Nobody else can hide: a span of air.

You think of following them. The sound of summer now
Falls only from an aeroplane that echoes somehow
In the soft sky. I'll find and interview
A lark with my machine ...
But will that comfort you?

Nature is leaving earth. The species one by one
Withdraw their voices. Soon the creatures shall have gone,
Leaving the subtle horns of rock for nitrogen
And oxygen and noble gas to play upon.

Alistair Elliot, 'Speaking of Larks'

In the opening chapter I highlighted an apparent contradiction between the existence of so many members of conservation organisations in the UK and the verdict of the *State of Nature* report in 2013. There are, we should recall, 8 million members spread across 15 voluntary societies (see also p. 10). Compared with the picture in other European countries, our devotion to the more-than-human parts of nature is remarkable. Only in the USA, a country with five times the population, could you possibly find comparable figures. By this measure, few nations on Earth care as much for their environment as the British.

Yet our attachment to wildlife is starkly at odds with the findings of the *State of Nature* report, to which many of the environmental groups contributed in 2013. Since that time an updated summary has been published entitled *State of Nature 2016*. The later document is more positive in its approach, noting increases as well as declines. Of approximately 4,000 species whose population trends have been measured over the last forty-three years, 56 per cent have incurred losses, but the other 44 per cent have risen in number. It also points out the remarkable human resource provided by the sheer numbers of competent British naturalists, as a result of whose records this country's wildlife is probably better documented than any other flora and fauna on the planet.

One refinement in the later report is the capacity to extrapolate from the disparate figures an overarching unified assessment of how nature fares in any country. This specific metric – called the Biological Intactness Index (BII) – calculates how complete a country's biodiversity is and how much has disappeared as a result of human activities going back centuries. It makes for uncomfortable reading. The index suggests that the UK has experienced a significantly greater long-term loss of nature than the global average. In fact, we are among the world's most nature-depleted countries. If one considers just England the figure is 80.6 per cent. The significance of the number is amplified when you learn how a BII value of less than 90 per cent indicates that national ecosystems may have fallen below a level when they can reliably meet society's needs. On this point one recalls those fenland peat soils blowing away at a rate of over half an inch a year. In a list of the 218 countries on Earth for which BII values have been calculated, England is twenty-eighth from the bottom.[1]

Alas, these grim findings are not the sum of all our environmental news. Dark tidings seem to pour in from all sides on an almost daily basis. Every year the collective human chimney puffs 38 billion tonnes of carbon into the atmosphere, raising atmospheric CO_2 to its highest level in 800,000 years. It is now calculated that we have taken over most of the planet's tropical grasslands, cut down half of all the temperate forest and converted a quarter even of the deserts for crop production.[2] In the oceans four-fifths of all fish populations are harvested to, or beyond, their sustainable limits.[3]

Extinction is the eventual fate of all living things, plant or animal, but the present background rate has accelerated to 1,000 times the Earth's average as revealed by the fossil record. Nor is it just loss of diversity that is intensifying. Decline of simple abundance in the last four decades is at unprecedented levels. In 2016 the Zoological Society of London published the *Living Planet Assessment*, which claimed that without radical intervention nearly two-thirds of global populations of animals will have gone by the year 2020.

All the time the drip-feed of doom is accompanied by an ever-growing population of one species – *Homo sapiens*. If you have an especially strong constitution you can call up the world clock (at http://www.census.gov/popclock) that shows you the moment-by-moment increase in human mouths and human souls. Given that each click of the rotating wheel signifies the same joyous moment which is etched into the heart of every parent, me included, it is very strange to see these births reduced to an accelerating mind-numbing number. As I type these very words it reveals a world human population of 7,343,514,500. At the end of day it will have gone up by 205,479. In a year the increase will be 75 million people.

Our species' success is so relentless, and the resulting diminution of all the other parts of life so inexorable, that some have switched attention away from ecological loss and towards its impact upon us. They have now given it a name: environmental melancholia. The overwhelming question assailing us all is: how do we remain optimistic for the future? Where is hope to be found? And what is there to feel good about so that we can be motivated to try to turn things around? For without encouragement won't we succumb to despair and give up?

I suspect something of this psychological malaise was implicated in the suicide of Tony Hare. When I see pictures of him before he died, campaigning against climate change at the Copenhagen summit in late 2009, standing there with fellow protesters, placards and banners in hand, smiling for the cameras, I can see the exhaustion in his face, sense the hollowness of his smile. Tone, who had devoted his life to living things, was overwhelmed by it all. It is a major problem, and the environmental community has been anxious for decades not to just be a source of bad tidings, lest it be accused of merely indulging in doom or, alternatively, of crying wolf. It has developed a range of strategies to stiffen the public's resolve and to encourage support.

The most frequent is to focus on a part of the story, so an organisation extrapolates from the big bad picture the single positive nugget. A heading from an article in *BTO News* (a publication of the British Trust for Ornithology) summarises the approach perfectly: 'Tree Sparrows in trouble? A local success story'.[4]* Another tale that has been the focus of frequent positive spin involves the water vole. The rodent is one of the most popular recipients of conservation effort in Britain, partly because of its characterisation as the loveable 'Ratty' in Kenneth Grahame's *The Wind in the Willows*. Water voles were so much a part of my Derbyshire childhood that I find it painful now to recall, given their catastrophic decline, with what indifference I once viewed them.

We would stop at almost any point along the River Wye – to scrutinise a dabchick, dipper or grey wagtail – and there overlooked at the edge of the tableau were the birds' gentle riverine neighbours. The creatures were supremely rotund, and invariably the jowls bulged and

---

* The tree sparrow is one of the species in the Farmland Bird Index, and has one of the most miserable stories to tell us about British agriculture. Since 1967 it has declined by 97 per cent, as the article, with its standard upbeat subtitle, goes on to tell us.

the jaws, with those extraordinary orange incisors, were grinding nonchalantly on some waterside vegetation. The voles' insouciance and our mutual disregard seemed to be rooted in an assumption that things would always be so. Alas, not.

In 1990 our mainland vole population was estimated at 7.25 million (and in the Iron Age it was an astonishing 6.7 billion).[5] Within eight years it had declined by 80 per cent, a loss of 6,419,000, largely as a consequence of predation by American mink, which have escaped and spread from fur farms. The solution to the problem is easy to write – rid our country of the offending mustelid – but complicated, relatively expensive and time-consuming to implement. Occasionally wildlife groups score big local successes, when they carry out relentless campaigns. In 2013 the author and *Guardian* journalist Patrick Barkham reported on just such a programme on the River Chess in the Chilterns.[6]

With some habitat restoration and by trapping and shooting the non-native predators, the Berkshire, Buckinghamshire and Oxfordshire Wildlife Trust saw the River Chess vole population return to almost 100 per cent of its pre-mink peak. The problem is that the background picture is not quite so rosy. Nationwide surveys completed in the last decade suggest that, regardless of local successes, we have lost a further fifth of our water voles this century.*

Another common strategy is to sound hopeful in the further hope that it will inspire affirmative action. Butterfly Conservation frequently resorts to this particular tone. One can understand why, given that the butterflies in this country have had an especially torrid time in the last century. Half of all species have undergone major losses and five have become extinct. What we have, as a result of the remarkable dedication

---

* There may yet be a happy ending to this particular tale from the riverbank because, while mink eat voles, otters probably kill and certainly displace mink, and otter numbers are now on the rise after decades of decline. The result of the otter's nationwide resurrection may, like some stirring chapter from *The Wind in The Willows*, herald Ratty's eventual restoration. The key background to this success is the banning of otter hunting and improvement in water quality over several decades. It is one of the major environmental achievements of the last thirty years.

of staff for Butterfly Conservation, is far fewer butterflies, but a lot of expertise and practical experience in helping them. It is this aspect that the associated news stories tend to emphasise:

It gives me great heart to know that just when butterflies and moths are at their most threatened, interest has never been higher (editorial in *Butterfly*, the magazine of Butterfly Conservation).[7]

Or (in the *State of the Nation's Butterflies* report) this:

Conserving butterflies is undoubtedly a large and difficult task, but we have never been better equipped to face the challenge.[8]

There is another element manifest in these examples that is a wider feature of conservation rhetoric. It is to salt the good news with the bad and vice versa, so that you get across the awkward truths while making them palatable with a spoonful of optimism.

Sometimes it extends to the use of what one might call white lies. A good example is the BBC television series entitled *Britain's Big Wildlife Revival*. For all the fabulous achievements of conservation, there is one acid test that measures the limits of its capacity and attainments. Not a single formerly abundant species – plant or animal – that has suffered major decline in this country as a consequence of habitat loss has yet been restored to its former status. The closest we have come are probably grey and common seals and several species of bird of prey, such as the common buzzard, red kite and peregrine. Yet all these were threatened not by habitat loss, but by direct persecution, or inadvertent poisoning from agrochemicals. A truer test would be the restoration of fortunes in the kestrel, which the common buzzard has now replaced as our most abundant raptor. Kestrels, by contrast, once numbered 100,000 pairs and are now down to 36,800.

The larger point to make is that to date there has been no big wildlife revival. The programme's title is untrue. There are episodes of wonderful achievement. And these stand in for and justify the programmer makers' initial dishonesty. Through the title, the viewer is enticed to watch and thereby absorb all the evidence of the problems, with the occasional good-news stories as moral fortification. In the end the hope is that the viewer will overlook the fact that the 'big revival' is merely hypothetical or, perhaps, an illusion.

Personally, I have a problem with hope, not because I don't feel it, but because it steadily becomes an objective in its own right, a distraction confusing and diluting the real issues. It also draws an imaginary line between those who are assumed to be able to face the truth and those for whom it must be replaced with calming reassurance. Ultimately a tissue of half-truths meshes with something far more powerful and potentially destructive – myth. Recall the words of the cleric Richard Holloway quoted in Chapter 7, who suggested that the importance of a myth was not whether it is true or false, but whether it still carries existential meaning for us in our time.

The myth that has so much content for us is the idea that the British countryside is in ineradicable good health: that in the now-clichéd words of William Blake's poem, this is still 'a green and pleasant land'. That axiomatic assumption is even now a reflex in public discourse about our countryside. It is almost impossible for a radio or television journalist to be located in a green setting, talking about countryside, without the phrase tumbling effortlessly from their lips.

We seem to need that myth because one of the stock purposes of nature, one of the values which we have long attributed to it, is its powers of restoration. As Richard Mabey argued in the passage quoted in this book's frontispiece, the fundamental goal of environmentalism is 'to renew the living fabric of the land so that it also replenishes the spirits of its human inhabitants'.

Replenishing our collective spirit involves our immersion in nature's unfathomable and obliterating otherness, so that it can purge the travails and toxins of our own making. Nature's great and irreversible continuities – the passage of the clouds, the turning of the seasons – measure all our smallnesses. They put things in perspective. They render us humble. Nature is the go-to place when life seems too full of self-generated woe – ISIS, bank bail-outs, recession, Brexit, terrorism, war. The case was made at the other end of the twentieth century by Thomas

Hardy in a poem called 'The Darkling Thrush'.* In a final verse, as the poet stood in awe at the song, as the season reaches its dead end, and when the whole century seems to be laid out before him like a corpse, he asks of the creature:

> So little cause for carolings
>   Of such ecstatic sound
> Was written on terrestrial things
>   Afar or nigh around,
> That I could think there trembled through
>   His happy good-night air
> Some blessed Hope, whereof he knew
>   And I was unaware.

Hope is written into all our connections with the rest of nature, and it is a two-way process. The other parts of life are our deepest sources of hope; and hope is part of the very fabric of our encounters. It begins the moment you open the door to go outside. You have only to have the sun on your back, the wind in your face and birdsong in your heart to know their rivet-bursting powers of liberation. It is perhaps partly what Henry Thoreau was tilting at when he wrote the words for which he is most famous and which are among his most ambiguous: 'In Wildness is the preservation of the world.'

It explains why we cling so tenaciously to the myth that this country continues inviolate. We don't want to hear that our final redoubt, the place where we go when our human condition is overwhelming, is itself in need. Alas, it is. In the twentieth century, the British drained their landscape of wildlife, otherness, meaning, cultural riches and hope. Yet because it is central to our purposes and to our relationships with each

---

* Hardy claimed that it was written on 31 December 1900. A remaining mystery of the poem concerns the species of thrush that he heard. The mistle thrush more commonly sings in late winter, but has a joyously melancholy song. By contrast the song thrush is a follower of Professor Pangloss and a believer that all is for the best in the best of all possible worlds. Its own song has the power to awaken a dead season and give hope to a new century. But which bird did Hardy hear?

other, we continue in denial. And what we have done to our country becomes the truth that dare not speak its name. However, hope lies, surely, not in perpetuating any myth, not in doctoring the facts, but in owning them squarely and with the whole of ourselves.

I list here ten interlocking Truths that are fundamental to the story of British nature in the twentieth century. They help to explain what happened, why it happened and, as far as possible, what needs to be done. They bear equally on the agents of destruction and those who oppose it. They are arranged, with a single exception, in a kind of chromatic scale from dark to light. They are, in my opinion, the antithesis of all the platitudes about a green and pleasant land.

1. In the twentieth century the British people devastated large areas of their environment, largely through the instrument of farming and forestry policies. Not only have the citizens of this country had to witness the processes, they also paid for them through subsidies. The losses took place largely over two generations, from 1940 to 1985, though their full effects span a century from 1920 to 2018. In that time 99 per cent of 4 million acres of flower-rich meadow were destroyed and 44 million breeding birds vanished from the countryside.

The loss is not evenly distributed. Our coastlines are still relatively intact, partly because of the National Trust's extraordinary Operation Neptune. Also parts of what Oliver Rackham called the 'Ancient Countryside', which includes a swathe from south Norfolk to Kent and westwards through Sussex and Hampshire, and then due north from Dorset to south Lancashire, have escaped some of the worst effects. Surrey and Kent, despite the large human population of the south-east, retain some of the highest levels of woodland, and Kent has more ancient woodland than any other county.[9]

Density of occupation is a significant factor, and since England holds all but 11 million of Britain's population, it has borne the brunt. Loss of landscape, however, is not necessarily always about human numbers. One need only drive through the sparsely occupied Borders areas from Alnwick in Northumberland to Lockerbie in Dumfriesshire to see a hill country burnt out and minimised to a continuous, sheep-grazed grass monoculture punctuated with conifer plantations. Yet to see in full the twenty-eighth most denatured landscape on Earth one should take the M6 or the A1 south of Cumbria and Northumberland. Then you can really bear witness to the hollow heart of this country, pretty much all the way south to Bristol or London. The arable areas are stripped bare of wildlife. In fact, it is now commonplace for bumblebee numbers and species diversity to be much greater in suburban and urban areas than in the countryside. So much so that it is almost meaningless to talk of it as *countryside*, and one recalls Tony Hare's prophetic words: 'Whenever people talk to me about the British countryside, I ask, "What countryside?"'

Finally, we must acknowledge that some of our agricultural landscapes – south Lincolnshire and south-west Essex spring instantly to mind – offer a vision of what the entire country will look like if the processes of intensification continue undiminished. It brings me to the next Truth.

2. Things are bad, but there is very little in present public life to suggest that they will not get worse. As a society, so far, we have done too little to turn the environmental ship around. The fundamental drivers of further loss are all intact. The fragmentation will continue: the implications of island biogeography, as outlined in Chapter 15, are still in train. No single generation since the First World War has bequeathed a healthier British countryside than the one they inherited. What special efforts have we made in recent years for us to assume that things are different today? They are not. As I noted in Chapter 1, the *State of Nature* report indicates a direction of travel, not a final location.

It is not just that the same forces are in play and bearing down on what remains of our wildlife. It is that we are facing new pressures, not least the need to build a million new houses to accommodate the large population increases mainly since the beginning of the millennium. The scale of demand has led to a loosening of planning regulations, so that new developments contest with the old environmental protections.

One of the most telling is a plan of Medway Council and Britain's biggest property developer, Land Securities, to erect 5,000 homes on the outskirts of Rochester, Kent, in an area called Lodge Hill. The site is Ministry of Defence land, long neglected and in transition from scrub to full-canopied woodland and perfect, it would appear, for nightingales. Today it holds 84 singing males and Britain's largest single population of the species, which since 1970 has declined by 90 per cent.

Each side is claiming that their need for the place is of overriding significance: 5,000 homes as opposed to one per cent of the British nightingale population. It is in many ways a rerun of the Cow Green reservoir debate about industrial water versus wild flowers. One precise difference, however, is the intervening precedent that involves a half-century of destruction that has brought the nightingale to its present plight.

Each side has supplementary arguments. The developers, who have cross-party support in the local council, point out that there are 20,000 local people on the housing waiting list in the Medway area. Lodge Hill is, according to them, the only large site where infrastructure can also be created, including three primary schools, a nursing home and a hotel, creating 5,000 jobs.[10]

The RSPB staff who are leading the challenge point out, meanwhile, that it is not just about nightingales. The place has 19 bat roosts as well as significant scarce reptile and plant communities and rare breeding butterflies, all of which are strong indicators of its wider importance for biodiversity (this MOD location is so little known because access has been highly restricted for a century). Most significant is that it is already an SSSI and thus, theoretically, protected by legislation. The developers, however, are claiming that they must build there and nowhere else and its legal status should be overridden in the national interest. For those championing wildlife in this dispute, Lodge Hill is an acid test of the very framework on which conservation has been based since the Second World War.

Regardless of the eventual outcome at Lodge Hill, which is only a trifling part of the full national impact, when all these fresh inroads into surviving biodiversity are audited in a generation's time they will reveal nature's inexorable decline.*

3. The third Truth is about understanding nature. Ecology as a formal scientific discipline has only been in existence for about 150 years. That is a short time for it to have influenced the ways in which we think and function. What ecology tries to bring into focus is the dynamic structures of natural systems – habitats, biomes etc. – which are infinitely complex. Essentially, ecology exposes how everything in an ecosystem impacts upon everything else. The usual form invoked to illustrate this level of interconnectedness is a sphere, rendered at its most simple in the 'circle of life' in *The Lion King*, which, for all its Disneyfied triviality, is still an ecological parable.

A circle may be an inadequate representation of ecological complexities, but the real issue for the British environment is that the dominant pattern in our thought processes is not a circle, but a straight line. Look at the page you are reading to appreciate the fundamental line-mindedness of our species. Recall the plough lines running through the Flow Country that Magnus Magnusson likened to claw marks made by an angry god. Recall Vermuyden's dead-straight ditch from Earith to Salter's Lode right through the middle of the Fen. Recall those machine-drilled GPS-spaced regiments of daffodils at Gedney.

Among our various capacities to express ourselves, only music, and possibly painting and poetry, come close to the complex interconnectedness of an ecosystem. *The Lark Ascending* or the song of a blackbird say

---

* To give a small sample sense of developments that typify the ongoing erosion of remaining wildlife areas, there are proposed motorway developments in the Gwent Levels, where a road would cut through five protected areas (see Chapter 5, pp. 78–9), and across Lough Beg in Northern Ireland, one of the region's most important wetlands. Phase one of the HS2 rail link between Birmingham and London will pass through fifty ancient woodlands, four Wildlife Trust reserves and ten SSSIs, as well as numerous local wildlife sites. Since this chapter was written, one positive development has been the withdrawal of the planning application at Lodge Hill in Kent. Environmentalists now hope that the original scheme to build 5,000 new homes will be permanently dropped. However, they expect at the least that smaller applications will be submitted in the future that will affect parts of the site.

more about the British landscape than any words ever written. Yet what we need to acquire is something that might be called 'ecological thinking': an ability to approximate, through our imaginations, to the processes of a real ecosystem. We need a way of thinking that apprehends the rhizome-like multiplicity of impacts that work through and upon land and nature. Farmers used to practise it because they managed a complex ecosystem – a blend of multiple, fluctuating, simultaneous harvests including hens, cattle, sheep, root crops, vegetables, fruit, pasture, hay and cereals – in one land unit. For four generations they have been urged to abandon complexity and ecological thinking in favour of the 'logical' straight line.

Straight-line thinking connects too few truths to be of value in appreciating ecological processes. The spraying of pesticides and the use of nitrate fertilisers are linear approaches to ecological issues. The assumption is that once the chemicals have fulfilled the single intention of a user – once they have gone 'away' – they will cease to operate within the ecosystem to which they were introduced. As Clark Gregory argues in William Bryant Logan's masterful book *Dirt*, 'There's no such place as "*away*"[my italics].'[11] We, the chemicals, the land, are part of a single system. The fertilisers continue journeying through the physical environment interacting in complex ways, fulfilling their unleashed ecological destinies.

While they boost crop production they also accumulate in the aquifers and must be stripped at high cost from our drinking water. They convert to nitrous oxide, a greenhouse gas 200 times more potent than carbon dioxide. Ecological thinking, as expressed by the European report discussed in Chapter 15, tells us that the true costs of that 'logical' and linear application of nitrogen is a downstream bill of between €70 and €320 billion per annum, double the value of the original boost to crops. The damage that we have inflicted on the land of this country in the name of logic requires that all of us acquire a capacity for ecological thinking.

Ecological thinking entails that we see ourselves *within* nature, and that we understand how everything we do has ecological consequences. We can, in truth, *never* escape nature. A convicted murderer, held in a concrete-and-steel cell in solitary confinement in the bowels of the most secure prison, encircled by nothing but razor-wire and linear arrangements of man-made material, who barely has the opportunity over

291

several decades to see a square of natural daylight, let alone walk upon the soil and enjoy all its manifold bounties, still lives within nature. Everything that he eats and breathes, all that he evacuates, everything about him, is part of an ecosystem. Ecology requires that all of us understand the privileges and blessings of those unending connections and the remorseless, possibly terrifying, scale of our responsibilities.

As our material and interior lives become supercharged with new sources of stimulation we have compensated by succumbing to another linear simplification. Our entire value system, the ways in which we think and talk about life, society, morality, etc., in any public and most especially in any political forum, have been rendered subservient to a single dominant scale as the capitalist model intensifies its hold on all parts of ourselves. It is as if the only qualitative measure of human happiness and experience is money. The entire national political conversation has been canalised into one debate. Yet the economy of a country is nothing but a way of disguising or, rather, one should say, a way of talking about, ecology – since all money comes *only* from nature. It is just ecology entirely devoid of responsibility for the rest of the living system.

We need somehow to recover a sense of responsibility for the non-linear structures of real life. We live on a planet where life is only to be found in about a fifteen-mile-deep veneer that is wrapped around the surface of the Earth. As far as we have been able to establish in the last 4,000 years, this is the only planet that bears life. We spend our days among the greatest event in all the galaxies; but many people would seem to prefer to play with their iPhones. Isn't it time that we built an appreciation of life into the very foundations of who we are?

4. The fourth horseman of the environmental apocalypse in our island is something identified in Oliver Rackham's *The History of the British Countryside*, where he wrote of 'all the little, often unconscious vandal-isms that hate what is tangled and unpredictable but create nothing.' Among the list of hateful measures, he included the destruction of ivy-tods or 'misshapen trees', the annual cutting of hedges down to the ground, the levelling of churchyards – and here I cannot help but recall the regime at St Mary Magdalene's in Gedney – and what he described

as 'pottering with paraquat'.[12] The real problem is that an ever-expanding arsenal of chemicals and equipment allows us all – not just farmers – to intervene almost to the point of nature's annihilation. In short, we are, as an entire people, guilty of excessive tidiness.

It is this that drives much of the sterilisation of Britain's public space, because what it aspires to is uniformity and, invariably, uniform lifelessness. The classic location is not farmland, but our gardens. The signature sound is the seemingly innocuous drone of the Sunday-morning mower, whose use is ritualised almost to the point of piety. Recall the sit-on mower near Gedney reducing ten acres to a short-back-and-sides of rye-grass monoculture. Ten acres could, correctly managed, support thousands of species of organism, in an explosive mix of colour and texture, across the full spectrum of life.

However, it must be added that lawnmowers are now possibly at risk, because the latest must-have of the tidy-minded is plastic grass, which is spreading with viral intensity. In London, where 3.6 million domestic gardens occupy about a quarter of the entire city area, an estimated third are already obliterated under concrete or other synthetic surfaces. And what happens in the capital happens everywhere. I have relatives who have just laid plastic grass.

If plastic grass is not ubiquitous already, then it soon will be, judging from the state of so many of our civic and public spaces – road verges, roundabouts, the curtilage to municipal institutions such as schools, offices, hospitals, churches and sometimes even our recreational parks, which all obey the same deep concern for rectilinear design and abiotic uniformity.* It is not uncommon to see, in such places, maintenance staff in white space suits, chemical drums upon their backs, spraying herbicides on the minute creases of green life that dare extrude from the cracks between concrete slabs. The closest thing that these outdoor

---

* But not, it must be added, the sides of many modern roads and motorways, which have been planted with rich varieties of perennials and now represent some of our most visible and even most beautiful flower-rich environments. There are glorious examples around Norwich and on the A11 through south Norfolk, which point to a brighter, more colourful, more nature-tolerant future. Such measures should be fast-tracked in all civic spaces.

spaces resemble is not anything in nature, but the interiors of buildings, which is presumably the largely unconscious intention.

As a result of the broad interpretations placed upon the word 'environment', which is taken to mean anything and everything connected to our surroundings, it is often assumed that tidiness is an important *environmental* goal in its own right. It finds expression in the mania for litter-picking and keeping Britain tidy, etc. Not that anyone should condone thoughtless litter; it is not just illegal, it is morally disgraceful, especially fly-tipping. Yet in a list of ten important environmental issues, litter would be tenth and in a list of twenty it would be twentieth. The perfect cure for this 'environmental' concern would be a visit to West Thurrock Lagoons and Canvey Wick nature reserves in Essex. They are two of Britain's most famous biodiverse brownfield sites, which are smothered in flowers and packed with rare bumblebees and beetles, but which are also described in Dave Goulson's recent book as a paradise of 'dog faeces, graffiti, discarded beer cans and broken bottles'.[13]

Litter may be a social problem, but it is seldom a real enemy of biodiversity. Excessive tidiness, however, entails a massive loss of potential wildlife. If we could free ourselves as a society from this neurosis then it offers an extraordinary and, as yet, barely tapped dividend for nature. We may have destroyed 4 million acres of flower-rich meadow. We could recover at least half that figure if only our gardens, both civic and private, were freed from chemical interventions and turned back primarily to native flowers and shrubs. Instead of the work-intensive grass monoculture, we could have virtually labour-free pocket-sized meadows that require only a single cut in late summer. Instead of fitted grass carpets we could have zones of colour and diversity, rich in pollinating insects such as bumblebees, butterflies and hoverflies.

One final observation is that our reluctance to live with nature's creative disorder is an attempt not just to subordinate the life around us, but also to control something within ourselves. This moral imperative is present on the first page of the Old Testament:

And God said, Let us make man in our image, after our likeness: and let them have dominion over the fish of the sea, and over the

fowl of the air, and over the cattle, and over every creeping thing
that creepeth upon the earth.

As troubling in its way, for me, is that these issues play out even in
the branding of the RSPB, which illuminates how human dominion
over nature is, in the words of John Livingston, concreted into 'the very
foundations of western thought'.[14] The organisation's present strapline
is 'Giving Nature a Home'. One can understand the very positive intent.
Permitting presence may be the absolute inverse of enforcing absence,
but both rely on the same basic solipsism that we are the agents and
nature is the passive external recipient of our agency. We cannot *give*
nature a home: nature is a home – *ours*. We live within it. As long as
we see ourselves as outside it, then in those powerful words of John
Fowles, cited in my frontispiece, 'it is lost both to us and in us'.

5. Environmentalism is part of what you might call soft politics in
Britain. Even writing this line of words is a form of political activity.
But hard politics in this country converges in a very specific form of
psychological architecture, which we know as the Houses of Parliament.
Those structures were designed to fulfil an eighteenth- and nineteenth-
century process, whereby two relatively similar landed communities
exercised power in their own interests. These tribal groupings were
known as the Whigs and the Tories, or the Liberals and the Conservatives.
Much later, at the beginning of the twentieth century, there was a process
of displacement as the Labour Party supplanted the Liberals as the
broadly progressive grouping in parliament. The pattern has obtained
until today.

Its fundamentally binary structure is indisputable. The very vocabulary of our system – both sides of the House, yah-boo politics, the
benches opposite, upper and lower chamber, Her Majesty's Opposition
and Her Majesty's Government, divisions, the ayes to the left and the
noes to the right, the contents and the not contents, the two-horse
race – reinforces the essential kinesis of our public life. If you cannot
hear the central dialectic in those words then conjure its physical
analogue: two rows of raked wooden benches in diametrical opposition.

At the heart of the process is a winner-takes-all, first-past-the-post arrangement. It squeezes the body politic of a twenty-first-century nation into an eighteenth-century whalebone corset. Some say this is beneficial since it delivers strong, disciplined government and has avoided internal civil conflict for the last 330 years (if one discounts the 'Jacobite' uprisings of the eighteenth century). And we had a chance to change it by referendum in 2011. By more than two to one we rejected the most basic form of proportional representation. Yet no one can doubt that our peculiar political dispensation acts as a powerful drag upon change in Britain.* Recall how it took 114 years and more than twenty separate submitted bills before people acquired a legal right simply to walk on non-productive land. Should we really believe that this legislative entanglement was a clear expression of the will of the nation?

The same restrictive process acts as an immense, regressive filter upon our entire imaginative life. It is very difficult to find ways to talk about environmental issues except outside the main architecture of hard politics because of the binary clamp that the system places over us. For 150 years 'green' politics have remained in the margins of our national conversation or have tried to adapt to the prevailing conditions. As one small illustration of the contortion that this entails, at the 2015 election it took 34,343 votes to elect each Conservative MP and 40,290 votes for each Labour MP, but 1,157,613 votes to elect a single Green MP. And spare a thought for the United Kingdom Independence Party, which needed 3,881,099 votes for its solitary representative.

---

* One cannot help noticing in a post-Brexit, post-Trump age a profound sense of broken politics among the English-speaking communities on both sides of the Atlantic. One can also see a shared trend towards increasing voter apathy. In the six US elections from 1896 to 1916 the average turnout was 67.25 per cent, compared with 53 per cent in the six elections since 1996. In Britain, the average voter turnout in the six general elections between 1951 and 1970 was 77.1 per cent, but 66.85 per cent in the six between 1992 and 2015. Does the downward pattern in each country – and in the USA only a little over half those eligible now bother to vote – indicate a pervasive sense that binary two-party politics changes nothing? And if it does, is it time that we addressed how the deepest reflex patterns in Anglo-Saxon thought, which seem rooted in the idea of an eternal antinomy between two equal forces, and which is perhaps also manifest in the dominance of the iambic poetic metre, are blocking modern politics?

6. This political system dovetails with another part of the country's political mindset, which we can call 'land-blindness'. As we have seen, the British, more than almost any other country in Europe, are a landless people. In excess of 53 million of us possess an average of just seven one-hundredths of an acre. In 1072, at the drawing up of the Domesday Book, 4.9 per cent of England's eleventh-century population controlled 99 per cent of the land. Today just 0.3 per cent of Britain's 65 million own 69 per cent of it all. In Scotland, which has the most concentrated pattern of land ownership in Europe, three-quarters of the entire country is held in estates of 1,000 acres or more.[15]

Land is the business of a tiny minority, and because it has been outside the mental horizon of so many people for so long, it seems not to register with the British public. How else can we explain the inertia and lack of a sense of injustice that for the last seventy years we have had, in the form of farm subsidies, a feudal system of transfer from the poor to the wealthy? At its worst this process delivers huge amounts of taxpayers' money to millionaire landowners for no other reason than the fact that they are millionaire landowners. In the twelve years to 2011 just fifty Scottish farmers received £230.6 million in subsidy between them, an annual average of £383,000.[16] Should we not even ask why?

It is odd that in all the brouhaha about Brexit, neither from the remainers nor the leave campaign has there been much if any discussion of the 40 per cent of the EU budget which still goes in these feudal payments. As we noted in Chapter 16, Kevin Cahill, in *Who Owns the World*, pointed out that at the heart of the annual giveaway of €46 billion are the 77,000 landowners in the EU area, who own 112 million acres and receive an annual €12 billion of taxpayers' money.[17] Nor is the CAP the only measure of our land-blindness. As Andy Wightman observes, 'Rural landowners have successfully secured the abolition of all taxes on land and, despite professing to be rural businesses, still enjoy exemption from business rates.'[18]

We have somehow contrived to discount land as a significant subject for public debate, yet continued to view land ownership as an instinctive measure of social and cultural merit. The landed lord it over us still. As I observed in Chapter 16, until the early part of this century,

750 hereditary peers sustained a central place in Britain's political life. Even now ninety-two of them – unelected and unrepresentative, except perhaps of the peculiar interests of their community – retain this same inexplicable privilege. Yet we seem embarrassed to talk about it.

Our land-blindness meshes perfectly with a peculiar characteristic of the landed themselves. It is their land secrecy. They, by contrast, jealously guard the precise details of their territorial possessions just as they might resist public knowledge of their private incomes or their personal sex lives. Recall the shadow Conservative minister who observed that the tax scam at the heart of forestry might attract the attentions of 'the *envious* and *malevolent*'. Recall also how the Forestry Commission, unlike comparable institutions in other European countries, publishes nothing and collects minimal information on the ownership structure of private forestry in Britain. Kevin Cahill has pointed out how, in a manner very similar to the latter agency, the UK government refused to reveal the names of those getting public farm subsidies from the public purse, despite being in breach of the EU's own Constitutional Convention.[19] Today one-third and possibly as much as half the acreage of England and Wales is still not recorded in the Land Registry. One estimate in 1999 suggested that just 25,000 acres of the 11.2 million acres that are unregistered, when they were released as building plots to the construction industry, were worth £40,000 an acre, with a total value of £10–17 billion.[20]

We need as a nation to end the bizarre taboo that nourishes our land-blindness. We should challenge the vested interests who would wish us *not* to be aware or to understand the uses and abuses of our countryside.

7. The discipline that has revealed the inner workings of the more-than-human parts of life is science. Ecologists and biologists were also the community who devised the system of land assessment that is at the very foundations of British conservation and which is elegantly articulated in the *Nature Conservation Review*.

None of this should change. In fact, I would go so far as to say that the only meaningful designations about land quality should be those rooted in an appreciation of biodiversity, and all others that rely upon aesthetic ideas about landscape – the designation of Area of Outstanding

Natural Beauty springs to mind – should be scrapped or radically reorganised. But these issues belong under Truth 8.*

Unfortunately, however, the dominant roles accorded to science and scientists in the ways that society ascribes importance to nature have led to a major undervaluing of nature's multiplicity of roles. For scientists have constructed all the arguments for nature in their own image. The Site of Special Scientific Interest is the classic motif of their mindset. The process was writ large in the battle to stop Cow Green Reservoir, as described in Chapter 12.

Setting aside that the other parts of marine and terrestrial life are the source of all the air we breathe and all the food we eat, nature is the regulator of human health. Recently the Wildlife Trusts have expressed these ideas through its Nature and Well Being Act, a proposed piece of legislation that places nature at the heart of the planning process and which takes account of the increasing evidence that access to nature is a crucial element of much preventative and treatment-based healthcare. Yet that ascription of central importance to nature says nothing about its fundamental place in all cultural activity.

What has also been overlooked is the way that diversity in nature is a primary driver for our creativity. Our relationship to the rest of life nourishes the sciences, the visual arts, sculpture, photography, poetry – indeed, all forms of literature, dance, music and cinematography. We are accustomed to the physical connections that flow through the web of life, but sometimes its impacts are immaterial. Our imaginations are, in part, a result of ecological processes. Soul and soil are genuinely and fundamentally interconnected.

Recall George Trevelyan's words that are cited in the frontispiece: 'By the side of religion, by the side of science, by the side of poetry and art stands natural beauty, not as a rival to these, but as the common

---

* I will add, however, that I once spoke with a Nebraskan farmer, whose 500-acre farm of GM corn was one continuous monoculture, on which, in 2008, he sprayed an estimated $500,000-worth of chemical fertilisers and pesticides annually. The farmer also thought his farm was beautiful, although he could not explain why. The point I would make is that 'beauty', while profound and real to its beholders, is a near-worthless measure of landscape quality. Recall also the imaginary couple described in Chapter 12 who professed how much they loved Cow Green Reservoir.

inspirer and nourisher of them all.' The only thing I would change would be to substitute *nature* for 'natural beauty'. 'Beauty' is unnecessary. The wings of a house fly, the eyes of an adder and the carapace of an edible crab are beautiful if you look at them for long enough.

The French anthropologist Claude Lévi-Strauss wrote of Amerindians that they found birds not only good to eat but also good to think with.[21] The same principle should be extended to include all nature and all peoples. Other life forms supply the basic fabric of our inner worlds. It is evident in the earliest human forays into what we now call art, especially the spectacular Palaeolithic cave frescoes involving images of aurochs, reindeer, horses, rhinoceros, bears, lions and owls.

Aldous Huxley once suggested that if you took birds out of English poetry you would have to dispose of half the nation's verse canon. I would go so far as to suggest that the single most important natural motif in all world poetry, yielding deeper and more profound insights into the quality of human experience, is the nightingale (see *Birds and People*, pp. 476–9). Tim Dee, chair of the judges for the Forward Prize for Poetry in 2005, noted how there were far more poems on blackbirds in that year than there were on the Iraq War or the 9/11 bombings of the Twin Towers.[22] Nature matters perennially. And these examples merely glance at the totality of our cultural indebtedness.

Go into any British village hall to look at any local art exhibition and you will find a very high percentage of the works depict the other parts of life. At the other end of the artistic continuum, if one had to redact the references to nature from William Shakespeare's collective canon, then one would have to disfigure virtually every single page he wrote and ruin whole plays.

What happens when a country destroys the very basis of its creative responses? We may well find out. But I suggest that, along with the biological deficits inflicted by the self-destruction of our land, we will incur systemic cultural loss. Go to South Lincolnshire if you want to experience what denatured landscapes do to the human spirit.

At present, there is a vector in our cultural life that seems to contradict this statement. It is the massive growth in what one might call environmental art, of which nature writing is a component. Never has the field been richer. Yet we must be careful not to assume that this upsurge of creative responses to our vanishing natural environment is an organic part of some societal awakening and perhaps the vanguard of corrective action. The danger is that it is a compensatory, nostalgic and internalised re-creation of what was once our birthright and is no more: the nature that we knew and are trying to retain through cultural re-imaginings. Ultimately, without the thing itself, without the under-lying biodiversity, these responses will be like the light from a dead star: they will persist for a while, maybe even decades, but they will travel onwards into the darkness that will eventually consume them.

8. In the sections on north Norfolk (see Chapter 5) and Kinder Scout (Chapter 8) I discussed at length the confusing multiplicity of landscape designations that have grown up in a thicket around the enterprise of environmental thought. Not only have we gone on adding additional layers as each new initiative sweeps us briefly away, but British environmentalism has also been dogged by what is called 'the Great Divide', which was instituted with the establishment of the national parks in 1950.

Essentially it turned on a particular question about nature. Do we cherish it for its manifest beauties measured by some arbitrary aesthetic code? Or do we value and protect wildlife diversity? At that time, we allowed two fundamentally separate systems to grow up. National parks were an answer to the first question, and SSSIs and national nature reserves were intended as the answer to the second. Recall the words of historian Michael Winter when he suggested that the division was intel-lectually flawed and 'a debilitating feature of the British arrangements'.

At present in the British landscape, places are classified as national parks, national nature reserves, areas of outstanding natural beauty, Ramsar sites, biosphere reserves, special protection areas, special areas of conservation, sites of special scientific interest, local nature reserves, county wildlife sites and so on. The truth is, it is maddeningly complicated.

And is it really necessary? Could we not call them just one name, from the most important to the least, from the World Heritage Site or biosphere reserve as designated by the UNESCO programmes, to the county wildlife site like my own Blackwater?

My version of that name would be 'special places for all nature' (merely as a token to allow discussion of this issue), with an acronym SPAN that recalls for us in perpetuity that the location's importance *spans* what it does both for the more-than-human parts of nature and for us. It would remind us that the process is a dual one: for people and for the other parts of life. And all constitute one thing. So, Blackwater would be a SPAN site. But anywhere that was previously an SSSI would become a SPAN1 site. If a place were an SSSI, but also an SAC and an SPA it would be SPAN3. And if it were additionally a Ramsar Site and a Biosphere Reserve it could be SPAN5. But there would be only one designation for all places important for nature.

Whatever anyone thinks of this idea, the underlying truth is incontrovertible: environmentalists have constructed a barrier to the general public's understanding of nature and of environmental activity. It should be pulled down to make life simpler. Naturalists and environmentalists need to recover the art of speaking plainly.

One other classic expression of the way in which environmentalists have functioned like the legal profession or a medieval priesthood – using language to ring-fence their profession – is in the matter of scientific nomenclature. Scientific Greek and Latin and the nomenclatural system originally devised by Linnaeus in the eighteenth century are undisputed cornerstones of all natural history. Unfortunately, many organisms are still unknown outside this complex vocabulary, and it inserts a major obstacle between the layperson and the other parts of life. British spiders (650 species), flies (>7,000 species) and lichens (>1,600 species) are especially shut out from our ken, partly because of this issue.

Just to give another small example, until very recently it was difficult to find any publications that use common English names for the 10+ British species of sphagnum moss, whose effects are discussed in detail in Chapter 17. They are still invariably referred to with titles such as *Sphagnum capillifolium* subsp *capillifolium*, or *Sphagnum denticulatum* or *Spahgnum fimbriatum*.* Yet they are, arguably, among the most important wild plants in all of British nature.

---

* There are mercifully common names for these species. The three listed are acute-leaved, cow-horn and fringed bogmosses.

Not all life forms can be incorporated into public knowledge. Some groups are just too complex, and reference to them only in scientific nomenclature is an unavoidable technical necessity. Massive strides have also been taken to introduce accessible names for all sorts of organisms that were previously behind the Latin wall. Fungi and moths, especially micro-moths, are two such large groups that have been rescued from oblivion. Both are now mainstream parts of British natural history activity. There is no more communal, nor more enjoyable wildlife excursion than a foray in search of mushrooms. I have been party to outings that comfortably accommodate scores of people. They are caravans of sharing and laughter and learning and intimacy with the October landscape.

On the other hand, there is a section of the community that wishes to cleave to the old ways. So often it is a matter of pride. It arises out of a mindset which insists that 'since I have mastered these complexities, so must you, in order to join the club.' I once attended an excellent entomological course focused on hoverflies, one of the most beautiful and important insect groups, which plays a fundamental role in pollination. When I suggested that common names should be devised and promulgated for the 280+ British species there were unanimous howls of opposition. How could they possibly function without the primacy of *Sphaerophoria scripta* or *Helophilus pendulus*? Both these species, which are in their ways as attractive, engaging and harmless as butterflies, probably occur commonly in your garden. I am guessing, however, that many will never have even heard of them.

9. The creation of common names for all parts of nature is probably the biggest low-cost change that environmentalists could implement. The most important single measure to improve all environmental effort would be to forge genuine systemic unity among all parts. All too often there is discussion of the 'environmental movement' or the 'green lobby', as if there were harmony and accord among its various constituents. The ninth Truth is that there is not.

The inability to combine over the course of the twentieth century and until today, is the cardinal failure of environmentalists in this sense: all parts of its resolution are in the hands of those who are all apparently on one side. There needs to be an NEU – a National Environmentalists' Union. The present government talks about our generation leaving a countryside richer than the one it inherited. If it is serious then the NEU needs representation at the highest levels equal to that of the NFU (National Farmers' Union).

The environmental campaigner George Monbiot has pointed out in his book *Captive State* that almost all the major industries that have impact upon the British environment employ sector-wide lobby institutions to fight their case in parliament and beyond. These collectives have names like the Construction Clients Forum, the Construction Industry Council, the Construction Confederation, the British Quarry Products Association and the National Council of Building Materials Producers.[23] Is it not odd that environmental organisations have no such voice?

There are indisputable alliances that have been long established and which yield major dividends. The organisation Wildlife and Countryside Link has provided a platform for collaboration in key campaigns. The ability of the different organisations to act in concert is seen by environmentalists elsewhere in Europe as a distinguishing feature of the British scene.[24] Equally, the *State of Nature* reports show an increased recognition of the need for collective impact and offer in themselves a vision of a more united future.

Yet it is not enough. There is no round table that regulates and intensifies the collective impact of the nature lobby. There is no evolving blueprint that sets out a common policy. There is no social forum that allows for the parts to mingle, to appreciate shared values, to forge common bonds. On the contrary, sometimes, as shown in Chapter 5, there is a sense of go-it-alone individualism and even competition.

Sometimes one sees how separate parts of the 'movement' function in ways that even look contradictory. A longstanding initiative for the Campaign to Protect Rural England is to safeguard the Green Belt, the encircling boundary between town and country that has curtailed the outward sprawl of development for decades. Dogged resistance to building on the outer green spaces has been a central plank of CPRE work almost since its foundation. The question that now hangs over this old fixture is what exactly is being safeguarded in the process, and where is the development directed if not into the countryside?

Alternative sites for development are commonly found in what are known as brownfield sites, the pockets of unused or under-used land lying within the urban boundary. These are part of the CPRE's answer to safeguarding the Green Belt. Such places, however, have often been shown to be rich in wildlife, and occasionally very rich. In 2008 BugLife, Britain's leading conservation charity for invertebrates, surveyed no fewer than 576 such places in the London and Thames Gateway region and found that half held significant biodiversity. A few, including the West Thurrock Lagoons in Essex, may be, proportionate to area, among the most biodiverse places in the entire country. Some environmentalists now question the value of kneejerk defence of Green Belt when such intensively managed agricultural land, which is what Green Belt land often is, can be nearly worthless for wildlife, irrespective of its greenness or its open character.[25] Protecting Green Belt only adds to the pressure on brownfield areas.

The two parts of this environmental conundrum should speak to one another and harmonise a common position.* A perennially attended round table of the NEU would allow this to happen.

The other loss incurred because of a divided house is well illustrated by the present efforts to halt a six-lane, 22,000-cars-a-day highway across one side of the marshes at Lough Beg, County Derry, which is a reserve protected not only as an ASSI (the Northern Ireland equivalent of a SSSI), but also as an SAC, a Ramsar site and a Natura 2000 site. It is, incidentally, at the heart of the bog landscapes that inspired Seamus Heaney's poetry discussed in Chapter 17.

A remarkable couple, Chris and Doris Murphy, at their own expense and initiative, are seeking to overturn the decision in the courts after all the major NGOs have failed to contest the construction. What the Murphys want is not to prevent the road, which all agree is necessary,

---

* This division in opinion over Green Belt versus brownfield biodiversity is, incidentally, a classic expression of the 'Great Divide' in British environmental thought. The healing of this split between those concerned with landscape beauty and those prioritising biodiversity would be a primary goal for any round table.

but to re-route it in a way that accords with the long-established environmental legislation. It is as much a test of the principles governing the development of the British countryside as the other 'hot issue' at Lodge Hill in Kent, discussed in Truth 2. Yet the RSPB, along with the Wildfowl and Wetland Trust, Birdwatch Ireland, the Joint Nature Conservation Committee and Ulster Wildlife (a Wildlife Trust affiliate) have offered no visible public support for the Lough Beg campaign.

In short, the Murphys are pretty much alone, although they have received backing from musicians and from poets and writers outraged at the idea of Heaney's poetic landscape being violated. One of the central functions of an NEU round table would be to ensure that each campaign could be eligible for support from the collective 7 million members of conservation groups.

10. The American farmer and writer Wendell Berry, in an essay from 1969 entitled 'Think Little', suggested that in matters of wildlife loss none of us is innocent. 'A protest meeting on the issue of environmental abuse', he wrote,

> is not a convocation of accusers, it is a convocation of the guilty. That realization ought to clear the smog of self-righteousness … and let us see the work that is to be done.

Every one of us is to blame. And there are no exemptions; not even Sir David Attenborough. Britain's contemporary capitalist society, from which it is impossible to disconnect, is a shared enterprise. It implicates us all. We *are* the problem. 'Nearly every one of us, nearly every day of his life,' according to Berry, 'is contributing *directly* to the ruin of this planet.'[26] No amount of opposition to it in our heads or on our Facebook pages will change those basic facts.

Berry's larger point is that, while we may be responsible, every one of us is, therefore, potentially part of the solution. We *merely* have to act to make a difference. It returns us nicely to the matter of hope, with which I began the chapter, because its supply is in direct proportion to the individual efforts made by any person. To have real hope is not to smear over the facts a higher gloss of optimism, as if the problems can be resolved merely by thinking about them in a particular way. The measures we take have to be ecological in nature; that is, they must travel from the head and heart to the hand. In Matt Howard's magnificently simple line of poetry quoted in Chapter 1, each one of us has 'to act with the whole body and mean it'.

The answer to our environmental problems may be societal in nature, but the solutions will not come if we wait until all of us resolve to act together. Change happens when individuals have the courage to do something independently, regardless of the opponents and even the indifference of supposed colleagues. We have only to contemplate the example set by Chris and Doris Murphy in their attempts to halt a motorway across Lough Beg to realise this. Octavia Hill was another such individual. Think also on Benny Rothman (see Chapter 6), or Margaretta Louisa Lemon (see Chapter 3) or Jake Fiennes (see Chapter 17). In truth there are thousands, if not tens of thousands of individuals acting as well as thinking in ways that can change the world by changing one small part of it.

Yet it is not all about founding momentous societies or attending dramatic court appearances. Most of the key decisions in matters of the environment are literally kitchen-sink choices: they are about which washing-up liquid we use, which shampoo, which detergent, what transport we employ, what food we eat, what pension fund we have, which energy source we pick and the level of acquisitiveness of our lifestyles. Wendell Berry further points out that most of the vegetables needed for a family of four can be grown on a plot measuring 40 × 60 feet. Our gardens are potential sources of high-quality food and of diverse habitat. How we manage them, he argues, can change 'a piece of the world'.

We all need to do more. For my tenth Truth is not really a truth at all, but a question. If the British – with all the privileges of our technology and our historical wealth, with our traditions of democratic government but also our long intricate attachments to nature and our self-proclaimed love for a green and pleasant land – if we cannot sustain a country equal to the love we bear it, then who on Earth can?

Notes

Abbreviations

COED – The Compact Edition of the Oxford English Dictionary, Oxford University Press, 1971.

Chapter 1 – My Place

1. Marren, 2012, p. 24.
2. Cocker and Tipling, 2013, pp. 125–8.
3. *State of Nature*, 2013, p. 7.
4. Avery, 2012, p. 112.

Chapter 2 – A Very Big Thing

1. Allison and Morley, 1989, p. 7.
2. Darley, 1990, p. 314.
3. Weideger, 1994, pp. 26 and 122.
4. Avery, 2012, p. 303.
5. Murphy, 2002, pp. 63–4.
6. Hopkins, 1986, p. 30.
7. Taylor, 1997, p. 124.
8. Murphy, 2002, p. 22.
9. Waterson, 1994, p. 37.
10. Waterson, 1994, p. 123.
11. Smout, 2000, p. 156.
12. Weideger, 1994, p. 92.
13. Weideger, 1994, pp. 93 and 168; Gaze, 1988, pp. 113 and 288. National Trust Annual Report, 2013/4.
14. http://www.breitbart.com/london/2015/04/07/why-id-rather-eat-worms-than-renew-my-national-trust-membership.
15. *Daily Mail*, 9 April 2015, p. 63.

16. Waterson, 1994, p. 78.
17. Weideger, 1994, pp. 120–54.
18. Darley, 1990, p. 309.
19. Waterson, 1994, p. 45.

Chapter 3 – RSPB Soap

1. Bloomfield, 1993, p. 9.
2. Doughty, 1975, p. 25.
3. Sharrock, 1976, p. 32.
4. Hopkins, 1986, p. 72.
5. Batchelor, 2000, p. 241.
6. Marren, 2002, p. 63.

Chapter 4 – A Large Number of Local Reserves

1. Moss, 2004, pp. 44–5.
2. Sheail, 1976, p. 44.
3. Fowler in anon, 1976, pp. 13–17; George in Taylor, Seago, Allard and Dorling, 1999, pp. 67–91.
4. Sheail, 1976, p. 175.
5. Rothschild and Marren, 1997, p. 42.
6. George in Taylor, Seago, Allard and Dorling, 1999, p. 71.
7. Fowler in anon, 1976, p. 16.
8. Sands, 2012, pp. 36 and 54.
9. Sands, 2012, p. 54.
10. Sands, 2012, p. 459.
11. Sands, 2012, pp. 219–27.
12. Sands, 2012, p. 521.
13. Wildlife Trusts, *The Status of England's Local Wildlife Sites 2014*, p. 5.
14. Rothschild and Marren, 1997, p. 7.
15. Rothschild and Marren, 1997, p. 42.
16. Sands, 2012, p. 14.
17. Sheail, 1976, p. 64.
18. Sands, 2012, p. 40.

Chapter 5 – A Bit of a Competitor

1. Richardson, 1995, p. 154.
2. Smith, 2007, p. 59.
3. Julian Hoffman, pers comm.
4. https://www.gov.uk/government/publications/2010-to-2015-government-policy-common-agricultural-policy-reform. Accessed 26 October 2016.
5. http://store.mintel.com/mens-and-womens-fragrances-uk-august-2014.
6. http://www.ctpa.org.uk/content.aspx?pageid=310.
7. Sands, 2012, p. 41.

8. Sands, 2012, pp. 59–60.
9. http://www.wcl.org.uk/what-we-do.asp.
10. Williams, 1976, pp. 219–24.
11. Adams, 1996, p. 148.
12. http://www.wcl.org.uk/legal.asp; accessed 14/10/16.
13. Cahill, 2006, p. 26.
14. Wightman, 2013, p. 242.
15. Wightman, 2013, p. 243.

Chapter 6 – We Don't Like Hill Walkers in Derbyshire

1. Avery, 2012, p. 197.
2. Rothman, 2012, p. 38.
3. Rothman, 2012, p. 19.
4. Rothman, 2012, p. 51.

Chapter 7 – The Legitimate Lord of the Landscape

1. Hoskins, 1988, pp. 150–51.
2. Hoskins, 1988, p. 154.
3. Mabey, 1980, p. 171.
4. Hopkins, 1986, p. 39.
5. Hopkins, 1986, p. 6.
6. Hopkins, 1986, p. 63.
7. Hopkins, 1986, p. 271.
8. Smout, 2000, p. 147.
9. Hopkins, 1986, p. 88.
10. Hopkins, 1986, p. 73.
11. Hopkins, 1986, p. 163.
12. Defoe, 1928, vol. II, p. 176.
13. Taylor, 1997, pp. 23–5; Cannadine, 1992, p. 14.
14. Taylor, 1997, pp. 121–2.
15. Smout, 2000, p. 155.
16. Taylor, 1997, p. 23.
17. Taylor, 1997, pp. 79–80.
18. Hey, 2014, p. 164.
19. Gaskell, 2006, p. 38.
20. Stephenson, 1989, p. 46.
21. Stephenson, 1989, p. 44.
22. Smout, 2000, p. 155.
23. Taylor, 1997, p. 260.
24. Stephenson, 1989, p. 153.
25. Stephenson, 1989, p. 153.
26. Stephenson 1989, p. 165.

27. Smout, 2000, pp. 151–4; Taylor, 1997, p. 122.
28. Mabey, 2015, p. 131.
29. Shoard, 1997, p. 130; Cahill, 2001, p. 6.
30. http://www.monbiot.com/2012/06/04/the-resurgent-aristocracy.

Chapter 8 – Things Are Going To Be Different after the War

1. Smout, 2000, p. 143.
2. Nicholson, 1970, pp. 29–30.
3. Moore, 2003, pp. 526–8.
4. Seaman, 1966, p. 419.
5. Nicholson, 1970, p. 183.
6. Seaman, 1966, p. 416.
7. Winter 1996, p. 88.
8. Winter, 1996, p. 200.
9. Sheail, 1976, pp. 75–6; Sheail, 1998, p. 21.
10. Brodie, 2013, p. 13.
11. Worster, 2008, p. 328.
12. Shoard, 1997, p. 475.
13. Tubbs, 1997, pp. 79–85.
14. Tansley, 1945, p. 63.
15. Peterken, 2013, p. 358.
16. Sheail, 1998, p. 9.
17. MacEwen and MacEwen, 1982, pp. 17–18.
18. Waterson, 1994, p. 233.
19. Waterson, 1994, p. 233.

Chapter 9 – Pluto's Dark-Blue Daze

1. Austin, 1988, p. 81.
2. Lawrence, 1994, p. 584.

Chapter 10 – One of Nature Conservation's Biggest Disasters

1. Sheail, 1998, p. 1.
2. Sheail, 1998, p. 36.
3. Sheail, 1998, p. 26.
4. MacEwen and MacEwen, 1982, p. 19.
5. Sheail, 1998, p. 33.
6. Sheail, 1998, p. 32.
7. Marren, 2002, p. 81.
8. Tompkins, 1989, p. 36.
9. Smith, 2007, p. 129.

10. Sheail, 1998, p. 207.
11. Shoard, 1980, p. 70.
12. Shoard, 1980, p. 70.
13. Smith, 2007, p. 133.
14. Smith 2007, p. 135.
15. Smith, 2007, p. 135.

Chapter 11 – The Chaotic Conditions of a Public Inquiry

1. Harvey, 1998, p. 146.
2. Gregory in Smith, 1975, p. 180.
3. Gregory in Smith, 1975, pp. 171 and 177.
4. Gregory in Smith, 1975, p. 153.
5. Gregory, 1975, p. 153.
6. Gregory, 1975, p. 156.

Chapter 12 – Irreparable Harm to a Unique Place

1. Gregory in Smith, 1975, p. 164.
2. Gregory, 1971, p. 133.
3. Gregory, in Smith, 1975, p. 171.
4. Gregory, in Smith, 1975, pp. 181–2.
5. Stamp, 1969, p. 71.
6. Stoddart, 2013, pp. 39–56.
7. Tansley, 1945, p. 5.
8. Adams, 1996, p. 90.
9. Sheail, 1998, p. 162.
10. Baker, 2010, p. 31.
11. Livingston, 2007, p. 48.
12. Adams, 1996, p. 95.
13. Adams, 1996, p. 95.
14. http://hansard.millbanksystems.com/lords/1967/feb/23/tees-valley-and-cleveland-water-bill.

Chapter 13 – Factory Flowers

1. Cobbett, 2011, vol. 2, p. 239.
2. Cobbett, 2011, vol. 2, p. 239.
3. http://countrysideinfo.co.uk/woodland_manage/tree_value.htm.
4. Grigson, 1996, pp. 415–6.
5. Dee, 2013, p. 3.

Chapter 14 – The Greatest Achievement of Our Ancestors

1. Rackham, 1996, p. 35.
2. Wheeler, 1868, p. 13.

3. Purseglove, 1988, p. 25.
4. Wheeler, 1868, p. 19.
5. Thirsk, 1953, p. 9.
6. Darby, 1974, p. 42.
7. Thirsk, 1953, p. 4.
8. Darby, 1968, p. 35.
9. Darby, 1968, p. 52; Wheeler, 1868, p. 69.
10. Ray and Willughby, 1678, p. 373.
11. Ekwall, 1960, p. 166.
12. See the COED, pp. 2379 and 2384, and Worthington et al., 2010, p. 375.
13. Thirsk, 1953, p. 9.
14. Thirsk, 1953, p. 27.
15. Thirsk, 1953, p. 26.
16. Thirsk, 1953, p. 6.
17. Rotherham, 2013, p. 128.
18. Darby, 1968, p. 69.
19. Darby, 1968, p. 55; Rotherham, 2013, p. 127.
20. Worthington et al., 2011, p. 4.
21. Browne, 1927, III, pp. 537–8.
22. http://www.gofishing.co.uk/Angling-Times/Section/News–Catches/General-News/July-2010/Extinct-burbot-spotted-in-River-Eden-and-Great-Ouse/, accessed 21 June 2016.

Chapter 15 – What Countryside?

1. Wilson, 2003, p. 14.
2. http://www.tradingeconomics.com/united-kingdom/agricultural-land-percent-of-land-area-wb-data.html, accessed 28 July 2016.
3. Smout, 2000, p. 80.
4. Harvey, 1998, p. 147.
5. Juniper, 2013, pp. 60–2.
6. Juniper, 2015, p. 64.
7. Smout, 2000, p. 80.
8. Smout, 2000, pp. 80 and 86.
9. Smout, 2000, p. 80.
10. Shoard, 1980, p. 15.
11. http://www.ecifm.rdg.ac.uk/maclab3.htm, accessed 8 July 2016.
12. Harvey, 1998, p. 113.
13. Body, 1984, p. 4.
14. Shoard, 1997, p. 112.
15. Harvey, 1998, p. 36.
16. Williamson, 1986, p. 310.
17. Jake Fiennes, pers comm.
18. Smout, 2000, pp. 78–9; pers comm Jake Fiennes.
19. http://www.birdlife.org/datazone/speciesfactsheet.php?id=3153, accessed on 4 August 2016.

20. Hayhow et al., 2015, p. 12.
21. Balmer et al., 2013, pp. 352–3.
22. Brenchley, Gibbs, Pritchard and Spence, 2013, pp. 200–201.
23. Wilson, 1992, pp. 220–27.
24. Andrew Chick, pers comm.
25. Taylor and Marchant 2011, pp. 176–7.
26. Brenchley, Gibbs, Pritchard and Spence, 2013, pp. 200–201.
27. Tapper, 1992, p. 42.
28. Jake Fiennes interview, 13 December 2016.
29. Hayhow et al., 2015, pp. 12–13.
30. Macdonald, 2013, p. 181.
31. Thomas and Lewington, 2010, p. 102.

Chapter 16 – Subsidies I: The Sorcerer's Apprentice

1. Cannadine, 1992, p. 93.
2. Cannadine, 1992, p. 14.
3. Williams, 1983, p. 186.
4. Winter, 1996, p. 79.
5. Blythe, 1969, pp. 11–13.
6. Blythe, 1969, p. 20.
7. Winter, 1996, pp. 101–2.
8. Winter, 1996, pp. 104–5.
9. Harvey, 1998, p. 118.
10. Winter, 1996, pp. 105–6.
11. Sheail, 1998, p. 199.
12. Marren, 2002, p. 140.
13. Shoard, 1980, p. 44.
14. Harvey, 1998, p. 7.
15. Harvey, 1998, p. 5.
16. Harvey, 1998, p. 128.
17. http://www.igd.com/Research/Retail/UK-grocery-retailing; https://www.gov.uk/
    government/uploads/system/uploads/attachment_data/file/515048/food-farming-
    stats-release-07apr16.pdf. https://en.wikipedia.org/wiki/Obesity_in_the_United_
    Kingdom https://www.theguardian.com/commentisfree/2010/jun/17/common-
    agricultural-policy-cap-rotten-system, accessed 8 November 2016.
18. Winter, 1996, p. 118.
19. http://ec.europa.eu/eurostat/statistics-explained/index.php/Agricultural_
    census_in_France, accessed 8 November 2016.
20. Winter, 1996, pp. 130–31.
21. Marren, 2002, p. 139.
22. Harvey, 1998, p. 85; Adams, 1996, p. 83.
23. Monbiot, 2014, p. 160.
24. Monbiot, 2014, pp. 164–6.
25. Harvey, 1998, p. 13.

26. Hayhow et al., 2012, p. 19.
27. Cahill, 2006, pp. 79–80.
28. Shoard, 1980, p. 201.
29. Harvey, 1998, p. 155.
30. Harvey, 1998, pp. 58–9.

Chapter 17 – Subsidies II: The Sequel

1. Adams, 1996, p. 59.
2. Jake Fiennes interview, 13 December 2016.

Chapter 18 – Bog

1. Lindsay et al., 1988, p. 12.
2. Lindsay et al., 1988, pp. 13–15.
3. Lindsay et al., 1988, p. 27.
4. Ratcliffe, 1990, p. 157; Stroud et al., 1987, p. 18.
5. Cocker, 2006, p. 138.
6. Lindsay and Thompson, 1996, pp. 15–18.
7. Glob, 1969, p. 73.
8. Stroud et al., 1987, pp. 5–6.
9. Lindsay et al., 1988, p. 58.
10. John Lister Kaye interview, 11 June 2016.
11. Ogilvy in Jenkins, 1986, p. 38.

Chapter 19 – A Loathsomeness of Conifers

1. Rackham, 2003, p. 1.
2. Grove, 1983, p. 48.
3. Rackham, 2006, pp. 457–8.
4. Rackham, 2006, p. 458; Leslie, 2014, p. 10.
5. Rackham, 2006, p. 444.
6. Winter, 1996, p. 288.
7. Marren, 2002, p. 161.
8. Condry, 1995, p. 29.
9. Winter, 1996, pp. 291–2.
10. Leslie, 2014, page 31.
11. Tompkins, 1989, p. 31.
12. See for example 'The fall and rise of Galloway and Carrick trout', by Andy Ferguson et al. (http://www.wildtrout.org/content/wtt-articles).
13. Rackham, 2006, pp. 460–61.
14. Tompkins, 1989, p. 12.
15. Marren, 2002, p. 161; Michael Winter thought it was 14.3 per cent by 1991: see Winter, 1996, p. 278.

16. Tompkins, 1989, pp. 160–63.
17. Shoard, 1997, p. 167.
18. Tompkins, 1989, pp. 47–9.
19. Tompkins, 1989, p. 50.
20. Thompson, Birks and Birks, 2015, pp. 406–9; Shoard, 1997, pp. 167–9.
21. Wightman, 2013, p. 260.
22. Wightman, 2013, pp. 259–60.
23. Tompkins, 1989, p. 85.
24. Shoard, 1997, p. 92.
25. Tsouvalis, 2000, p. 71
26. Tsouvalis, 2000, p. 81.
27. Tsouvalis, 2000, p. 82.
28. Marren, 2002, pp. 165–6; Tompkins, 1989, p. 20.
29. Lindsay in Thompson, Birks and Birks, 2015, p. 444.
30. Lindsay in Thompson, Birks and Birks, 2015, p. 445.
31. Hunter, 1995, p. 27.
32. Stroud et al., 1987, p. 24.
33. Stroud et al., 1987, p. 8.
34. Tompkins, 1989, p. 26, Thompson, Birks and Birks, 2015, p. 412.

Chapter 20 – The Most Massive Single Loss of Important Wildlife Habitat

1. Stroud et al., 1987, p. 9.
2. Stroud et al., 1987, p. 106.
3. Smout, 2000, p. 20.
4. Thompson, Birks and Birks, 2015, p. 415.
5. Thompson, Birks and Birks, 2015, p. 415.
6. Tompkins, 1989, p. 170.
7. Tompkins, 1989, p. 168.
8. Marren, 2002, p. 165.
9. Thompson, Birks and Birks, 2015, p. 428.
10. Mabey, 1999, p. 165.
11. Tompkins, 1989, p. 133.
12. Tompkins, 1989, pp. 126–7.
13. Tompkins, 1989, p. 49.
14. Wightman, 2013, p. 257; Thompson, Birks and Birks, 2015, p. 407.
15. Leslie, 2014, p. 28.
16. Pete Mayhew and Mark Hancock interview, 17 April 2015.
17. Thompson, Birks and Birks, 2015, pp. 422–3.
18. Pete Mayhew and Mark Hancock, interview, 17 April 2015.
19. Leslie, 2014, p. 7.
20. Leslie, 2014, p. 169.
21. Leslie, 2014, p. 95.
22. Leslie, 2014, p. 29.

23. Thompson, Birks and Birks, 2015, p. 426; Sheail, 1998, p. 247.
24. http://www.independent.co.uk/news/people/obituary-lord-ridley-of-liddesdale-1495860.html.
25. Waterson, 1994, p. 227.
26. Marren in Goldsmith and Warren, 1993, p. 291.
27. Ridley, 1991, p. 114.
28. Marren in Goldsmith and Warren, 1993, p. 293.
29. Wightman, 2013, pp. 143 and 166.
30. Winter, 1996, p. 217.
31. Clements in Maclean, 2010, p. 174.
32. Marren in Goldsmith and Warren, 1993, p. 288.
33. Sir John Lister-Kaye interview, 11 June 2016.
34. Avery, 2015, pp. 139–42.

Chapter 21 – Our Green and Pleasant Land

1. Hayhow et al., 2016, p. 3.
2. Balmford, 2012, p. 3.
3. Balmford, 2012, p. 160.
4. Su Gough, *BTO News*, January – February 2012, pp. 16–17.
5. Gregory, 2016, pp. 150 and 191–4.
6. https://www.theguardian.com/environment/2013/sep/06/water-vole-population-slump.
7. *Butterfly*, Summer 2005, p. 3.
8. Fox et al., 2001, *The State of Britain's Butterflies*, p. 16.
9. Rackham, 2000, p. 3.
10. https://www.theguardian.com/environment/2014/sep/25/-sp-nightingales-lodge-hill-sanctuary-conservation-britain.
11. Logan, 1995, p. 47.
12. Rackham, 2000, p. 28.
13. Goulson, 2017, pp. 156–79.
14. Livingston, 2007, p. 69.
15. Wightman, 2013, p. 107.
16. Wightman, 2013, p. 243.
17. Cahill, 2006, p. 80.
18. Wightman, 2013, p. 107.
19. Cahill, 2006, p. 80.
20. Cahill, 2001, p. 14.
21. Levi-Strauss, 1963, p. 89.
22. Dee in anon, 2006, p. 9.
23. Monbiot, 2000, p. 150.
24. Matt Shardlow interview, 26 February 2014.
25. Goulson, 2017, pp. 156–7.
26. Berry, 2017, p. 50.

Select Bibliography

Place of publication is London unless stated otherwise.

Adams, W. M., *Future Nature*, Earthscan, 1996.

Allison, Hilary, and Morley, John (eds.), *Blakeney Point and Scolt Head Island*, National Trust, 1989.

Austin, Mary, *The Land of Little Rain*, Penguin, New York, 1988.

Avery, Mark, *Fighting for Birds: 25 Years in Nature Conservation*, Pelagic, Exeter, 2012.

—, *Inglorious: Conflict in the Uplands*, Bloomsbury, 2015.

Baker, J. A., *The Complete Works of J. A. Baker*, Harper Collins, 2010.

Balmer, Dawn, Gillings, Simon, Caffrey, Brian, Swann, Bob, Downie, Iain and Fuller, Rob, *Bird Atlas 2007–11: The Breeding and Wintering Birds of Britain and Ireland*, BTO Books, Thetford, 2013.

Balmford, Andrew, *Wild Hope: On the Front Lines of Conservation Success*, University of Chicago Press, Chicago, 2012.

Batchelor, John, *John Ruskin: No Wealth but Life*, Chatto and Windus, 2000.

Berry, Wendell, *The World-Ending Fire: The Essential Wendell Berry*, Allen Lane, 2017.

Bishop, Billy, *Cley Marsh and its Birds*, Boydell Press, Woodbridge, 1983.

Bloomfield, Andrew, *The Birds of the Holkham Area*, Fakenham, 1993.

Blythe, Ronald, *Akenfield*, Folio Society, 1969.

Body, Richard, *Agriculture: The Triumph and the Shame*, Temple Smith, 1984.

Bradshaw, Margaret (ed.), *The Natural History of Upper Teesdale*, Durham Wildlife Trust, Durham, 2003.

Brenchley, Anne, Gibbs, Geoff, Pritchard, Rhion and Spence, Ian, *The Breeding Birds of North Wales*, Liverpool University Press, Liverpool, 2013.

Brodie, Ian, *Why National Parks?* Wildtrack, Sheffield, 2013.

Browne, Sir Thomas, *The Works of Sir Thomas Browne*, vol. 1–3, John Grant, Edinburgh, 1927.

Cahill, Kevin, *Who Owns Britain*, Canongate, Edinburgh, 2001.

—, *Who Owns the World: Hidden Facts behind Land Ownership*, Mainstream, Edinburgh, 2006.

Cannadine, David, *The Decline and Fall of the British Aristocracy*, Picador, 1992.

Clapham, A. R. (ed.), *Upper Teesdale: The Area and its Natural History*, Collins, 1978.

Cobbett, William, *Rural Rides*, vols 1–2, Cosimo, New York, 2011.

Cocker, Mark, *A Tiger in the Sand*, Jonathan Cape, 2006.

Cocker, Mark and Tipling, David, *Birds and People*, Jonathan Cape, 2013.

Cole, G. D. H. and Postgate, Raymond, *The Common People: 1746–1946*, Methuen, 1968.

Condry, William, *Wildlife, My Life*, Gomer, Llandysul, 1995.

Darby, H. C., *The Medieval Fenland*, David and Charles, 1974.

—, *The Draining of the Fens*, Cambridge University Press, Cambridge, 1968.

Darley, Gillian, *Octavia Hill: A Life*, Constable, 1990.

Dee, Tim, *Four Fields*, Cape, 2013.

Defoe, Daniel, *A Tour Through England and Wales*, vol. II, Dent, 1928.

Doughty, Robin, *Feather Fashions and Bird Preservation*, University of California Press, Berkeley, 1975.

Edwards, K. C., *The Peak District*, Bloomsbury, 1990.

Ekwall, Eilert, *The Concise Dictionary of English Place-Names*, Oxford University Press, Oxford, 1960.

Ennion, E. A., *Adventurers Fen*, Herbert Jenkins, 1949.

Foot, David, *Woods and People: Putting Forests on the Map*, The History Press, Stroud, 2010.

Fox, R., Warren, M. S., Harding, P. T., McLean, I. F. G., Asher, J., Roy, D. and Brereton, T., *The State of Britain's Butterflies*, Butterfly Conservation, Warham, 2001.

Gaskell, Elizabeth, *Mary Barton*, Vintage, 2006.

Gaze, John, *Figures in a Landscape: A History of the National Trust*, Barrie & Jenkins, 1988.

George, Martin, *Birds in Norfolk and the Law, Past and Present*, Norfolk and Norwich Naturalists' Society, 2001.

Glob, P. V., *The Bog People: Iron Age Man Preserved*, Faber and Faber, 1969.

Goldsmith, F. B. and Warren, A. (ed.), *Conservation in Progress*, John Wiley and Sons, Chichester, 1993.

Goulson, Dave, *Bee Quest*, Jonathan Cape, 2017.

Gregory, Christine, *The Water Vole: The Story of One of Britain's Most Endangered Mammals*, Vertebrate Publishing, Sheffield, 2016.

Gregory, Roy, *The Price of Amenity: Five Studies in Conservation and Government*, Macmillan, 1971.

Grigson, Geoffrey, *The Englishman's Flora*, Helicon, 1996.

Grove, Richard, *The Future for Forestry*, British Association of Nature Conservationists, Cambridge, 1983.

Harvey, Graham, *The Killing of the Countryside*, Vintage, 1998.

Hayhow, D. B., Bond, A. L., Eaton, M. A., Grice, P. V., Hall, C., Hall, J., Harris, S. J., Hearn, R. D., Holt, C. A., Noble, D. C., Stroud, D. A., and Wooton, S., *The State of the UK's Birds 2015*, RSPB, Sandy, 2015.

Hayhow, D. B. et al., *State of Nature 2016*, The State of Nature Partnership, 2016.

Hey, David, *A History of the Peak District Moors*, Pen and Sword, Barnsley, 2014.

Hopkins, Harry, *The Long Affray: The Poaching Wars in Britain*, Papermac, 1986.

Hoskins, W. G., *The Making of the English Landscape*, Hodder and Stoughton, 1988.

Hunter, James, *The Making of the Crofting Community*, John Donald, Edinburgh, 1995.

—, *On the Other Side of Sorrow: Nature and People in the Scottish Highlands*, Birlinn, Edinburgh, 2014.

Jenkins, David (ed.), *Trees and Wildlife in the Scottish Uplands*, Institute of Terrestrial Ecology, Huntingdon, 1986.

Juniper, Tony, *What Has Nature Ever Done For Us?*, Profile, 2013.

—, *What Nature Does For Britain*, Profile, 2015.

Lawrence, D. H., *The Complete Poems of D. H. Lawrence*, Wordsworth, Ware, 1994.

Leslie, Roderick, *Forest Vision: Transforming the Forestry Commission*, New Environment Books, Bristol, 2014.

Lévi-Strauss, Claude, *Totemism*, Beacon Press, Boston, 1963.

Lindsay, Richard, Charman, D. J., Everingham, F., O'Reilly, R. M., Palmer, M. A., Rowell, T. A. and Stroud, David, *The Flow Country: The Peatlands of Caithness and Sutherland*, Nature Conservancy Council, Peterborough, 1988.

Lindsay, Richard and Thompson, Des, 'Bogland Brilliance', *Birds*, Spring 1996, pp. 15–18.

Livingston, John, *The John A. Livingston Reader*, McClelland and Stewart, Toronto, 2007.

Logan, William Bryant, *Dirt: The Ecstatic Skin of the Earth*, W. W. Norton, New York, 1995.

Lymbery, Philip, *Dead Zone: Where the Wild Things Were*, Bloomsbury, 2017.

Lymbery, Philip and Oakeshott, Isabel, *Farmageddon: The True Cost of Cheap Food*, Bloomsbury, 2014.

Mabey, Richard, *The Common Ground: A Place for Nature in Britain's Future*, Hutchinson, 1980.

—, *Selected Writings, 1974–99*, Chatto and Windus, 1999.

—, *The Cabaret of Plants: Botany and the Imagination*, Profile, 2015.

Macdonald, Helen, *H is for Hawk*, Jonathan Cape, 2013.

MacEwen, Ann and Malcolm, *National Parks: Conservation or Cosmetics?*, George Allen and Unwin, 1982.

McEwen, John, *A Life in Forestry*, Perth and Kinross Libraries, 1998.

Maclean, Norman, *Silent Summer: The State of Wildlife in Britain and Ireland*, Cambridge University Press, Cambridge, 2010.

Marren, Peter, *Nature Conservation: A Review of the Conservation of Wildlife in Britain 1950–2001*, HarperCollins, 2002.

—, *Mushrooms*, British Wildlife Publishing, 2012.

Monbiot, George, *Captive State: The Corporate Takeover of Britain*, Macmillan, 2000.

—, *The Age of Consent: A Manifesto for a New World Order*, Flamingo, 2003.

—, *Feral: Rewilding the Land, Sea and Human Life*, Penguin, 2014.

Moore, Norman, 'Max Nicholson CVO CB', *British Birds*, 96:526–8, 2003.

Moss, Stephen, *A Bird in the Bush*, Aurum Press, 2004.

Muir, John, *The Eight Wilderness Discovery Books*, Diadem, 1992.

Murphy, Graham, *Founders of the National Trust*, National Trust, 2002.

Nature in Norfolk: A Heritage in Trust, Jarrolds, Norwich, 1976.

Newton, Alfred, *A Dictionary of Birds*, A. & C. Black, 1896.

Nicholson, Max, *The System*, Hodder and Stoughton, 1967.

—, *The Environmental Revolution: A Guide to the New Masters of the World*, Pelican, Harmondsworth, 1972.

Niemann, Derek, *Birds in a Cage*, Short Books, 2012.

—, *A Tale of Trees*, Short Books, 2016.

Peterken, George, *Meadows*, British Wildlife Publishing, Gillingham, 2013.

Purseglove, Jeremy, *Taming the Flood: Rivers, Wetlands and the Centuries-Old Battle Against Flooding*, HarperCollins, 1988.

Rackham, Oliver, *Trees and Woodland in the British Landscape*, Phoenix, 1996.

—, *The History of the British Countryside*, Phoenix, 2000.

—, *Ancient Woodland: Its History, Vegetation and Uses in England*, Castlepoint Press, Dalbeattie, 2003.

—, *Woodland*, HarperCollins, 2006.

Ratcliffe, Derek (ed.), *A Nature Conservation Review*, 2 vols, Cambridge University Press, Cambridge, 1977.

—, *Birds of Mountain and Moorland*, Cambridge University Press, Cambridge, 1990.

—, *In Search of Nature*, Peregrine Books, Leeds, 2000.

Ray, John and Willughby, Francis, *The Ornithology of Francis Willughby*, 1678.

Richardson Jr, Robert, *Emerson: The Mind on Fire*, University of California Press, London, 1995.

Ridley, Nicholas, *My Style of Government: The Thatcher Years*, Hutchinson, 1991.

Rotherham, Ian, *The Lost Fens: England's Greatest Ecological Disaster*, The History Press, Stroud, 2013.

Rothman, Benny, *The Battle for Kinder Scout*, Willow, Altrincham, 2012.

Rothschild, Miriam and Marren, Peter, *Rothschild's Reserves: Time and Fragile Nature*, Harley Books, Colchester, 1997.

Samstag, Tony, *For Love of Birds: The Story of the RSPB*, Royal Society for the Protection of Birds, Sandy, 1988.

Sands, Tim, *Wildlife in Trust: A Hundred Years of Nature Conservation*, Elliott and Thompson, 2012.

Schama, Simon, *Landscape and Memory*, HarperCollins, 1995.

Seaman, L. C. B., *Post-Victorian Britain 1902–51*, Methuen, 1966.

Sharrock, J. T. R. (ed.), *The Atlas of Breeding Birds in Britain and Ireland*, T. & A. D. Poyser, 1976.

Sheail, John, *Nature in Trust: The History of Nature Conservation in Britain*, Blackie and Son, Glasgow, 1976.

—, *Nature Conservation in Britain: The Formative Years*, The Stationery Office, 1998.

Shoard, Marion, *The Theft of the Countryside*, Temple Smith, 1980.

—, *This Land is Our Land: The Struggle for the British Countryside*, Gaia, 1997.

Shrubb, Michael, *The Lapwing*, T. & A. D. Poyser, 2007.

Smith, Peter (ed.), *The Politics of Physical Resources*, Penguin, Harmondsworth, 1975.

Smith, Ted, *Trustees for Nature: A Memoir*, Lincolnshire Wildlife Trust, Horncastle, 2007.

Smout, T. C., *Nature Contested: Environmental History in Scotland and Northern England Since 1600*, Edinburgh University Press, Edinburgh, 2000.

Spowers, Rory, *Rising Tides: The History and Future of the Environmental Movement*, Canongate, Edinburgh, 2003.

Stamp, Sir Dudley, *Nature Conservation in Britain*, Collins, 1969.

State of Nature 2013, State of Nature Partnership, 2013.

Stephenson, Tom (ed. Ann Holt), *Forbidden Land: The Struggle for Access to Mountain and Moorland*, Manchester University Press, Manchester, 1989.

Stoddart, Andy, *Shifting Sands: Blakeney Point and the Environmental Imagination*, self-published, 2013.

Stroud, David, Reed, Tim, Pienkowski, M. W. and Lindsay, Richard, *Birds, Bogs and Forestry: The Peatlands of Caithness and Sutherland*, Nature Conservancy Council, Peterborough, 1987.

Tansley, Arthur, *Our Heritage of Wild Nature*, Cambridge University Press, Cambridge, 1945.

Tapper, Stephen, *Game Heritage*, Game Conservancy, Fordingbridge, 1992.

Taylor, Harvey, *A Claim on the Countryside: A History of the British Outdoor Movement*, Keele University Press, Edinburgh, 1997.

Taylor, Moss and Marchant, John H., *The Norfolk Bird Atlas*, British Trust for Ornithology, Thetford, 2011.

Taylor, Moss, Seago, Michael, Allard, Peter and Dorling, Don, *The Birds of Norfolk*, Pica Press, Mountfield, 1999.

The Forward Book of Poetry 2006, Forward, 2005.

Thirsk, Joan, *Fenland Farming in the Sixteenth Century*, University College of Leicester, Leicester, 1953.

Thomas, Jeremy and Lewington, Richard, *Butterflies of Britain and Ireland*, British Wildlife Publishing, Gillingham, 2010.

Thomas, Keith, *Man and the Natural World*, Allen Lane, 1983.

Thompson, Des, Birks, Hilary and Birks, John, *Nature's Conscience: The Life and Legacy of Derek Ratcliffe*, Langford Press, Narborough, 2015.

Thoreau, Henry, *Collected Essays and Poems*, Library of America, New York, 2001.

Tompkins, Steve, *Forestry in Crisis: The Battle for the Hills*, Christopher Helm, Bromley, 1989.

Tsouvalis, Judith, *A Critical Geography of Britain's State Forests*, Oxford University Press, Oxford, 2000.

Tubbs, Colin, 'A Vision for Rural Europe', *British Wildlife* 9(2):79–85, 1997.

Warren, Martin, 'Spreading our Wings', *Butterfly*, Summer 2005, p. 3.

Waterson, Merlin, *The National Trust: The First Hundred Years*, The National Trust, 1994.

Weideger, Paula, *Gilding the Acorn: Behind the Façade of the National Trust*, Simon and Schuster, 1994.

Wheeler, W. H., *History of the Fens of South Lincolnshire*, Simpkin, Marshall and Co., 1868.

Wightman, Andy, *The Poor Had No Lawyers: Who Owns Scotland (And How They Got It)*, Birlinn, Edinburgh, 2013.

Wildlife Trusts, *The Status of England's Local Wildlife Sites Systems 2014 Report*, pp. 1–29.

Williams, Raymond, *Keywords: A Vocabulary of Culture and Society*, Flamingo, 1976.

—, *The Country and the City*, Hogarth Press, 1985.

Williamson, Henry, *The Story of a Norfolk Farm*, Clive Holloway, 1986.

Williamson, Tom, *England's Landscape: East Anglia*, Collins, 2006.

Wilson, Edward O., *The Diversity of Life*, Belknap Press, Cambridge, Mass., 1992.

—, *The Future of Life*, Abacus, 2003.

Winter, Michael, *Rural Politics: Policies for Agriculture, Forestry and the Environment*, Routledge, 1996.

Worster, Donald, *A Passion for Nature: The Life of John Muir*, Oxford University Press, Oxford, 2008.

Worthington, T., Kemp, P. S., Osborne, P. E., Howes, C. and Easton, K., 'Former distribution and decline of the burbot (*Lota lota*) in the UK', *Aquatic Conservation: Marine and Freshwater Ecosystems*, 20:371–7, 2010.

—, 'A review of the historical distribution and status of the burbot (*Lota lota*) in English rivers', *Journal of Applied Ichthyology*, 27 (Suppl. 1), 1–8, 2011.

INDEX

Abercrombie, Patrick 69*n*, 115
Access to Mountains Act (1939) 95
Access to Mountains bill (1884) 109
Adams, Bill: *Future Nature* 7, 70, 151, 155, 156
Addison Report (1931) 100
afforestation 246–60, 248*n*, 249*n*, 250*n*, 251*n*, 258*n*, 261–78, 261*n*, 264*n*, 265*n*, 266*n*, 268*n see also* woodland
Agricultural Research Council (ARC) 127
agriculture: Agriculture Act (1947) 209–10; Agricultural Revolution 85; agri-environment schemes 222–30, 224*n*, 225*n* 228*n*; biodiversity and 8, 62, 113–18, 133–5, 160–71, 178–85, 186–205, 211–12, 215–20, 221–31, 287–8; Corn Laws and 206–7, 208, 209; depression in (1870s–1930s) 106, 206, 207–8; enclosure and *see* enclosure; fen drainage and 178–85; fertilisers, use of 137–8, 137*n*, 150, 187–9, 188*n*, 199, 217, 224, 250, 279, 291, 299*n*; First World War and 208–9; land-owning/farming lobby and possibility of change within 219–20, 220*n*; landscape and 113–18, 160–71, 191, 287–8; mixed farm 194–5, 228*n*; NFU and government, relationship between 210; pesticides, use of 6, 141*n*, 151–2, 189–90, 199, 224*n*, 250, 291, 299*n*; producers, concentration in hands of small number of 192–3, 192*n*; production/yields, increased 85,

193–4, 193*n*, 214; Second World War and 209–10; specialisation in 194–5; subsidies 66, 72, 117, 206–31, 211*n*, 217*n*, 218*n*, 220*n*, 251, 252, 253, 256, 265, 267, 268, 269, 287, 297, 298 *see also under individual subsidy name*; Third Agricultural Revolution (1945–80) 116, 137; tractor and 191–2, 191*n*; transformation/intensification in 20th-century 187–95; 'value' adding and economy of 212–13; woodland destruction and *see* woodland
alder 2, 3
Alderfen Broad, Norfolk 50
Aldreth, Cambridgeshire 184
alpine bartsia 124
alpine bistort 124
alpine cinquefoil 124
alpine meadow-rue 124
alpine penny-cress 124
alpine rush 152
ammonia 137, 188*n*
Annual Investment Allowance 210–11, 211*n*
Anti-Corn Law League 207
Area of Outstanding Natural Beauty (AONB) 11, 70, 298–9, 301
ash 121, 246*n*, 248
Askham Bog Nature Reserve, North Yorkshire 50–1
Atlas of Breeding Birds in Britain and Ireland, The (1976) 198, 200
Attlee, Clement 109, 126
Audubon Society 190
Austin, Mary 124–5